FOSSIL COVE PRESS

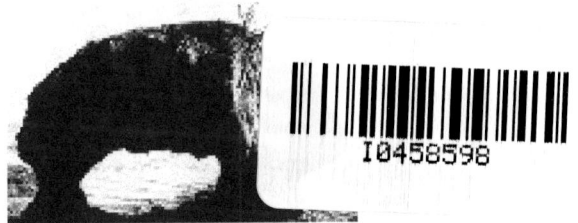

I0458598

The Second PIRATES History of Doctor

by

D. G. Valdron

The Second PIRATES History of Doctor Who, Volume II

© 2014 by Denis George Arthur Valdron. © 2022,Second Edition, revised and updated, by Denis George Arthur Valdron. The right of Denis George Arthur Valdron (D.G. Valdron) to be identified as the author of this work is asserted. All rights reserved. This Book is a work of review, commentary, and criticism. Reviews and commentaries are the opinions of the author.
Note: This volume was formerly titled 'The Greatest Unauthorized Doctor Stories, Volume II,' – But has been substantially revised, edited and updated.

'Doctor Who' series Copyright © British Broadcasting Corporation 1962-2016 'Daleks', 'Cybermen,' 'Master,' 'Sontarans' and others Copyright © to the creators. Copyrights of the individual works reviewed acknowledged. All uses of copyright materials, including quotes, are for historical and review purposes, and for criticism and commentary, recognized by and permitted under fair use, but remain as applicable under copyright to third parties. 'Doctor Who,' 'The Doctor,' 'Tardis,' 'Gallifrey,' and other marks, trademarked to the BBC, and no infringement is express or implied. Only nominative use for purposes of review and criticism is used.

Fossil Cove Publishing, 90 Garry Street, Suite 1301
Winnipeg, Manitoba, Canada, R3C 4J4
http://www.denvaldron.com

Cover: A group of youths out to make their own version of Doctor Who, dressing up as Monsters and Aliens, and busily painting a traditional red British phone booth blue. Art and Design by Roberto Gonzales Lara
http://www.robertogonzalezlara.com/

Issued in print formats ISBN: 978-1-998453-33-7 (IngramSpark print);

No part of this book may be used or reproduced in form or by any means, including electronic or mechanical, or by any information storage and retrieval system, any manner whatsoever without the prior written permission of the publisher, except in the case of brief quotations embedded in reviews.Text set in Garamond

The Second Pirates History, Page iii

THE SECOND PIRATE'S HISTORY
OF DOCTOR WHO
TABLE OF CONTENTS

INTRODUCTION

A Word about Redundancy.

This book, and the others in the series, are not necessarily meant to be read in order. You can if you'd like, that's just fine. But you can read in any order you want.

They consist of chapters and reviews which are by and large stand-alone, so it's perfectly fine, and I completely encourage just wandering back and forth, reading the bits that strike your fancy in whatever order you want.

The world of Doctor Who is a timey-wimey, wibbly-wobbly place and often things overlap, so I've built a degree of redundancy and repetition into the various chapters and articles, touching on the same information in different places to make your reading experience easier and more satisfying.

The downside is that after a while, you may be afflicted with flashes of déjà vu the more you read. Don't sweat it, just relax and keep on going.

The Actual Introduction

Fan Films? This Book? Why bother?

Seriously, that's the question. Why would anyone want to write about fan films?

And why would you want to read it?

If you've bothered to get this far, then I figure I've got at least half a shot at convincing you.

Let's start here: I'm a Doctor Who fan. I suspect that you are too. For me, it was walking through the TV lounge of the Student Union building, and glimpsing some program about two very different starships, phased into each other, and a tall curly haired man in an impossibly long scarf who was trying to sort it out. I was hooked. I loved the show. I loved its quirkiness and charm, its wit and characterization, the intricacy of the stories, the room given to supporting characters to grow, the originality of the production design, its sprawling stories.

Fast forward a few years. At a Doctor Who fan club I ended up watching the *Wrath of Eukor*. This was a full episode length production, shot on 16 millimeter film, with amazing production values and talented actors, featuring a female Doctor.

I had never heard of fan films.

I had no idea what they were.

But I was watching a Doctor Who story as good as anything I'd ever seen on the regular show. It was witty and twisty and brilliant in a Doctorish way.

So I got interested in fan films.

And then, I lost interest.

Most fan films, it turns out, aren't actually all that good. I hate to say this. They're made by people out of love, and a lot of hard work goes into them, and often a lot of creativity and imagination. But mostly, they're made without money, by people without a lot of experience or skill. It tends to show. But they pretty much wear their amateur status on their sleeve. That's okay. There's nothing wrong with that. It's a labour of love by people who want to make a tribute to a show that they enjoy. I admire that spirit.

Fast forward a few more years, and I ran across something called *Phase Four*, a four part serial where a young Doctor, played by Rupert Booth, confronted an army of very authentic Cybermen. This was professional quality, nearly indistinguable from the real series. There was a whole series of stories featuring the Booth Doctor.

And I ran across something called *Star Trek Continues*, where Vic Mignona and Todd Haberkorn recreated the original Star Trek series with such perfect fidelity that initially, I literally couldn't tell the difference. It was that good.

So I got interested again, this time systematically.

I'd realized something. There was a continuum, a range for fan films. From the appalling, to the mostly amateur and mundane, to a handful of genuinely brilliant films - productions so smart, so polished, so well done that you could place them alongside the original show. They were worth watching, a lot of them had something interesting going for them, even if it was only naïve enthusiasm and pure love. But more than that, the best of them were worth seeking out.

That was the problem. There may be around a thousand Doctor Who fan films out there. They're all over the map, and ninety per cent of them perhaps, really are mostly for the people who made them. A lot of them are really tedious; I'm not being a snob, that's what it is. Maybe five or ten per cent are really good, they match or approach the level of the original show, they're the ones that knock you on your butt, the ones that you really want to see, the ones that elevate the entire genre.

But finding them is actually pretty hit or miss. If you just go looking randomly through YouTube, then you end up wading through a lot of dross to find the gems. That's tedious and most casual fans, even most hard-core fans, are just not up to it. If only there was some way to bypass all of that, to help identify and seek out the best of it, the stuff that's worth watching. The stuff that was cool and amazing.

As I researched, my scope widened. I started digging into stage plays, finding a world of official and unofficial productions, and even bootleg recordings of a stage play. Doctor Who's *Ultimate Adventure*, where Colin Baker and Jon Pertwee both played the Doctor.

I delved into the hidden corners of the show, the stories that were abandoned or never made, the projects that went in strange directions, the way the BBC almost threw hundreds of episodes away, and the work that fans did in recovering lost episodes, and making audio recordings of episodes unrecovered. Fans, fan films and Doctor Who history intersected in fascinating ways, stories that needed to be told.

So I started writing reviews, and they turned into these books.

I even explored the gray-market stuff, the copyright skaters that found loopholes in copyright law, to make movies with Who characters and monsters, to create Doctor Who without the Doctor. It crystallized something for me.

I didn't love a piece of legal intellectual property. I loved Doctor Who. I didn't watch the show for the BBC's official licenses and trademarks. I watched because it was a show about a kind hero, a hero who believed in people, brought out the best in them, who could talk to the monsters, whose weapons were intelligence, compassion and conviction. If that was there, if those were the qualities of the Doctor, then it didn't matter to me whether it was BBC approved, so long as it was true to the spirit of the show.

That's what this is about.

This is about the overlooked and ignored stuff, and specifically, the very best, the most interesting, the most significant unauthorized Doctor Who. The stuff that you would want to seek out and watch, the stuff you would enjoy.

This isn't just reviews, but recommendations, a guide to identify and hunt down, so you don't have to wade through mud to find the gems. Here are the gems, on a silver platter, just for you, and you can read these reviews and decide if you want to hunt them down. And maybe learn a few things about the history of the show as you go.

These are the things I want to share with you. I promise you that if you love the show, you will love these. You will be amused and amazed, enthralled, entertained. I offer you the thrill of discovery, a chance to learn about hidden corners, and strange quirks and secret treasures. I will show you things you've never seen things you never imagined. I will show you that it's bigger on the inside.

So come with me. You won't regret it. All you have to do is step through the blue door...

CHAPTER 9: ON STAGE TREADING THE BOARDS

A History of Doctor Who Stage Plays

Doctor Who has always been a television series, but you know how it goes. Things drift, a popular television series gets made into movies, or gets taken up as a comic strip, novels are published, there are audio adventures, board games, trading cards, you name it. Basically every successful franchise inevitably crosses over into other mediums, either because it's cheap and easy, as in the case of comic strips and novels, or because there's the promise of big money in movies and merchandise.

Which explains why, over the years, Doctor Who has a long, but rather patchy history on stage, both as professional and fan productions.

There are the big well known officially licensed productions – Curse of the Daleks, Seven Keys to Doomsday, the Ultimate Adventure. We'll be covering those.

In the modern era there's been *Doctor Who at the Proms, Crash of the Elysium, The Monsters Are Coming, Doctor Who Live*, a *Muppets Revival Show* where David Tennant and Peter Davison appeared for a sketch as the Doctor on alternate nights. The Chuckle Brothers did a parody called *Doctor What and the*

Return of the Garlics. We won't be covering those. I think they're pretty fresh.

There has been an assortment of recognized semi-pro or amateur productions, restaging of *Seven Keys to Doomsday* for instance, *Empress of Otherwhen*, the *Trials of Davros*, the *Karnak Trilogy*, and Scovell's Bedlam plays. There's probably more than we can ever fully track down. But that's all right.

There are Doctor Who plays that never made it onto the stage. Back in the 1980s, comic book writer Jon Ostrander attempted to mount his own production of Doctor Who, *Inheritors of Time*, for the stage in California in the mid-eighties. Last year, a young writer named Andrew Hawcroft wrote a Doctor Who play, *A Light in the Dark*, so far unproduced, but shared with fans.

Doctor Who on stage has always been a thing.

That said, I don't recall a lot of *Star Wars* or *Star Trek* stage plays. But then, this is the British. They've always had an affinity for stage, so that probably has something to do with it. The British are crazy for theatre both amateur and professional, in the way that Americans are crazy for guns, or Canadians are addicted to clubbing seal pups on ice floes.

Now, you're probably thinking that this is all very interesting, but what does it have to do with Doctor Who fan films?

The really short answer is that many of these stage plays are recorded, or remade, or have documentaries made by fans, and some of them end up available on YouTube or elsewhere, so they end up being fan films through the back door.

I think that Doctor Who stage and Doctor Who fan films have very similar roots. Both arise from a fascination with the television program, and a desire to re-create in a new format, to tell new stories.

There are differences. The stage productions are often official, or semi-official. The BBC itself is not in the business of producing Theater of course. But they can and have allowed others to use their product. If a stage production is not formally licensed by the BBC, there's usually some kind of formal letter of permission or authorization granted. In this section, we'll cover a number of stage plays, and almost all of them have either a license or at least a letter.

There are very few Doctor Who stage plays that take place with no permission granted. Whereas pretty much every fan film is a renegade production without permission or authorization.

Part of that difference is that stage productions typically sell tickets – there's a commercial aspect to it, even if that's often nominal. The stage tradition is much more formal and much more mindful of rights, so they're more inclined to seek permission, even for small productions. On the other hand, it's a self-limiting venue, so maybe the BBC is more tolerant. There are always only a finite number of performances. And the BBC is probably much more used to dealing with Theatre people and Theatre matters, so there's a comfort there.

But beyond the legal issues, stage plays and fan films have a key thing in common. Inspiration. Both are inspired by the TV, and they exist as recreations and interpretations of the TV show in their mediums. They are made for fans of the show, and they're almost exclusively made by fans. Even the big commercial productions are ultimately driven by a fannish urge.

There's also a key distinction between stage and film. Stage is ephemeral.

Curse of the Daleks lasted barely a week. *Seven Keys to Doomsday* ran a few weeks. *Ultimate Adventure* ran a couple of months.

Empress of Otherwhen ran four performances. *Planet of Storms* three nights.

It comes, it goes, it's gone.

Theatre as we've mentioned is ephemeral. The curtains go up, the boards are tread for a handful of performances, then the curtain goes down and they're gone forever.

I had a friend who did a fringe festival show. He worked on the script for a year, cast six months ahead, for two months his cast and crew worked hard, rehearsing, building sets, getting ready. Then opening night comes along, and a few days later, it's over.

Done.

Gone.

All that work, all that time and energy spent, and nothing to show for it but a couple of reviews and some leftover handbills and paperwork.

Planet of Storms played for three days and then apparently vanished from the earth.

That feels shocking, doesn't it?

We've gotten used to performance as an ageless form - nowadays, we can save our video games, listen to golden oldies, binge on reruns, we watch fifty year old episodes of William Hartnell, listen to Jazz or blues recorded seventy years ago on vinyl, and watch century old silent skits by Charlie Chaplin or Harold Lloyd.

The notion a performance could simply happen and be lost the moment it's completed, that this was the way it was for most of human history, that it is probably still this way for so much that is performed live... It seems... subversive, even disturbing.

And really, I suppose that's the crucial difference between Theatre and Film or Video. We can go back and watch William Hartnell recite lines spoken fifty years ago, televised Doctor Who has this immense record or body of work going back half a century.

Empress of Otherwhen simply evaporated away with its final performance.

Except...

That's not always the case.

Technology's changed that. Back in 1983 and 1984, the first domestic Camcorders came on the market, quickly pushing Super8 out of the way. They were expensive and crude, but they steadily got better, cheaper and more accessible over the next decades.

Now the thing with these Camcorders was that they made filming convenient, and portable. There was no painstaking loading film rolls or popping in film cartridges capable of only a few minutes at a time, there was no processing and development, no special equipment was required to play.

And, very importantly, they had a lot of running time. Maximum time on your Super8 was three minutes, twenty seconds. But you could pop a tape in your Betacam, and assuming you were fully charged up or connected to a power line, you could go for an hour or two.

You could, if you were minded, videotape an entire play. Sometimes the players did that themselves. It was nice to have a record of their own performance after all. Sometimes it was an audience member being sneaky. But it could be done.

The same technology that drove an explosion in fan films in the 80s and 90s also drove recording stage plays, particularly through the 90s and beyond.

So a lot of Doctor Who stage plays ended up being recorded, and some of them have ended up on YouTube or in circulation.

There were handicaps with recording stage plays of course – it's not the same as a real movie. Movies are edited, they have a variety of shots and camera angles, close ups, establishing shots, you name it.

For recordings of plays, the camera stands in for the audience usually. The camera is stationary, it might swing to follow action, or it might zoom in or out, but it's pretty fixed. Stage plays are often dim in recordings; the stage lighting isn't designed for the camera. Sound is often muddy, again, built in camcorder microphones are not the greatest, and the voice projection of stage actors sometimes is only partial compensation for that limit.

You can always tell the difference between a deliberate film or video shot as a movie, and a videotaped performance of a stage play. And you can usually tell the difference between a video recording of a stage play by the players or theatre, and one snuck in by a fan.

But then again, a lot of fan films can struggle with the technical requirements of their production. So the gulf, while distinctive, is not insurmountable. Fans learn to forgive a bit here and there.

If you're willing to make those allowances, what you've gotten is often surprisingly watchable. And the existence of these recordings basically amounts to something so close to a fan film, there's not really a lot of meaningful difference.

Almost every Doctor Who stage play, official or unofficial has intersected with the world of fan films. They re-created *Curse of the Daleks*, they made a documentary for *Seven Keys to Doomsday*, they recorded the *Ultimate Adventure*, somewhere out there, there are video recordings of just about every Who stage production from the last thirty years.

So why not cover the official and unofficial world of Doctor Who Theatre?

Curse of the Daleks Remade (1965)

The First Official Stage Play, 1965, and 2000's CGI

Believe it or not, the first Doctor Who stage play didn't feature even feature the Doctor. No Doctor, no companions, no Tardis, not even a police box, no time travel, nothing.

Nothing but his nemesis, the Daleks.

This was *Curse of the Daleks*, running from December 21, 1965, to January 15, 1965, written by David Whittaker, the story editor for Doctor Who, and along with Terry Nation, creator of the Daleks.

The difference between script editor, Whittaker, and Nation, or BBC designer, Ray Cusack, and Nation is simple. They were BBC employees, so their work was owned by the BBC. Nation was a free-lancer, so he owned his own contribution to the Daleks.

And since the BBC couldn't use his 'contribution' to the Daleks without his permission, that effectively meant he owned the Daleks.

1965 was the middle of *Dalekmania*, back when Dalek songs were on the radio; they were in comics and cartoons, television and movies. Daleks filled toy stores and Daleks were practically celebrities on their own, and made public appearances, and every child was running around with arms outstretched screaming 'Exterminate!'

They dominated the two Doctor Who feature films with Peter Cushing, so much so that Doctor Who wasn't even mentioned in the title of the second film.

There was even talk of an American television series to be called *The Destroyers*, built around the Daleks. *Mission to the Unknown* - Doctor Who's famous single-episode story, which also doesn't happen to have any of the regular cast, was supposed to be a sort of backdoor pilot. The Daleks were well on their way to being a multimedia empire, so why not a stage production?

Hence, Curse of the Daleks, written by David Whittaker: The Doctor and his time machine had no part in the story, the BBC didn't license that use. But due to a quirk of BBC's copyright policies, Terry Nation, had the rights and the influence to license them for a stage play.

But then, wouldn't Nation have written the stage play? How did Whittaker end up writing it? I have no idea. In fact, I really have no idea who produced this, or why, apart from Dalekmania, someone decided that a Dalek play was just the thing. Whittaker did contribute the scripts for the two Dalek movies. Apparently, Nation was busy with other things, so he could just cash the cheque and let Whittaker do the work.

There's an interesting movie connection. The stage play apparently commissioned at least four Daleks, from the same company that made the movie Daleks. Once the play was over, it wasn't like they were going to be needed for the stage, so they were sold off. Terry Nation, creator of the Daleks, swooped in and bought them. Apparently, the plan was to use them for his American spin-off space opera, *The Destroyers*.

After that fell through, Nation then rented them to AARU productions, for the second Doctor Who movie, Dalek *Invasion Earth 2150 AD*. As it turned out, the movie didn't do particularly well, so AARU cancelled any plans for a third movie.

It may well have come full circle, some of the AARU Daleks were rented for the BBC television series, and may well have been Terry Nation's original stage play Daleks.

But Nation kept his little army of Daleks, and for the next couple of decades he had a nice side line in exhibiting or renting them out.

A thorough history of Terry Nation's Daleks, and in fact a thorough history movie and television Daleks is available from *Dalek 63-88*, an absolutely brilliant, incredibly enjoyable web site, podcast and YouTube series. Check them out.

The *Curse of the Daleks* told the story of far future human colonists on Skaro, a future so distant that humans have forgotten what they were. Skarro is still full of Daleks, but without power, they're dormant, basically, just a lot of ancient statuary. Some bright guy gets the idea of reviving the dormant Daleks. At first, the Daleks play along and make nice, but eventually their true nature comes out.

Obviously, there's no video record of the stage play. Neither film nor video were accessible enough to allow for a record of the performance. All we have are the scripts, a few playbills, and maybe some camera stills, if that.

But there is a fan film connection: Many, many years later, in the early 200s, a fan group called Altered Vistas, as part of its Dalek Chronicles, remade the play as a full length CGI Adventure. Their gig was doing crude CGI figure animation with existing software. If you look at the Altered Vistas web site, you can find their feature material – a detailed photo gallery for the production, and a set of very enthusiastic reviews. It's no longer available from them. But I suspect that if you look hard enough, you can find it out here somewhere. Sometimes it seems that nothing ever truly goes away on the internet.

Altered Vistas appears to still be active, they maintain a detailed web site, and they've made a number of CGI movies based mostly on Dalek or Cyberman appearances in comics, including *Absalom Daak* stories (a character unique to comic strips – Daak was a criminal brute who, together with a few allies, waged a bloody and violent campaign killing Daleks). They've given life to Grant Morrison or Alan Moore stories, usually traded or run off on DVD roms.

Daleks seem to be very CGI friendly, I notice. They're basically just ornate cylinders that glide around a lot. That's easy to animate, especially compared to critters with limbs and joints and features all akimbo and going in different directions. A lot of CGI people or animal animation is often ponderous and clunky, with all these limbs with awkward joints and projecting heads, jaws and tails, sticking out all over, their movements stiff and mannered. But Daleks? Man, they just glide around smoothly.

Sadly, as I've said, the *Altered Vistas* production is no longer easily available. In 2008, Big Finish Productions, in its ongoing and very laudable quest to expand the Doctor Who universe, eventually followed up with an audio version and Altered Vistas withdrew theirs. Still, the Big Finish Production is commercially available, and worth tracking down.

Review: Remembering Seven Keys to Doomsday (1974)

The 1974 Official Stage Play and the 2017 Documentary

The next stage production came in 1974. It was officially Doctor Who, authorized and licensed by the BBC. *Seven Keys to Doomsday* took place in the gap between Jon Pertwee and Tom Baker. Indeed, Pertwee was originally going to play the Doctor, but either due to scheduling, or just being sick of the role, he declined.

Instead, the part went to Trevor Martin. Martin actually had a connection to the show; he had appeared in Troughton's *The War Games*, as one of the Time Lords who puts the 2nd Doctor on trial.

Pertwee did agree to have his image used, however. So the opening scene of the play featured a sequence of 48 flashing slides in two alternating carousels, depicting Pertwee regenerating into Martin. This was the beginning, as I understand it, *Seven Keys* did a lot of this kind of thing; it was a highly technical play that utilized a lot of visual effects.

It premiered two weeks before Tom Baker's first appearance as the Doctor, which technically makes Trevor Martin the first actor to appear before the public as the fourth Doctor.

Another key component, Wendy Padberry, who had played Zoe in the Troughton serials, returned as a new companion, Jenny. Once again, the Daleks were a big part of the story written by Terrance Dicks.

Terrance Dicks, was a Script Editor during the Troughton days, and wrote eight serials, running from the Troughton to the Davison era. He also wrote an immense whack of Doctor Who novels, and was involved in several fan productions, from *Shakedown* and *Mindgame* to *Death Takes a Holiday*.

This time out the newly regenerated Doctor's Tardis materializes on stage, where he picks up two teenage audience members, obviously plants. That's actually a fun "meta" idea, blurring the lines between stage and audience before taking off.

Together with his new companions, Jenny and Jimmy, the Doctor goes off for a jaunt to Karn where he has to foil the Daleks and their crab monster henchman, 'clawrantulars,' as they search for the seven jewels which will give them universal domination. Oddly, it seemed to be aimed more at children than Pertwee's family oriented adventures. It was literally a re-creation of the show on stage, with familiar old tropes. At one point, Wendy's character hides in a Dalek… we'd only seen that a handful of times before. The natives of Karn were reminiscent of the Thals of original Dalek serial. There seemed to be a lot of recycling of previous elements.

Terrance Dicks, would re-use the planet Karn for Tom Baker's Brain of Morbius. When the new series of Doctor Who rebooted, Karn would become increasingly important to the mythology of Who.

Well, Karn begins here.

The play was hampered by excessive technical requirements - a lot of special effects, as I've mentioned - which made for a difficult stage production. Ambitions were high; the intention was to take it on tour, eventually end up playing the summer at Blackpool. The production was too expensive to make a profit, the sets too large to go on tour, and audiences were scared away by an IRA bombing campaign that year. One bomb, in fact, exploded so close that it was heard by the audience and cast during a performance. The production lost money, earning only twenty-seven thousand pound, but costing thirty-five thousand pounds.

Technology had moved along somewhat. Super 8 cameras were commonplace, but that wasn't good for more than two and a half minutes at a pop, and frankly it's hard to imagine a Super 8 enthusiast being allowed to record. Video was still big heavy studio cameras on reel to reel tape. Television news had location cameramen, but odds were they'd never have taken more than a snippet. There's simply no record of any film footage of the play.

And from the sounds of it, it wasn't likely. This was an extremely technical, special effects oriented play, so any kind of news filming or super 8 would be like giving away secrets. Plus, because it was so technically difficult, they were literally working right up until opening night to get it right. Not even the Daleks were ready for publicity shots.

If you search online, you can find publicity stills, mostly Trevor Martin hanging out with Daleks. Interesting factoid: The stage production built its own Daleks, but those weren't ready in time for the publicity shots. So Martin is actually posing with Terry Nation's Daleks, the ones from the stage play and Cushing movie.

Although there is no video record of the play itself, there is a fan made student documentary, **_Remembering Seven Keys to Doomsday,_** by Thomas Jedski, which is well worth searching out. Although lacking live footage, it features a treasure trove of black and white stills which showcase the fearsomely ridiculous clawrantulars, half lobster, half cyborg

Frankenstein, half glam rocker; the Grand Master of Karn is a skeletal ten foot tall figure whose bulbous skull glowed with internal light; blue skinned natives with long white hair; and a fascinating new version of the Tardis console, and of course the Daleks.

Still photos, and compositions of black and white still photos, with lines from the script recited, re-create a vivid feeling of what the play must have been like. Meanwhile, interviews with Trevor Martin, Terrance Dicks, director Mick Hughes, other actors, technicians, and Kevin Davies (at that time a young audience member), give us windows into the theatrical experience.

Rear projection for instance, then comparatively rare in the theatre, was a huge part of the show, with three rear projection screens on stage, including a central one which lifted to become a doorway, and other rear projection screens suspended in the air.

An actor notes that the sets were designed to move, so you had to be careful or you could be run over by your own set. Another technician recalls 'flying' objects, lowered from the ceiling. Simon Jones, who plays the Grand Master recalls that his costume was essentially a stepladder on wheels— he stood at the top, flowing robes concealed his pedestal, and a hidden stagehand pushed him around, so he effectively glided across the stage with unearthly effect. An actress, who was a Dalek operator, recalls being spun too fast and falling into the orchestra pit.

These experiences and memories, the stories and the images bring the story to life. It makes you want to find a time machine so you can go back and watch it, the way it was originally meant. Despite the pedestrian story, it feels like a spectacle.

Seven Keys has had a few more turns at bat after that initial run.

In December, 1980, Colin Jones starred as the Doctor, in a restaging of the play in Buxton, England by a local theatre group. Unfortunately, there's not much more information than that. We don't even know where they got their Daleks.

Then in November and December, 1984, there was a production in New Zealand, with Michael Sagar as the Doctor. It just missed the boat, home camcorders didn't come onto the market until 1984/85, so there was no opportunity to record either of these. However, the New Zealand production was well documented online, and if you poke around, you can see their own distinctive versions of Daleks, Clawrantulars and Grand Master.

Finally, Big Finish released an audio re-creation of the play. Trevor Martin returned to the role of the Doctor some forty years later. Wendy Padbury's daughter, Charlie Hayes, took up the role of Jenny.

With all due respect to Big Finish, which has done an extraordinary job of following up on these lost aspects of the show, I don't think the Audio play really cuts the mustard on this one.

Curse of the Daleks? Sure, fine as a stage play.

But *Seven Keys?* As originally mounted, it was intended to be a visual spectacle, full of special effects, striking costumes, with ten foot tall skeletal menaces with gigantic heads, and giant stompy cyborg lobsters, rear projection effects everywhere, and showmanship. You can't capture all of that in audio. This is one of those things that needs to be visual.

The story in *Seven Keys to Doomsday* seems rather threadbare, but it must have been a wonderful spectacle. Sadly, the bottom line was that it was a financial bust, which may explain why there wasn't another original Doctor Who play for a full ten years.

Review: Recall UNIT, The Great Tea Bag Mystery (1984)

Sargent Benton's Lost Fringe Festival Production

Perhaps for that reason the next effort was rather less ambitious, and once again Doctor-free: *Recall Unit: The Great Tea Bag Mystery* played at the *Edinburgh Fringe Festival* in 1984. The story behind the story is kind of interesting though.

UNIT and its characters, particularly Brigadier Lethbridge Stewart, played by Nicholas Courtney, actually had their origins in the Troughton Era serials, *Web of Fear* and the *Invasion*. The concept is pretty simple, if there are bona fide alien invasions in modern day London, someone is going to call out the army, for sure.

When Jon Pertwee became the Doctor, the new production crew decided on a new format. The Doctor would be exiled to Earth by the Timelords, and he would fight alien menaces from home. This was supposed to save costs - past and future settings and alien planets were expensive to build.

If you're setting a lot of the action on Earth, it stands to reason that there's going to be a specialized military force to contend with all those alien invasions. To help out the Doctor, the Brigadier and UNIT came back into play.

To round out UNIT, Richard Franklin came in as Captain Yates, and John Levene as Sergeant Benton. Caroline Johns was added as Doctor Liz Shaw, UNIT's scientific advisor, resident skeptic, and eventually the Doctor's sidekick.

The Liz Shaw character lasted only a year, before being replaced by Jo Grant. A generation later, she's make a comeback in the BBV's PROBE series.

But the rest of the UNIT crew proved pretty steady through Pertwee's tenure. The Brigadier and Benton in particular, were steady through the end and beyond. The series changed format again when Tom Baker came in. UNIT was eventually written out.

Nicholas Courtney's Brigadier had a few appearances with Tom Baker, notably *Robot* and *Terror of the Zygons*, appeared in *Mawdryn Undead*, in the Davison years, and in Sylvester McCoy's *Battlefield* in 1989. He popped back in *Dimensions in Time*, and was even referenced in the new era.

Sargent Benton's last official appearance, on the other hand, was Baker's *Android Invasion* in 1975.

Although UNIT ceased to be an active part of the Doctor's stories in the Pertwee era, they were still part of the Doctor's universe, and revisited from time to time by subsequent Doctors. In the new series, they were referred to in the Tennant era, and have appeared in Smith and Capaldi stories.

The Brigadier appeared in the *Sarah Jane Adventures*, and was referred to a few times in the main series. Nicholas Courtney passed away, but somehow, his character managed to return one last time. The Brigadier's mantle was also handed down to his 'in universe' daughter, Kate Lethbridge who now runs UNIT.

Levene's and Franklin's characters did not have the same extended life as the Brigadier.

Franklin's, Captain Yates was written out at the end of the Pertwee Era. Captain Yates did wobble off the beam at the end of Pertwee's term, in *Invasion of the Dinosaurs* and was written out in *Planet of the Spiders* in 1974. And that was the end. There may have been appearances in Audio or Books, but he disappeared from the main series.

Levene's Sargent Benton lingered briefly in Tom Baker's reign, appearing in *Robot,* and then later in the Android *Invasion* in 1975.

By 1984, the roles of Captain Yates and Sargent Benton were almost a decade in the past; their final appearances had been 1974 and 1975. Normally, that would be the end of things. Both of these guys were essentially just supporting characters, and the format had left them behind.

Normally, you don't really feel a lot of impulse to return to a supporting character you did ten years ago.

But by the 1980s, Doctor Who was going over big in the United States, and consequently, any actor connected with the Tom Baker or Jon Pertwee eras were in demand at conventions. Suddenly, even minor recurring actors, including Levene and Franklin, were being invited to appear in America. They were meeting people for whose experience of their work was as recent as a few weeks or months ago. For the American fans, Levene and Benton weren't a decade old; they'd just watched them a few weeks ago.

It was at one of these conventions that Richard Franklin got the notion of reviving his Captain Yates character for the stage. John Levene and Nicholas Courtney came on board with Sargent Benton and the Brigadier. Courtney dropped as a result of scheduling conflicts.

The story featured the UNIT regulars facing off against the Master, the Supreme Dalek and a race of evil Margaret Thatcher clones called Dragoids. It sounded pretty tongue in cheek. As a fringe festival entry, it played in a field of some eight hundred and forty fringe plays, so it's not surprising that it got lost in the crowd.

I assume that Levene and Franklin got permission from the BBC and the copyright owners to re-use their characters and series concepts in their play. This was the troubled 80s era of who, John Nathan-Turner was the showrunner, Colin Baker was just beginning his tenure and the cancellation crisis was bare months away. But that storm had not yet broken and this does seem like the sort of thing that Nathan-Turner might support. I suspect he would have seen it as a bit of free advance publicity for the 1984 season then in production.

I like the thought of some confused bureaucrat in the BBC's legal department coping with the request of an actor who played a supporting character in a children's show a decade earlier asking to revive his character for the stage.

Recall Unit vanished almost without a ripple. It was never remounted anywhere again. This one is especially lost, there was no video record, no fan video remake, no Big Finish audio, I'm not sure that a copy of the script even exists any more. It's remembered mainly for an article or two and a few photographs in fanzines.

But it may have had one important consequence. It established Doctor Who's subordinate characters as independent creations with something like a life of their own.

That may have opened the door for Sargent Benton to return three years later. In 1987, John Levene would reprise, Sargent Benton in Reeltime's production of *Wartime*. *Wartime* didn't feature any other Doctor Who elements except Sargent Benton.

And it really isn't a substitute for *Recall Unit*, which had its tongue firmly in its cheek. This is serious, even mopey. The half hour drama had Benton confronting the ghosts of his past. Frankly, it's not my cup of tea.

But it was the first video production to take advantage of the BBC's screwy copyright situation with respect to Doctor Who's characters and creations. This in turn would eventually lead to an entire genre of Pseudo-Who productions from 1991 onwards by Reeltime, BBV and Dreamwatch.

As for John Levene's Sargent Benton, no more official appearances in Doctor Who or its official spin offs. But he did reappear as his character in a fan film or two, and possibly some audio adventures.

Review: The Ultimate Adventure, Bootlegged (1989)

The 1989 Extravaganza, Two & 1/2 Doctors, No Waiting

Along the long way around 1988, the classic series last Script Editor, Andrew Cartmel, was for a time involved in a possible Doctor Who play, *War World*. This would have involved a race of insect-like aliens called the Metatraxi.

This fell through, in favour of *The Ultimate Adventure*.

If you're interested, Cartmel recycled his Metatraxi for a Big Finish 'lost adventure' audio production.

Instead of bug eyed monsters, Doctor Who's next big stage production was 1989's *The Ultimate Adventure*, an officially licensed BBC production, written once again by Terrance Dicks. This time the Doctor would confront both Daleks and Cybermen, pair up with a nightclub singer, sit through musical numbers, visit revolutionary France and a low rent version of the Star Wars cantina, dodge meteors, gain a furry alien companion called Zog, face off against flying critters and other aliens including a Vervoid and a draconian, all on a mission from Margaret Thatcher herself.

The Second Pirates History, Page 27

If that's not enough, there are a few things that make this outing particularly memorable. One is the cast - both Jon Pertwee and Colin Baker returned to play their own versions of the Doctor. Pertwee played the role from March 3 to June 3. Colin Baker assumed the role and returned to a variation of his old costume from June 5 until August 19.

A third man, David Banks, who had played the role of the Cyber-Leader in the 1980s, was the understudy for the lead role and played the Doctor for two performances. Banks was also a Doctor Who series semi-regular, but more on him later.

This was very close to the last hurrah for Doctor Who. Sylvester McCoy's final season would begin to air in September, a few weeks later, and conclude in December, 1989, after which the series would go on its long hiatus.

Something else that made the *Ultimate Adventure* memorable was that we finally have a record of it. By this time, camcorders were now cheap enough that they were practically ubiquitous, and sophisticated enough that you could, if you were of such a mind, bring one to a theatre and quietly record the proceedings.

Which is what happened.

Who would have thought? Who would do such a dastardly thing? Shocking!

There are at least three, and possibly more, versions of the *Ultimate Adventure* stage play, including both Jon Pertwee and Colin Baker versions floating around as bootleg videos, shown quietly at conventions, traded and sold among collectors, available for download or online viewing on YouTube and popping up in the strangest places. There's even an audio version of one of David Banks performances.

I gather that it's probably terribly bad form to videotape stage plays, or at least for audience members to do so. It's kind of like bringing your own food to eat at a restaurant. I'm not sure what the actors would have thought of this, probably very little.

I don't know though.

There's another side to the coin:

Colin Baker's tenure as the Doctor was brief enough and tragically controversial enough that it's probably a good thing that there's some record of his work here. He got such a raw deal on the show, it's nice to see him having a bit of fun with the role, and showing what he could do with it.

And Jon Pertwee, that grand old gentleman, passed away in 1996, and is lost to us forever now. Watching his turn here is a journey back to happier times.

I can't find it in my heart to consider these videos as unmitigated evils.

So maybe it shouldn't have been recorded by fans. Maybe it shouldn't exist at all. But we have them available to find and enjoy, if we look hard enough. I'm not going to complain.

Technically, these recordings are not quite fan films, not in any proper sense of the word. The Ultimate Adventure was a thoroughly above board, professional, licensed production, it wasn't a fan made play.

On the other hand, it was certainly made for fans. It's a celebration of Doctor Who, a call back to the glories and foibles of the show, awash with warm nostalgia and affection. The illicit videos were recorded by fans, for fans, distributed among fans, and wouldn't exist or be accessible at all but for fans. So it does approach the borderlines of being a fan film, or a fan record.

What they are is unique: Amateur recordings of real Doctors playing their roles in a real BBC authorized reproduction. So it's worth talking about, and I certainly encourage you, the reader, to hunt it down. Your Pertwee or Baker collections aren't complete without it.

And for the record, I believe Big Finish has done an audio version, so you can legitimately seek that out, if your conscience troubles you.

But with all due respect to Big Finish, which has done amazing work, it's like *Seven Keys*. Both Seven Keys and *Ultimate Adventure* are visual extravaganzas. An audio play just doesn't do them justice. I'll stick with the bootlegs.

As to the videos?

As always, it's not perfect. Technically, we're seeing the limitations of late 1980s era camcorders, they've only been around for a few years. It's possibly dubbed a couple of times on VHS before it made it to YouTube. The image isn't great; the sound quality is kind of muddy and hard to follow. This is a bootleg, live with it.

We have a stationary camera; the lighting is kind of tough. That's kind of the way it is with video recordings of stage plays – the play isn't really designed for it, it's got its own lighting cues, and the camera seldom moves much. Again, it's the sort of thing we accept and live with.

Let me recap the story. Normally, I'd just do a teaser, but the sound is pretty rough and it can get hard to follow. Fair warning, I may go off on a little tangent. So here goes:

In the intro, we discover that the Cybermen and Daleks have gotten together for a fiendish plot to destroy the Doctor. The Doctor is summoned by Margaret Thatcher, who wants him to look after an American envoy to world peace talks. The envoy is absolutely vital and, it seems, there are possibly unearthly agencies out to abduct him from a nightclub.

If that 'special diplomat for world peace' thing seems familiar, you're probably remembering Pertwee's *Day of the Daleks* which used an identical shtick – villains meddling with a peace conference.

The Doctor, and his companion, Jason, head off to the nightclub, but too late. Cybermen and Space mercenaries have abducted him. Lots of pyrotechnics. The Doctor is off on the chase. Unknown to the Doctor, a nightclub singer named Crystal, has snuck aboard the Tardis. Cue the comic relief revolving around a stowaway who can't quite believe she's travelling through time and space. This has happened to the Doctor a few times in the TV show.

By the way, in the nightclub scene, just before the Cybermen and Space Mercenaries showed up to do some kidnapping, Crystal managed to get off a nightclub song. Obviously, they weren't fast enough on the draw. So fair, warning.

The end up on some alien planet where the Doctor is assaulted by winged bat-men who drop down from the ceiling in some impressive wire work. Turns out the Doctor knows them, he helped them out in the past. So when the Cybermen show up to take the Doctor prisoner, he just sends the bat-men at them and while he makes a getaway.

It's a kind of pointless filler of a scene - but on the other hand, it's got guys in bat costumes dropping down from the ceiling, flapping their arms. And frankly, I love that kind of crap!

Afterwards, the Cybermen meet up with the Daleks and they get all passive aggressive, blaming each other for things not going according to plan.

But still, our heroes need to find the envoy. The Doctor realizes the Space Mercenaries left a radiation trail. He follows it back to the Bar Galactica, a sort of low budget riff on the *Star Wars* Cantina. Lots of aliens, including a Draconian and a Vervoid.

Draconians are one of those fan favourite races in Doctor Who. Reptile men fond of dressing up like pseudo-Japanese samurai. I remember in documentaries, Pertwee would rave about them as the best aliens ever, because the half masks really allowed the actors to give a performance. I was, as a young fan, duly impressed.

So I was shocked to discover that the Draconians had only ever appeared once in the show's history, in *Frontier in Space*. If you'd have asked me back then, from the way Pertwee went on about it, I would have been sure that they'd practically been regulars on the show. Maybe not as steady as Daleks and Cybermen, but showing up as often as the Sontarans. At least a few times.

But no, just once, and they still haven't made it into the new series.

But in *Frontier in Space*, they were a big deal - a rival space Empire to Earth, an old and noble civilization, and a people that the Doctor had dealt with in the past. He was an honorary Draconian noble. They had nuance!

And let's face it. Not a lot of nuance to Doctor Who aliens mostly. Daleks just want to destroy. Cybermen... do whatever Cybermen do. Sontarans are militaristic. There's not a lot of depth or inner life to most Doctor Who monsters. Their basic motivation is to go 'Arrr! Destroy!' and the Doctor's motivation is to stop them.

So I guess when the Draconians showed up and actually had something like an inner life; a history, aspirations, a point of view; that was pretty compelling.

Come to think of it, Pertwee's Doctor, in particular, did that a fair bit – if you look at the Silurians or Sea Devils for instance, they're not straight up monsters, they're people. People on the other side from us, but people in a sense. The Troughton Doctor was inclined to send the whole Ice

Warrior fleet plunging into the sun without a care or qualm. The Pertwee Doctor often had a certain sympathy for the monsters and tried to find alternatives.

Anyway, Draconians turned into a bit of a fan favourite. They showed up in the comics. They showed up in the *Absalom Daak* stories, and in CGI renderings with *Altered Vistas*. They featured in *Mindgame* and *Mindgame Trilogy*, and in the video clips with *Trial of Davros*.

So anyway, there's a Draconian here, and he's an extra. No lines. But... it's cool to see him.

And as for the Vervoid – they had only one appearance, in *Trial of a Timelord's* story, *Terror of the Vervoids*, written by Pip and Jane Baker. The story was Mel's first appearance, by the way, but don't hold that against her, because Bonnie Langford gives her one good performance as Mel. After that, the subsequent writers and directors just savaged her character all to hell.

Anyway, the Vervoids were plant men from outer space - and oddly, there's a long tradition of that, going back to Howard Hawk's *The Thing*. The Vervoids had actually been created to be slaves to humans (when did that ever turn out well?), but had kind of woken up en route in a space liner, and were slowly taking over and killing off the passenger. The Doctor comes along and wiped them all out.

This, when you think about it, kind of creates a problem. I mean, *Terror of the Vervoids* ends with the Vervoids all being extinct, kaput. It was officially genocide. And they'd just been created. So what's a Vervoid doing here? Doesn't seem possible

You know what? I don't care. The Vervoids were the one genuinely interesting alien created during the Colin Baker era. Better than the obnoxiously shrill Sil, better than those big slug-moths from *Twin Dilemma*, certainly better than the campy Androgums from *The Two Doctors*. The costumes were excellent, with built in Freudian overtones (there was a certain 'genitalia' quality to them) but allowed the actors within free movement, their backstory was interesting and even sympathetic.

So, Vervoid cameo! That's a plus in my book.

There are a few other aliens to spice things up, but nothing too dramatic. Except for a weird furry child-like critter named Zog. Zog was created exclusively for the *Ultimate Adventure*.

Interestingly, Zog does sort of show up again - the costume was re-used in 1993 for *Dimensions in Time* - Zog appears as one of the aliens that the Rani uses to bedevil the Doctors. It's a blink and you'll miss it appearance, but it's there.

Keep an eye on Zog, it'll be part of the action from here on in, whether you like it or not.

Oh, and fair warning, there's another 'Nightclub Song,' this one sung by the proprietor of Bar Galactica, Madame Delilah.

I'm not sure why there are nightclub songs, I think maybe someone had pictures of Terrance Dicks with a goat and they made him put them in. Or maybe the actresses just demanded it, they had the pipes, they wanted to use them. Stuff happens like that. The songs don't seem to have anything in particular to do with Doctor Who. They feel pretty generic. If you shook the theatre really hard and they fell out and dropped into another play, they wouldn't feel out of place there, and you wouldn't feel like you were missing something in Who. So... Go figure. They're pretty brief, and not all that painful. So I guess I'm okay.

Anyway, turns out that Bar Galactica is yet another trap for the Doctor. As the Doctor flirts with Madame Delilah, Karl the Space Mercenary shows up. Only the intervention of Zog saves the Doctor from being taken prisoner. They flee in the

Tardis, with Zog joining the crew. The Doctor is really accumulating companions this time out.

Unfortunately, as they're escaping, the Daleks have been standing by to capture the Tardis with their tractor beam, and the Doctor is finally a prisoner. Cue some sarcastic sniping between the Doctor and the Daleks. Luckily, a convenient meteor storm, conveniently projected on a very big screen for the audience, allows the Doctor to play a quick game of 'dodge the Asteroid' and break free from the Daleks.

This is almost as exciting as watching someone play Asteroids on an Arcade video game, and at least as relevant to the plot. But, you know, they had a giant rear projection screen, so they needed to put something snazzy up there and pretend it was dramatic. I'll let it pass.

Besides, Asteroids was a really popular video game back in 1989. It's actually got a bit of retro charm.

Back in the 1960s and early 70s, Space travel movies almost always had a meteor shower. I suppose because otherwise, space travel was dead boring. So they'd throw meteors in, and the actors would sit in their rolling chairs and crash couches and suck their cheeks in to look concerned while meteors clanged off the hull, or flaming balls of fire would flash by. You don't see that around nowadays, but back in the day, it was definitely a B-movie thing. So, along with playing on the Arcade Video game motif for the teens in the audience, they're also throwing a nostalgic nod to their parents.

Or maybe it doesn't work. For act two, the Daleks are still mucking about the Tardis and getting on the Doctor's nerves. He learns that the Daleks can't kill him, since the Dalek Emperor wants him alive. He finally gets rid of them by tricking them into thinking the thing is going to blow up.

Karl the Space Mercenary reports back to the Supreme Dalek, and they spend some time blaming each other. You know, the

Doctor's enemies could be so much more effective if they didn't spend all the time bitching each other out and playing passive aggressive games. Just saying.

By the way, David Banks plays Karl, the Space Mercenary. Banks is a big strapping fellow, 6'3", who is famous for playing the Cyber Leader through the 1980s. Seriously - *Earthshock*, the *Five Doctors*, *Attack of the Cybermen*, *Silver Nemesis*... that's all him, in a slightly different helmet than the rest of the Cybermen, saying *"Excellent!"*

Banks got right into it, actually writing a non-fiction book about the Cybermen in 1988, pitching scripts to the show, and even writing a Doctor Who novel for virgin books. He was the Cyber-guy.

I think the Cyber Leader was a little bit of an attempt to do Davros again. An effort to give the Cybermen a central face, a central focus, a personalized villain. Both the Cybermen and the Daleks are pretty faceless and generic when it comes right down to it, and sometimes that undercuts their charm as villains. There's no distinctive identity for the Doctor to banter and match wits with. I think that's why Davros became so successful and dominant in Dalek stories, because he was such a distilled personification of the Daleks. So why not repeat that success and create a Cyber-Leader. If so, it failed, I think largely because they refused to take the bucket off the head - ultimately, the Cyber-Leader's characterization amounted to saying 'excellent' a lot. They were just another Cyberman. Still, Banks got to be the guy, and he rode that pony like there's no tomorrow.

So I suppose it's weird, in this play, there's a Cyber-Leader, and Banks isn't playing him. Instead, there's another actor in the role, and Banks is Carl, the Space Mercenary, swishing about in S&M gear and a cape. Why? I imagine that there was a conversation that went something like this:

Hi, I'm David, you wanted me for the role of Cyber-Leader. Here's my resume, you can see that I've played him several times and written a book about Cybermen.

Terrific, you're perfect. Now, we were just casting these other roles. Could you recommend someone for the part of Karl, the swashbuckling space mercenary?

Hey wait a second, stop right there! You mean there are parts available where I don't have to spend 90 minutes a night for three months sweating inside a flight suit with a giant bucket on my head???

For the record, the Cyber-Leader here is played by the improbably named Wolf Christian, who, a quick IMDB check reveals is a real actor. Go figure. The other Cybermen were played by Paula Tappenden, Oliver Gray and Gavin Warwick. It's hard to believe David didn't sneak his head into the bucket even once, just for old times sake. But there you go. Even the Cyber voices were someone else, Oliver Gray, again.

David Banks was Pertwee's understudy, and actually played the Doctor himself for two nights, when Pertwee was ill. There is apparently an audio record. But sadly, I don't think that a video exists of those performances. Still it's enough to qualify David as a semi-official, BBC licensed and approved, Doctor.

Anyway, where was I?

The Doctor Ditches the Daleks and departs with his damaged device to dire deviltry. Well, basically, the Daleks were trying to take apart the Tardis, when he escaped, so he's fixing it. They land on an unknown planet somewhere in space and time.

They don't know whether it's dangerous or not. Jason decides that there's one way to find out: He decides to go for a walk. Wait! What? I mean, what the hell? Unknown world, no idea where it is, or even when it is. Atmosphere could be

The Second Pirates History, Page 37

poisonous, could be Daleks, monsters, terrible creatures, poisonous critters, you name it, could be anything out there, could be nightclub singers, might be Australia. And Jason just decides that the way to find out is to go for a walk unarmed, no communicator, no nothing. Crystal decides to go with him.

They're immediately eaten by a giant Rat-Bat-Spider Monster rear projected in from *Angry Red Planet*!

Sadly no. Jason and Crystal have a romantic interlude where he reveals he's a refugee from the French revolution, and she reveals she's a nightclub singer, and does another song. And then... and then... And then he joins in, and it's a duet! The horror!

The danger was inside the Tardis all this time!

Well, at least it's really short. But seriously, just because a person can sing doesn't mean they ought to. It's like guns, just because you own one, doesn't mean you should whip it out and shoot someone.

I dunno. Maybe someone likes that sort of thing. It all culminates in Yodeling, which causes them to flee the angry planet. I'm not making this up. The Doctor fixes the Tardis, and to test it out off they go. Once they land, the Doctor invites Jason to step outside to see if it's safe, which tells me that he's getting tired of having Jason around.

As it turns out, they've landed in the middle of the French Revolution. Why the French Revolution? I don't know. Maybe the Theatre Company had the costumes lying around from a previous play. Maybe the French Revolution is theatre friendly, consisting of sloppily dressed people running around and shouting.

And also: Time Travel. Doctor Who travels through time and space. It's pretty meaningless if the Doctor drops in on the past or future of some other planet we've never heard if. So

The Second Pirates History, Page 38

basically, to fulfill the advertising, the Doctor has to go someplace in Earth's history. Otherwise, he's just travelling through space.

Whatever. There's a nifty guillotine prop that gets used a few times. Jason is caught and dragged onto it. But he's saved in the nick of time by an old woman ... who turns out to be the Doctor in Disguise!

That's right folks! Here, ten years before *Curse of Fatal Death*, the Doctor goes gender-bending! Or at least cross dressing. The Doctor dresses up as a woman as a cunning disguise! Take that, Jodie Whittaker! Take that, all you misogynists!

So why couldn't the Doctor be a shoe salesman, or a guillotine repairman, or a rotten fruit vendor. I mean, it's a play, any cockamamie disguise would do.

Truth is, you see a lot of English comedians in drag. Lily Savage, Mother Riley. Hell, you needed a crowbar to get the Pythons out of their dresses. It's a British thing, like conquering India, or inedible food with colourful names, there's something about the English character where the men just have to try on women's clothes.

Oh, and if you're interested in sweet transvestite Doctors, the British Drag Queen, *Lily Savage*, did a five minute Doctor Who sketch for her show, back in 1997. It's on YouTube.

Moving on, Zog throws a bomb, there's a swordfight between Jason and a Revolutionary (Pertwee being a bit too old for such nonsense) and they escape.

Back to Bar Galactica, and Madame Delilah, where the Doctor flirts with Delilah. Fortunately, before anyone is tempted to break into song, she rings in Karl, the Space Mercenary, and a pair of Daleks. Things go south, Delilah dies; the Daleks are killed; Karl has a change of heart, or maybe not...

The Second Pirates History, Page 39

Next scene, Karl and a Dalek is delivering the Doctor and his friends to the Dalek homeworld. But wait, it's a trick. The Dalek is being piloted by Zog. Which means it's an actor playing an alien in an alien costume playing another alien inside another alien costume. Weird. They're all off to rescue the Envoy, and eventually find him, trapped in a force field where he's being brainwashed by recordings from the Emperor Dalek, possibly singing nightclub songs to him. The Doctor goes off to get a doodad to free the Envoy. Meanwhile, the Daleks figure out that they've been infiltrated and sound the alarm. This leads to a bit of Houdini-type magical illusions with the Doctor and Crystal. Why? I have no idea. They were throwing in the kitchen sink, so why not do a bit of David Copperfield?

Ultimately, it doesn't work. Karl switches sides once again. The Daleks capture the Doctor where he's taken to the Emperor. The Emperor Dalek reveals its evil plan to blame everything on the Cybermen and Space Mercenaries. That's right; the great cosmic plan is to be passive-aggressive dicks. Well, it is kind of in character for Daleks.

Understandably, the Cybermen are upset to learn this, and fighting breaks out between the Daleks and the Cybermen. The Doctor and crew escape back to Earth.

Next scene is the peace conference. It turns out that the Envoy was brain washed and activates a bomb. After some panic, the Doctor defuses the bomb by putting it in a teapot.

This might be a callback to Recall Unit: The Great Tea Bag Mystery, which I think solved its problem in a similar way.

But then again, maybe not. Defusing a bomb in a cup of tea is a pretty British solution. After conquering India, inedible food and dressing in women's clothing, having a nice cup of tea is what the British are really known for.

That's about it.

There's a denouement back at the nightclub, where Crystal almost sings again, but is mercifully stopped. The Doctor and Jason show up, and after some dithering, she decides to go off with them.

The End.

Purists will loath the *Ultimate Adventure*. It plays rather too broadly, camps it up a bit, there are musical numbers. It feels less like Doctor Who than a mockery. That's if you are taking the show too seriously.

The reality is it wasn't a television production, it certainly wasn't a serial. Doctor Who in its classical run adopted a serial format of multiple episodes, which in turn required cliff-hangers, a twisty web of subplots maturing steadily to keep the cliff-hangers going, and vivid supporting characters and situation to support the subplots, all of which made for intricate and eccentric storytelling.

Well, sorry, this is theatre. You had two acts and an intermission, and everything had to be fit into that. You couldn't edit or do cutaways, have multiple locations and sets, you had one stage, and everything and everyone had to work around it. You didn't have close ups or fancy camera shots, every actor had to play to the back row as much as to the front row. So of course, it's going to be broad and more than a little tongue in cheek.

You know what this is? This is a medley. Back when I was younger, medleys were a thing. The idea was, you'd take forty seconds of a popular song, and staple it to forty seconds of another popular song, and so on, until you had a play-list length four or five minutes that could be put on the radio. There were all sorts, Star Wars had a medley, I think some popular bands put out medleys of their work. They were so recognizable, you'd be listening, it would be music you'd groove to, you'd be smiling and bobbing along, and then it would change to something else that was also really cool, and you'd just get carried on by the pleasures of familiarity and recognition. They were ungainly Frankenstein pieces of music, but they were oddly compelling. And they were popular, medleys actually made top forty lists, they'd play at dance clubs, people were really into it. It was a strange time.

This is like that. This is and it is not classic Doctor Who, it's both. It's a classic Doctor Who kind of story; it's got all the elements. It has the elements in spades. Fundamentally, it's a story about the Daleks and Cybermen getting together to blow up the Earth, and the Doctor gallivanting around time and space to stop them.

It feels like Doctor Who's greatest hits, a little of this, a little of that. There are all kinds of callbacks. At one point the Doctor actually says 'reverse the polarity on the neutron flow.' Another point, Sara Jane and Jo Grant are mentioned. The Doctor reminisces about teaching Houdini magic and feeding Winston Churchill his 'blood sweat and tears' speech. We got us Daleks, we got us Cybermen, we got an intergalactic space bar with Draconians and Vervoids, Zog rides inside a Dalek (honestly, if they weren't evil, they'd make a killing hiring themselves out for rides), we have the Doctor being rescued from a jam because he's made friends with the aliens in a previous adventure, it's all just nostalgia. More than that, it's played deliberately for the nostalgia.

It's not so much a story in and of itself, as a series of callbacks to previous eras, previous episodes, to tropes and iconic images and ideas about the Doctor, put together in the framework of a story. I'm surprised they didn't include a deliberately wobbly set. It's called the Ultimate Adventure, because it's really a distillation or a compilation of everything that is who.

Even the parts that aren't necessarily Doctor Who callbacks are referencing genre or cultural touchstones. Bar Galactica is inspired by Star Wars, Zog by everything from Ewoks to ET, the Asteroid field is video games and old movies, the drag scene is a British tradition.

Doctor Who, particularly in the Pertwee and the Colin Baker eras, took itself pretty seriously. It had to. You have to sell your menace, your situations to the audience. But the Ultimate Adventure always has a wink and a nod for the audience.

It's a naked appeal to old pleasures, old memories. Remember the time they got out of a jam by capturing a Dalek and riding inside one? Remember the time when a perfect stranger walked into the Tardis by mistake and got caught up in the adventure? Or how about they can't quite pilot the Tardis properly so they end up in places where they get into trouble? That sort of stuff. It's not serious. But then again, it's not mocking. It's not even ironic. It's almost naïve in its innocence. There's a fondness to the proceedings. It's like looking back through a photo album to enjoy the memories.

So in the end, as I've said, what we've got is something that both is and isn't Doctor Who. In many ways, the *Ultimate Adventure* really is a fan production at heart; it's infused with fannish nostalgia, in jokes, the tropes and the icons. So I guess it belongs here.

It's peculiar - less ambitious stage productions, *Planet of Storms, Hellblossom, Vox Dei, Empress of Otherwhen;* I think all came closer to emulating classic Doctor Who, to being something like what we were watching on television, the sort of standard straightforward adventures. But Ultimate Adventure went off that path, to do something both broader and less pure.

I think the *Ultimate Adventure* has to be understood in the context that Doctor Who had become a cultural institution by 1989. By that time, a generation of British children had grown up watching it, it was an integral part of the cultural landscape.

But it was also a cultural institution in decline, on its last legs, its audience almost gone, reduced to a handful of episodes and serials, teetering on the edge of self-parody. These were the dying days of Doctor Who. Literally, within a month after the last performance of the stage play, the decision was made to cancel the series. I think that there was a strong desire to turn back the pages, to go back to when it was fun, and to try and replicate that fun. To when the whole family sat on the couch together, silhouetted by the blue glow of the television set, waiting to see what would happen next for the Doctor.

I think that for a stage audience, particularly for that era, that's the way you had to play it. Particularly for a big stage production. There was no point in just playing it straight - that was already on television, it was in its decline, and no one was watching. You had to play to that cultural institution, and you had to play to memories, to that evocation. You had to distill. You had to write it for a theatrical audience that knew Who as a cultural institution. That's a delicate thing.

But I'll tell you a secret: I kind of liked those old musical medleys. Sure, it was ungainly, bolted and stitched together Frankenstein music, pieces of dead melodies jolted back to half-life. But they made me smile, even if it was just the memory of better real songs.

I watch the *Ultimate Adventure*, and what I see is Colin Baker, for once, having a good time as the Doctor. I watch the *Ultimate Adventure* and I see, once again, Jon Pertwee bringing his archness and dignity to the role. It's Doctor Who in the ways that count for me.

That said, there are shortcomings in the recordings - the sound recording is pretty crap, the image resolution is poor and it's always from a fixed vantage point so the camera doesn't move. Understandable given the limitations of the technology and the circumstances of recording.

But that doesn't take away from the fact that we're watching something that shouldn't even exist for us in the first place. It's kind of a miracle that we have it. Doctor Who's history is littered with things perhaps lost forever – 96 missing episodes, abandoned stories, even abandoned seasons, the *Journey into Time* radio pilot, *Ocean in the Sky* and other ambitious early productions.

So, it's kind of a miracle.

Oh, and small footnote – Of course, Big Finish Productions has done an Audio version of the play, starring Colin Baker. And if you have no idea what Big Finish Productions is… stick around.

CAST: *The Doctor* -*Jon Pertwee (to 3/6, except 29/4 - David Banks understudied) Colin Baker (from 5/6);*

Jason - Graeme Smith (to 15/7, except 22/4 - David Bingham understudied) David Bingham (from 17/7); Crystal - Rebeca Thornhill; Delilah / Mrs T(hatcher) - Judith Hibbert; Zog - Stephanie Colburn; U.S. Envoy - Chris Beaumont; M.C. - David Bingham (to 15/7, except 21-23/4), Oliver Gray (from 17/7); Envoy's Wife - Claudia Kelly; Bell Boy - Stephanie Colburn; U.S. Bodyguards - Troy Webb and Deborah Hecht;

Bar Galactica: *Waitress - Deborah Hecht; Ant-Person - Claudia Kelly; Insect Men - Claudia Kelly, Troy Webb and Alison Reddihough; Vervoid - David Bingham (to 15/7, except 22-23/4) and Gavin Warwick (from 17/7); Chicken-Headed Alien - Paula Tappenden; Hairy Alien - Chris Beaumont (except 29/4); Draconian - Wolf Christian; Customers - Wolf Christian, Claudia Kelly, Troy Webb, Paula Tappenden, Oliver Gray (to 15/7), Alison Reddihough and Gavin Warwick (from 17/7);*

Mercenaries: *Karl - David Banks (except 29/4 Chris Beaumont understudied); Martial Arts Mercenary - Troy Webb; Mercenaries -*

Terry Walsh (to 24/6), Alison Reddihough, Oliver Gray (26/6 to 15/7) and Gavin Warwick (from 15/7);

Daleks: *Emperor Dalek - Troy Webb; Dalek Voices -Chris Beaumont andTroy Webb; Chief Dalek - Paula Tappenden; Dalek Scientist - Chris Beaumont; Daleks - David Bingham (to 15/7, except 21-23/4), Oliver Gray, Troy Webb, Deborah Hecht and Gavin Warwick (from 17/7)*

Cybermen: *Cyberleader - Wolf Christian; Cybermen Voices - Oliver Gray; Cybermen - Paula Tappenden, Oliver Gray (to 24/6) and Gavin Warwick (from 17/7);*

French Revolution: *Executioner - Alison Reddihough; Execution Victim - David Bingham (to 15/7, except 21-23/4), Gavin Warwick (from 17/7); Ragamuffin - Claudia Kelly; Duelling Guards - Terry Walsh (to 24/6),Wolf Christian and Oliver Gray (from 26/6) French Women - Paula Tappenden, Deborah Hecht and Judith Hibbert; French Men - Chris Beaumont, Troy Webb, Oliver Gray (to 26/6), David Bingham (to 15/7, except 21-23/4) and Gavin Warwick (from 17/7);*

CREW: *Written by Terrance Dicks; Directed by Carole Todd; Designer Paul Staples; Music Composer Steven Edis; Daleks Created by Terry Nation; Cybermen Created by Kit Pedler and Gerry Davis; 'Flying by Foy'; Lighting Chris Boyle; Sound by Stage Electrics; Settings built by Suffolk Scenery; 'Zog' mask by Susan Moore; Laser Design Steve Playford; Creative Consultant John Nathan-Turner*

Review: Empress of Otherwhen (1994)

By Permission of Her Majesty, or at least, the BBC

This is a stage play made with the official permission of the BBC, which means it's sort of semi-pseudo something-legitimate.

There have been a few other plays produced with BBC permission. Nick Scovell's *Planet of Storms* and his other Bedlam Productions, Ian's *Karnak Trilogy*, the *Trial of Davros*.

I'm not sure of the legal status or relationship of these plays to the official BBC, or to the big productions - *Seven Keys* and *Ultimate Adventure*. I think, but don't quote me, that mainstream productions like *Seven Keys* and *Ultimate Adventure* had official formal licenses issued by the BBC.

Whereas these other production were in grayer legal territory, something along the lines of the BBC sending a letter saying *'permission given, go ahead, we promise not to sue you.'* Something like that.

Which makes them sort of official, but sort of not. Maybe.

I have the impression that the first great Who fan film, *Ocean in the Sky,* had the benefit of that kind of permission - the BBC telling DWAS *'go ahead, you have our permission, so long as it's just for showing in your club and suchlike'*, which might make *Ocean* semi-official.

Anyway, it's fairly nice of the BBC when you think about it. A lot of American rights holders tend to be a bit more aggressive and combative in asserting their rights. Disney, for instance, had a reputation as acting like piranhas.

In contrast, the BBC seems to have been pretty laid back about the whole thing. Part of that, I suspect, is simply that for a lot of the critical period - the 1990s and early 2000s, Doctor Who was a moribund property, off the air for years, with no prospects of renewal, so they weren't taking it too seriously.

The *Empress of Otherwhen* dates to 1994, and once again, I'm just struck by the amazing creativity and productivity from fans and fan groups during these dark years, 1989 to 2005, when the show was off the air. This was when you had the *Millennium Trap, Phase Four, Regenesis, Resurrection of Evil, Downtime, Shakedown, The Stranger series, the Auton Trilogy,* Timebase Productions, *Reign of Turner,* the Federation's second wave, *Trident,* and just on and on. You had fan films. You had audio adventures pioneered, among others, by the *Audio Visuals* in the mid-eighties. You had the *Reconstructions.* You had all this utterly amazing work produced by people out of sheer love. Wow.

And you have a scattering of semi-official stage plays.

The *Empress of Otherwhen* is the product of one Peter Vialls, who got the idea to do Doctor Who for the Huntingdon Drama Club.

Being in Canada, I have no idea where that it, or how significant or insignificant it is.

Stage drama just tends to be one of those things in England, I suppose, like beating seal pups with clubs is in Canada. Everyone does it.

I would say that after inedible food with colourful names, conquering India, dressing in women's clothes, and tea, that theatre is what the English are really known for.

Empress of Otherwhen is pretty obscure now. Unlike the *Karnak Trilogy*, the script isn't available online, although I suppose it could be.

According to playwright Peter Vialls, one of the performances was recorded on videocamera, and he's still in possession of that recording. But unlike *Planet of Storms* or the *Ultimate Adventure*, that recording hasn't been digitized or uploaded online, so there's no way and no place to see it. Unless you want to track Peter Vialls back to his home, and you really shouldn't.

Information seems to come mainly from a web site established by Peter Vialls himself, back around 2005. Two web pages contain a reasonably detailed synopsis of the plot, a sort of production history of the stage play, and a fair number of photographs.

Beyond that, the Google-Fu gets pretty thin - there's an online newspaper clipping from the Huntington Drama Club, and a few mentions here and there in obscure corners of the internet, but not a lot.

The basic plot: The Doctor and Companion show up in London in the 1960s, and discover its part of the Roman Empire. Turns out that somehow, the Roman Empire never fell and is currently ruled by the Eternal Empress, who has been around... forever. Worse, the Empress has a warrant out for the arrest of the Doctor, which seems prescient, since all this is news to him.

Can you say "Someone's been messing with the timestream?"

I bet you can!

There's some to and fro with the Romans and the Rebels, and eventually we learn that at some point, the Doctor's Tardis collided with a Cyberman time ship and knocked it into ancient Rome. A Roman Empress, Livia, got herself partially cyber-ized to be immortal, killed the Cybermen, killed the Doctor, and lived happily ever after...

I like her, actually.

This story actually anticipated a similar Big Finish audio adventure starring Sylvester McCoy. *Colditz*, from 2001, involved a story where the Seventh Doctor, discovers himself in an altered timeline. It seems that he and Ace were killed in 1944, the Nazi's used her walkman technology to win the war, and create a new future, forcing the McCoy Doctor to try and set things right.

But anyway, back to *Empress of Otherwhen*. Time paradox, Cybermen, Doctor killed, altered timeline...

'Well,' says the Doctor, *'I gots to fix that!'*

So he goes back in time to the Roman era. Turns out the Cybermen are already there, posing as Gods arrived in a flaming chariot. The Doctor gets embroiled in the cut-throat Roman politics of the time, as everyone tries to curry the Emperor Augustus' favour. Meanwhile, although their time ship is incapacitated, the Cybermen are up to a fiendish plot. The Doctor has to avoid being arrested, avoid assassination or execution, and stop both Livia and the Cybermen, which he does by being the Doctor and quite the sneaky bastard.

You're probably thinking, *'Wow, that's a hell of a lot of plot for what must have been a pretty tiny stage, for the Huntington Drama Club.'*

Yes. Yes it was.

It was so much plot, that they actually built an extension to the stage, a sort of platform or balcony which the actors could stand on for certain scenes away from other scenes. They also built themselves a Tardis materialization effect, did a couple of pyrotechnics, and constructed sets and props for Roman Londinium 1960s, the Roman era, and the Cybermen's lair, as well as costumes for both eras.

Contributing to the production value were two *Earthshock* style Cybermen costumes. Either original costumes or very very high quality reproductions. These had been supplied by an outside party, Alex Richards, who was running a company called *Who Books*.

This is an impressive amount of work.

Especially impressive when you consider that there were only supposed to be four performances.

Just four performances.

Due to Alex Richards enthusiasm, it was mounted again, for a fifth performance at Aylcon2, a Doctor Who Convention in Birmingham (the British one), in February, 1995. And since then... passed into history.

So now you know what I know.

Without actually seeing the performance, or seeing a video recording, or reading the script, it's hard to do a review. It's like working blindfolded. But it seems extraordinarily audacious and creative. There's a lot of story here, and there's a lot of ideas, and I'm always impressed by that. Beyond that, what we know of the production design, the effects, the Cyberman suits and the photographs suggest that this would have been enjoyable.

With a critical eye, I think it strikes me that the *Empress of Otherwhen*, is actually two stories, which don't appear to mesh terribly well. The first story has the Doctor trying to evade Romans and Rebels and figure out what's going on in an alternate universe Earth. The second story, the second act goes back to the beginnings of that alternate earth, and the events that created it, but I don't get the sense that the Doctor specifically derails the events that allowed Livia to kill the Doctor and enact her two thousand year rule.

Nevertheless, this actually compares favourably to a lot of the classic era stories. I could see Colin Baker giving his left arm to have been able to do a story like this - or Davison, or McCoy. It's fun, complicated, there's a lot going on, a bunch of twists and turns, room for characters to develop, and the stakes rise continually. You don't know where it's going to go, which is fun.

Of course, a lot comes down to the quality of the writing. I can't say much about that, except that Peter managed to get the entire Drama Club to go along with him, and Alex Richards was enthusiastic enough to arrange an encore performance.

Peter seems to have started writing this around 1991/1992. They asked for rights well in advance, and experienced a long delay, receiving them in May, 1994. Given the play dates to November, 1994, that seems like a long gestation, and probably, a reasonably polished piece of work.

Several years later, Vialls wrote a second Doctor Who play, called *Sleepers in the Marsh*, about 18th century smugglers and sea devils. The idea sounds fascinating, this is a rich era that the Doctor hasn't visited since the Hartnell days, and the Sea Devils feel like a perfect match.

Unfortunately, this time the BBC declined to give permission, and so the play has gone unproduced and unpublished. He shows no impulse to put that one on line either.

I would note that following *Legends of the Sea Devils*, I asked to read *Sleepers in the Marsh*, and Peter was kind enough to provide me with a copy.

Legends of the Sea Devils is the penultimate Jody Whittaker Doctor story, and to be as kind as possible, it's a dumpster fire composed of farts and medical waste, filled with screaming kittens thrown in there by laughing sadists who are getting paid to squat over keyboard. It's sub-par and awful, especially the writing in every possible way short of randomly smearing excrement over the walls of an art gallery. It's actually amazing that it could go so horribly wrong in so many different ways.

So I asked for *Sleepers in the Marsh*, knowing it was a Sea Devils story in order to get the lingering residue of *Legends* out of my brain. It was actually quite a good piece of work, better than *Legends of the Sea Devils* by full kilometers, and quite a shame it was never produced.

The story is set in a small coastal community in the smuggler's era. It seems that some smugglers, in extending their tunnels, have woken a small group of Sea Devils. The reptilians are pretty appalled by how things have turned out, but they've hatched an ingenious plot to set things right – they're going to build a time machine, go back in prehistory and make sure that all these stinky apes don't evolve. That'll show em.

It's kind of a stupid plan and well beyond their abilities, but it feels authentic, like something they came up with, knowing it's unworkable, but desperate to have a reason to keep from killing themselves because their situation is so hopeless. Honestly, it feels like the situation could have been resolved if they'd just had a good therapist. Of course, their half-baked experiments with time cause the Tardis to hiccup, which brings the Doctor in.

The story is complex but well constructed. The human characters are nicely drawn and diverse, particularly a mysterious woman with a book that seems to lay out the future. Even the Sea Devils are well done, each one a distinct character, some of whom are quite likable.

In short, I'd have much rather watched this one. Oddly, and I'm not sure why, it feels very much a 6th Doctor adventure.

Peter Vialls has published four fantasy novels, *Impcatcher*, *Sorrel in Scarlet*, *Sorrel in Silver* and *Sorrel Snowbound*, which are available from online stores. Feel free to buy them. Seriously, check them out, pick them up, support a fellow Who fan.

Apart from writing Doctor Who plays, and fantasy novels, Peter appears to be a dedicated fan, role playing gamer, amateur artist, figure painter, husband, father, barrister, cat owner.

CAST: The Doctor - Robert Pugh; Gwen (the companion) - Rachel Greaves; Cormac (celtic rebel/ new companion) - Andy Kibbey; Rhiannon (celtic rebel) - Ruth Cooper; Siobhann (celtic rebel) - Beth Pugh; Rhodri - Bob Kretowicz; Livia (Eternal Empress/Augustus' Wife) - Maggie Redgrave ; Emperor Augustus - Jack Hyde; Maecenas (Emperor's friend) - Gerry Davison; General Varus (Livia's Henchman) - Adrian Riglesford; Julia (Emperor's niece) - Debbie Mather; Tiberius - Ivan Mahon; Cyberman #1 - Paul Sweeney; Cyberman #2 - Adam Greaves; Roman Soldiers - ? [ED: Sharp eyed readers will note the name Adrian Riglesford, playing Empress Livia's Henchman, General Varnus. Is this the same Adrian Riglesford who wrote "Lost in the Dark Dimensions", the almost produced 1993 anniversary special? One wonders.]

CREW: Ruth Morgan - Director; Christopher Hunnam, Bob Beattie, Karen Beattie, John Morgan - Production crew; Bob Wilson - Sound Expert; Nick Thompson - Original Music; Alex Richards (Who Books) - Cyberman Costumes;

Review: The Karnak Trilogy (1999-2002)

Hellblossom, Vox Dei and Warsmith

So, what's this all about then? Today, I thought I'd talk about the *Karnak Trilogy*. I'm not sure that anyone else uses that term. But so what?

The *Karnak Trilogy* is a trio of Doctor Who stage plays: *Hellblossom, Vox Dei* and *Warsmith,* with the continuing companion, Karnak, Prince of Jocasta, written and performed between 1999 and 2002, by Ian Wheeler of Broken Suitcase Theatre Company. All apparently produced, with BBC permission, back when the BBC was pretty relaxed about this stuff, so it's semi-pseudo official.

Wheeler seems to have been a prolific playwright. Apart from his Doctor Who plays, he did a series of *Buck Rogers* inspired dramas about *'Crash Morgan'* which started as a mock radio play, and turned into a trilogy of theatrical serials. Other plays included *Sherlock Holmes* and the *Devil's Tallyman, Theatre Blood and Tales from the Jungle Book, Power League Murders* and *Pyramid of Death*. He was a director, an actor, a graphic artist, designed costumes, composed music and CGI and occasionally cross dressed. He seems like a fascinating guy and his inventive riffs on pop culture are right up my alley.

Wheeler, sadly, passed away in February, 2005, at the age of thirty-six, from meningitis.

I'm really sorry that he passed, I'm sure he would have kept on doing interesting things. I would have loved to have met him.

All too often, good people, talented people fall away from us, leaving no real trace. The world is full of marvelous works abandoned and forgotten. Even now, I'm not giving Ian full due. I'm not paying attention to *Crash Morgan*, or any of the rest of his body of work. I'm just looking at his Doctor Who. Which is a shame, and perhaps sometime, I'll go back and explore the rest of this remarkable man's legacy.

But Ian was lucky, in that he had friends and associates who cared about him enough to try and preserve his legacy. So, there was a tribute web site maintained for well over a decade, with all his stuff on it. Seriously, a ton of stuff. His scripts, production photographs, posters, bio, you name it. That's really a testament, that people cared that much.

When I go, my only legacy will probably be a well-used wood-chipper. Makes me sad.

But anyway, I'm not sure if it's still up, but while it was, you could actually go and read Ian Wheeler's original Doctor Who scripts, you can see the posters, see photographs of the actors, the costumes, get a little info on the history of the scripts. Just google '*Crash Morgan*.' Even now, I'm sure that you could probably track that stuff down with a little work. Wheeler's friends are still out there.

There was actually an invitation on the site for anyone who was interested to take this and do their own production, and they'd even provide you with graphics and titles.

I mean, wow. That's just cool.

Ian even made videotapes of some of the performances, and they've circulated a bit here and there. They're not online anywhere that I know of. So it's one of those that you'd have to do some legwork.

But another company, Exit Theatre, actually mounted two of these productions, recorded them on video. And uploaded those Videos to YouTube! So you can actually watch these plays.

I think that this is unbelievably cool. Along with the two versions of *Ultimate Adventure*, the *Planet of Storms*, this means that there are at least five Doctor Who stage plays available to watch and download.

So let's talk about them. Overall, as I've said, the unifying element is Prince Karnak of Jocasta. He's got a bit of history alluded through the plays, last survivor of the Jocastan royal family, refugee from a civil war, an ungainly lout with a rather high opinion of himself, but with a good heart deep down, and he's got a bit of an arc as he tries to find his way through the world. He's blue or green skinned, depending on the production.

Now, the thing is, these are stage plays, so heavy on dialogue and banter, characters bouncing off each other. The dialogue is the nicest thing about these. The Doctor has always traded on eccentricity, and it captures that feel nicely. Williams Doctor(s) have quite a bit of Oscar Wilde in their DNA, always ready with a knowing quip. And to be fair, good guys and bad guys are just as light on the feet and ready with retorts. It's genuinely fun to read.

There's a scene in *Vox Dei* where a character introduces herself as Jet Turbo, for instance and Karnak's reply is '*No you're not!*' It's a dumb name, what sort of mother would call her child Jet Turbo. Later, a character called Deathsbane comes and once again, Karnak gives him the gears. It's fun.

The stage productions that we're able to see aren't bad. For one thing, the video quality, particularly for *Vox Dei*, is a lot better than we've seen for either *Planet of Storms* or *Ultimate Adventure*. There are a couple of reasons for that - first the technology is simply better, period. And of course, this was an acknowledged not illicit taping, so the camera didn't have to hide, was probably mounted on a tripod, they used zooms and even camera movements. In *Hellblossom*, the camera actually shifts position for different scenes, giving a slightly more cinematic feel

There are downsides. This is a recording of a stage play, and so you have all those limits. The actors being confined to a fairly narrow stage, the lighting being oriented for the stage cues, everyone is doing 'theatrical acting' so there's a lot more projection than there is nuance, and of course the sound is pretty rough, with lots of reverb.

Look, it's one of those things. You either accept these limitations, get past them, and proceed to enjoy the production on its own; or you don't. If you can't, just read the scripts, they're not bad at all.

Now, if we're ready...

HELLBLOSSOM
(January 26-29, 2000,
Stage Play, United Kingdom)

First appeared at the New Theatre Royal, in Portsmouth, by Broken Suitcase; Mounted again by Arena Arts & Entertainment in Perth, Australia in 2003; Mounted for a third production by Exit Theatre Productions, 2010, videotaped by Exit Theatre in 2013.

It's Victorian England in the 1890s, and Springheel Jack is on the loose. Inspector Potts is on the job, and recruits consulting detective Professor Gardner to help him. The Doctor shows up with his companion, Valkyrie warrior woman, Sha'Atara, from New Asgard, to help out. Meanwhile, an 'Elephant-man' like hybrid is trying to hold it together, making a living as a side show exhibit, and plagued by dreams of murder, as gangsters blackmail her and her manager...

From the photographs of the original production, it looks like they built a half decent Tardis console, and the Hybrid ended up being creepy looking as all hell. The original production was videotaped, and a few copies of these are floating around with collectors, but don't seem to be uploaded anywhere. There's a photograph of the cast from the Australian production, but I don't know if there's a video record, certainly it hasn't been uploaded.

The available video of the Exit Theatre production, which isn't bad. There's electronic opening titles and some rear screen projection in one sequence, I believe designed by Williams, with music by Mark Ayres. The sets pieces are fairly elaborate - a couple of faux walls and a rather free form Tardis console, particularly given the size of the stage. This is one of those 'Indy' theatres, so the audience literally goes right up to the edge of the stage. Literally, an audience member could stick their foot out and trip an actor, that kind of close. The lighting involves soft yellows and browns, giving it the look and feel of old time photographs.

Obviously, there are differences - a different cast. Professor Gardener undergoes a gender change and is, played by a woman. The hybrid's design also shifts, less malevolently creepy, and more plant-like.

Of the two Exit Theatre productions, this is more overtly cinematic. The camera changes location several times, giving us scenes from different angles, there's more pans, and occasional close ups. You can't get away from the fact that this is a stage play, but some of the shifts are quite effective.

This is classic Victoriana - with allusions to everything from *Sherlock Holmes* to the *Talons of Weng Chiang*, from *Terror of the Vervoids* to *Seeds of Doom*. Karnak, Professor Gardener, Sha'Atara and Inspector Potts are all nicely fleshed out, the plot moves along briskly, with a suitable number of twists.

It's a fun script, full of banter and twists, and it nicely captures the feel of Doctor Who. This is one of those stories that feels like it would fit in both the classic and the new era. It's enjoyable, and worth searching out.

VOX DEI
(April 18 to April 23, 2001, Stage Play, United Kingdom)

Originally appeared, at New Theatre Royal, Portsmouth, by Broken Suitcase. It was re-mounted by Exit Theatre, in 2003. At that time, the BBC was getting sticky with its permissions, so the Doctor was renamed the Exile, a mysterious wanderer in Time and Space, the Tardis became a regular Time Machine, and it was called a 'Doctor Who Homage.' It was uploaded to YouTube in March, 2014.

A squad of Colonial Marines is trapped aboard a space station about to blow up; a mysterious Chimera monster is decimating their ranks, killing their pilot and bomb technician. Things are looking grim.

More grim than they realize - the station is built on the edge of a black hole, and it's created a point singularity as a weapon - a universe waiting to go 'big bang' - with unfortunate results for this one. The Time Lords send the Doctor and Karnak in to stop it.

When they get there, and hook up with the Colonial Marines, they learn that one of the station's scientists has gone rogue and is hiding somewhere. It seems that he was a religious fanatic bent on blowing up the universe to replace it with something better. Meanwhile, the alien race that humanity is fighting is on its way to the station. With aliens invading, a monster on the loose and a renegade scientist skulking about, the Doctor has his hands full.

Who can he trust?

The Second Pirates History, Page 61

This really does play like the Doctor Who version of *Aliens* - particularly the scenes with the Colonial Marines. There's a dead ringer for Bill Paxton's Hicks going 'we're gonna die!' There's the untrustworthy corporate type. There's a 'Xenomorph' and even an android. It's definitely a more ambitious play, far more action oriented, and more nakedly sci fi.

Hellblossom took time out to flesh out its characters, and even kindle a romance, it structured like a Victorian mystery. Vox Dei is an action movie, with characters reduced almost to stock. It's floated by a witty script, with the Doctor and Karnak bouncing easily off each other.

Again, the original production apparently was recorded, and copies ended up with collectors, but it was never uploaded. There is an uploaded video rendition of the performance by Exit Productions makes use of extensive CGI cutaways by Ian Williams showing the exterior of the space station, corridors, and even gives us a new version - the Time Machine resembles an old WWII sea mine, rather than the police box. But in every respect, this is straight up Doctor Who. Hell, the 4th Doctor's gigantic scarf is clearly visible in the background.

Despite the more cinematic quality of the script, Exit Theatre's production feels much more stage bound than Hellblossom. The camera, as far as I can tell, doesn't shift position at all. It might zoom in once or twice, but overall, it's pretty stationary. The lighting is brighter and oddly flatter, without that moody quality that we saw in Hellblossom. The static camera and lighting takes a little bit away from the proceedings. This is an action movie kind of script, and so we're used to a livelier camera, swoops, zooms, set ups and shots that emphasize the action component, the fact that events are ceaselessly unwinding.

In other ways, though, the more straightforward narrative works well with the production. This is a play about people going places and doing things, with the clock ticking away relentlessly. The performers give proceedings an urgency and a conviction, and the confined space of the stage provides a certain amount of claustrophobia.

Here, the acting is especially stagey, with characters practically shouting their lines, and the echo of the theatre space can be distracting. All I can say is fair warning - you live with it.

The principal weakness of the production is the Chimera, which looks pretty sad. The photograph of the Chimera from the original production, in contrast is terrifying. Also, the costume for Deathsbane is at best middling, whereas the original production was all Flash Gordon splendour. Still, these are minor objections, you take the good with the bad.

Again, witty banter, lots of twists, it's a kinetic story that races along, and manages to have that Doctor Who feel.

WARSMITH
(November 6 - 9, 2002,
Stage Play, United Kingdom)

Warsmith appeared at the New Royal Theatre, Portsmouth, for its one and only production, so far as I know. There is a two minute YouTube clip uploaded in 2006, featuring a mix of live action and CGI animation which was done for the production - Warsmith: Dogfight. Again, this was recorded but never uploaded. The script and a fairly detailed website is online.

The story is set in WWII. A mysterious drone is kidnapping scientists from England and spiriting them away to England where they are being put to work by the Nazis. An alien warrior is behind it, using the scientists to help repair his spaceship and promising to reduce London to ruins in exchange for Nazi assistance. One of the scientists has a device to summon the Doctor, who shows up with Karnak in tow. But things go awry from the start when the drones kidnap both Alan Turing and the Doctor. It turns out that the stranded warrior is a Jocastan, from Karnak's world, caught up in the civil war that arose from the Prince's abdication. Karnak's fate is catching up with him....

Sadly, except for the clip, I've not seen video to this one. It's a fun script which plays with a historical celebrity, and resolves Karnak's arc. There are some production photographs. Decent Tardis console once again. The Warsmith's armour is impressive. Not much more to say. As a bonus, there is an online comic 'The Women Warriors of Mantubu' featuring the further adventures of the Doctor, the Contess and Karnak.

Review: Trials of Tara (1998)

The Kandyman Returns

The only known Canadian Doctor Who stage production, *Trials of Tara* began innocently enough with a novella published by Paul Cornell, in *Decalogue 2*, in 1995.

The story was a bit of a lark. It's a sequel to Tom Baker's *The Androids of Tara;* but also a sequel to *The Happiness Patrol;* since the Kandyman from that serial makes an appearance. There's also a fair bit of borrowing (inspiration) from Shakespeare's *Midsummer Night's Dream*, with Oberon and Titania, as well as Miranda from *The Tempest*, and the witches from *MacBeth*. Cornell wrote and structured it as a play, and just to show off, he did the whole thing in iambic pentameter.

Fast forward a couple of years to a young actor in Winnipeg, Manitoba, named Tim Webster. Webster and his wife, Xam, had a small production company. He was also a major sci fi fan, and had been a member of the local Doctor Who club.

He found the story, thought it was absolutely brilliant, fresh and fun. He realized it was producible. You could actually produce *Trials of Tara* as a stage play. Convinced it could be a fringe hit, he mounted it at the Winnipeg Fringe, in July, 1998. The production was immensely ambitious.

Local actor and musician, Roger Leeder played the Seventh Doctor. They reproduced the costume, down to the sweater vest with all the question marks. He'd open up by playing the Doctor Who theme on a ukulele before someone would take it away from him in a visual gag.

The cast was immense - thirty-two people, with some double casting roles. Tim Webster himself would sneak in, playing various non-speaking parts at different showings. The Kandyman costume was made with a great many coloured bath sponges. But for the rest, Tim was able to borrow period costumes from another production company he worked with.

Already full of homages through Cornell, Webster added more from various science fiction franchises. Two are especially worth mentioning.

One is the character of Grendel, the antagonist. Visually, he was modeled after Matt Wagner's comic book character *Grendel*, with a black and white mask, and forked spear.

The other homage was stage Jawas. Through the course of the play, a lot of characters (androids) get killed. This is basically a one act play on a fringe stage, so the problem was how do you remove the dead bodies? Do they just clutter up the stage and the actors have to keep stepping over them? Do the 'dead' actors just get up and walk off? That ruins the illusion.

The solution was stage ninjas, who were dressed as Jawas from the first *Star Wars* movie that come out, bickering and squabbling away like in the movie, load the bodies onto dollies and cart them off. It was an exotic and comic way to deal with the problem and entertain the audience at the same time. At the end of the play, the Jawas would be behind the actors, and they'd get a second ovation.

The play's musical cues were also borrowed from a number of different science fiction films and television shows. Something that fans recognized.

I actually had the pleasure of seeing at the Fringe that year. It was bold and unique, Doctor Who crossed with Shakespeare, with everyone declaiming in Shakespearean English and iambic pentameter. I even got to meet the cast.

Disaster almost struck. While the production was getting underway, a local Winnipeg Doctor Who fan notified Paul Cornell.... Who hadn't actually given permission. Webster had been a bit naive and enthusiastic, assuming that having bought the book would be authorization enough to put on the play.

It doesn't quite work like that.

Fortunately, Cornell was tickled pink by the idea of someone mounting a stage production of his play. So he had his agent give permission for a nominal fee, and that problem solved itself.

A decade later, I ended up meeting Cornell at a World Fantasy Convention, and when he found out I was from Winnipeg, the first thing he wanted to know was whether I'd ever heard of his play there!

I don't think that they actually got the permission of the BBC to use Doctor Who. But frankly, I'm not sure that anyone in the BBC could have found Winnipeg on a map. This was in 1998. Doctor who had been dead on television for nine years, the movie had flopped two years before, and it was still seven years from revival. Big Finish hadn't really begun to ramp up. The franchise was as close to dead as it had ever been. So it's not like they were going to go ballistic over a small production company's fringe show in an obscure city somewhere out on the Canadian prairie.

It ran, I believe, eight performances. When all was said and done, they had made a net profit of about two hundred dollars - a hundred pounds. It wasn't quite the hit they'd hoped for. They got decent crowds for the venue, but it was an expensive production, huge cast, and a very crowded fringe with lots of competing shows.

When it was over, Webster called the cast together, asked if they wanted to divide the money up, or just use it for a pool party. Everyone opted for the party, which is very Canadian. That's about it.

In case you're wondering, it was recorded on video. That's apparently still around in Webster's library, but it's never been digitized. I'm not sure that the machine to play that particular videocassette is still operating. But at least it's hypothetically there waiting. I'm trying to encourage Tim to do so. I think Paul Cornell would love and certainly deserves a copy, and I'd definitely put in for one.

Tim and his wife continued on in theatre, and have raised lovely children. They're still friends with most of the cast.

Review: The Three Trials of Davros (1989, 1993, 2012)

Intuitively, the *Trial of Davros* seems like a terrible subject for a stage play.

Not the trial part. Trials are almost always good cheap drama. Basically, a single set, clearly defined roles of protagonist, antagonist, defender, prosecutor, judge and witness. Everybody knows the format, we all know what a Courtroom looks like and how it works. There's a long and vivid history of court-room drama in theatre, television and movies. It's just hard, but not impossible, to screw up.

On the other hand, Davros seems like death for an actor. Think about it, the character is literally immobile, trapped in a high tech wheelchair, barely able to move one palsied limb. Actors emote with their eyes, their facial expressions, but Davros is blind, his face is a latex fright mask. An actor's voice is their tool, but Davros voice is never less than a barely modulated psychopathic shriek.

Yeah, I want that on my stage. That's got hit written all over it.

It just shouldn't work. It's like writing a stage play with a wooden block as a character. It would be like playing a twitchy, malicious block of wood on stage.

It makes you wonder what they were thinking?

And why bother?

But it actually does work out, because Davros is such a vivid creation. I still remember that scene in *Genesis of the Daleks* where the Doctor debates Davros, and the father the Daleks literally goes into orgiastic rapture at the thought of a genocidal virus. I don't think anyone who's watched it will ever forget it.

There's something about Davros. He's just pure unalloyed evil; there are no redeeming qualities, there are no doubts, there are no second thoughts. He just is. He's savagely intelligent, treacherous and ruthless, and without a trace of remorse. He's terrifying. And he's almost pitiable. Scarred, blind, paralyzed, in a wheelchair. His only weapon is his mind. He's this strange combination of dangerousness and helplessness. Crippled brilliance and malevolent genius.

He's like Evil Steven Hawking.

Or since he came first, perhaps Steven Hawking was Good Davros.

Davros strange combination of physical helplessness, cunning and unrestrained malice is unique. This is a character who is unapologetically the personification of hatred. He's weirdly compelling. He was supposed to die in his first story, a disposable one off character. But he was so arresting, they brought him back against Tom Baker, Peter Davison, Colin Baker, David Tennant and Peter Capaldi. He literally outshone his own Daleks, and permanently rewrote Dalek canon.

He is one of only two great recurring Villains that Doctor Who ever produced. It's him and the Master.

Still despite all that, when you factor in the latex mask, blindness, complete lack of expression, immobility and hysterical voice, you'd figure he'd be complete death to play on stage.

The Second Pirates History, Page 70

Go figure. Nevertheless, the idea that somehow, somewhere, someone decided that the Davros would be a good subject for a stage play seems incredible.

And not just once, but three times.

THE FIRST TRIAL
(Dalek Con, 1989)
Stage Play, United Kingdom)

The first appearance of Davros on stage was at Julian Vince's Dalek convention, and we barely know much more than that.

Julian Vince is a major Doctor Who fan. He was involved in several Super 8 fan films in the late seventies – *The Destructors, the Thosian Strategy, the Image Makers and Mission of Doom*. He was a prop and model builder extraordinaire and a true Dalek fanatic. His work can be seen online in clips and photographs from *Mission of Doom*.

Back in September 2, 1989, he almost singlehandedly put on a Dalek Themed Sci Fi Convention, featuring a number of actors from the show, including Dalek operators.

To quote from Julian Vince's website: "*I managed to get personal appearances from original (and best) Davros actor, Michael Wisher, his 'sidekick' Nyder, actor Peter Miles,*

Just as an aside, in the original *Genesis of the Daleks*, Davros was just a creepy paralyzed guy with an immobile rubber face. I'm not sure that anyone expected him to become an iconic recurring villain. He could barely move his arm. To flesh the character out, he was given a sidekick / henchman / patsy, the character of Nyder, played by Peter Miles.

Nyder doesn't survive the end of Genesis of the Daleks. For that matter, neither did Davros. But Davros was weird and creepy so they kept bringing him back. While Nyder... Nyder was surplus to requirements, and killed off in his first story. Still, *Genesis of the Daleks* is one of those iconic Who stories, so the character of Nyder and his actor, Peter Miles, still had some cachet.

September 2, 1989. This was just weeks after the *Ultimate Adventure* concluded, and four days before *Battlefield*, the first serial of the final season, began on September 6, 1989, to conclude on December 6, 1989, with *Survival*. There's an element of melancholy to that, these were the dying days, the final gasps of Doctor Who.

Still, he gave it his all.

"I also commissioned a young Paul Cornell, another new series writer, to write a couple of brief plays starring Davros and Nyder, which were performed by the respective actors, to the audience at the event."

And thus, the first stage appearance, the first of three Davros stage plays.

Paul Cornell was barely 22 years old then. This may have been some of his earliest work. His Wikipedia bibliography lists a couple of Doctor Who comics credits from 1990. Since, then, he went on to write Doctor Who novels and Screenplays and a substantial career as a writer, including episodes of Doctor Who and *Primeval*.

We don't know that it was a trial actually. We don't know much of anything about it, except that the two original actors went on stage to play their original characters, with a real writer with a genuine feel for the show providing the script and dialogue. That's impressive.

I doubt that there's any record of those early plays. Maybe someone switched on a camcorder for posterity. Maybe the scripts are still around somewhere in Cornell's or Vince's old files. It's more than possible it may have amounted to very little, a few minutes of tomfoolery. Or possibly, Cornell and the actors tried for something more substantial.

There is a possibility - in 1993, Cornell was writing a Doctor Who comic strip which featured Davros being put on trial. No sign of Peter Miles' character Nyder, but it did feature the Sixth Doctor and Peri, and was an elaborate attempt to bridge the serials *Remembrance* and *Revelation*. The comic were collected as a graphic novel called *Emperor of the Daleks*, so it's just possible that Cornell recycled some of his work from his old plays from 1989 and incorporated them into the comic strips.

And of course, in 1921, a fan with the username Dalek Seth, used the trial sections of the graphic novel to create a twenty-two minute *Emperor of the Daleks* CGI fan film.

With only four years separating them, it's tempting to connect the two, and I suppose someone ought to ask Paul Cornell someday.

But for now, they're one of these tantalizing lost bits of history.

THE SECOND TRIAL
(Hyde Fundraiser, 1993, Stage Play, United Kingdom)

The second appearance was the *Trial of Davros*, back at a Doctor Who convention on November 14, 1993. This time the production was the brainchild of Nigel Peever.

Back in the late eighties, early 1990s, Nigel Peever and his friends were at the center of a group of interlocking fan production 'companies', called variously Planet Video, Pacific UK and Ad-Lib films. It looks like it was the same overall group of people involved, and the differences seemed chiefly who was spearheading a particular project. Collectively, they made a number of Doctor Who fan films of various styles and quality, some of which were brilliant, some not so much, some were vignettes, and some ended unfinished and abandoned.

Nigel Peever was responsible for two brilliant fan productions - *The Experiment*, a recreation of the *Sontaran Experiment*, with Cybermen in its place, and *Spectre From the Past*, a 'Hammer-esque' two-part serial, featuring the 2nd and 5th Doctor, where Peever played the 2nd Doctor. Peever had a third major project, *Second Spawn*, involving the 7th Doctor, the rescue of Adric, Nazis, the Master and a plot involving Krynoids, that was partially shot. He later helped out on Simon Williams's Timestealers series, featuring the Master. And he's been a successful English Actor and writer, beyond Doctor Who.

Other alumni from Planet / Pacific-Uk / Ad-Lib were Stuart Glazebrook, who played a version of the fourth Doctor in

Ad-Lib's Labyrinth of the Blud Devils, as well as Kevin Taylor and Hylton Collins.

Nigel Peever and Kevin Taylor were on record as the Producer. The script for this version of *Trial of Davros* was written by Kevin Taylor and Michael Wisher.

Wisher starred as his original character Davros, Peter Miles reprised his role as Nyder, Davros henchman from Genesis of the Daleks, Stuart Glazebrook played a prosecutor, and the cast was rounded out by Jean Rodgers as Inquisitor, and Keith Noble as another Prosecutor.

The story is straightforward: The Time Lords abduct Davros from just before his apparent death at the end of *Genesis of the Daleks*, and put him on trial for his crimes against the universe. The position of the 'Inquisitor' by the way is from Colin Baker's Trial of a Time Lord.

This seems like a dickish move by the Time Lords, since at that point, Davros' Daleks are just getting started, and neither Davros nor his Daleks have actually committed any of their interstellar evil. Literally, they're putting him on trial for things he hasn't actually done yet. Does anyone else see a problem with that?

Davros takes things in stride however, arguing brilliantly in his own defense, making the Time Lords look like fools, and generally having fun with proceedings.

And as it turns out, the whole thing was just a clever ruse. The whole trial was actually Davros running a Trojan horse scheme to buy time while he opened up a worm hole to Gallifrey so his Daleks could come and kick Time Lord ass. The proceedings have basically amounted to Davros running the clock until he was ready to make his move.

Which doesn't really make sense, when you think of it. Unless some much later version of Davros somehow switched out with his earlier self at the very start, right under the Time

Lords noses, without them noticing. We don't know, but I'd hope there was at least a line of dialogue to that effect.

Sorry to spoil the ending for you, but this was 1993, get over it.

Also, WWII? Hitler lost.

One thing that's fascinating is how neatly this story fits in with the whole backstory of the Time War that would play a prominent role when Doctor Who re-launched in 2012. For over a decade, the new series continually referred to the Great Time War between the Time Lords and the Daleks. But here it is twelve years earlier.

I can't help but be impressed - we have Wisher returning along with Peter Miles, to the roles they originally created. Literally, these are the original actors from Genesis of the Daleks, come home to recreate their parts. Wisher takes it a step further, helping to write the character. That's enthusiasm.

And to guild the lily, Nigel Peever actually shot a three minute short of a Dalek trundling around London murdering a group of very young UNIT soldiers, for an introduction, making this something of a multi-media production. This segment is actually still available, should you care to hunt it down on YouTube.

How did a group of fans, even fan film makers, managed to persuade a series of real working actors to come together so enthusiastically in a stage play?

Charity.

There was something called a Hyde fundraiser, dating back to 1985. Basically, fans would dress up in costumes, and put on a production of some sort. Over the years, there have been Star Wars and Star Trek themed productions, probably a few anime, whatever is popular. In thirty-five years, I'd have expected that they'd have covered everything a few times, particularly Doctor Who. It's not clear what the productions are, possibly pantomimes and sketches, musical variety shows, or displays. I have the impression that stage drama was fairly rare.

So far as I know, apart from the three minute Dalek invasion of London segment, no audio or video record exists of this production. The technology was there back in that day, but there's no indication it happened. This was a one night only, blink and you miss it production.

Otherwise, Copies of the original script might survive in the possession of Peever or a few others, as well as photographs, playbills and the usual detritus of the stage. But mostly, it exists as just a memory.

I suspect that for all intents and purposes, it's mostly gone.

THE THIRD TRIAL
(Hyde Fundraiser, 2012,
Stage and Video, United Kingdom)

The third iteration came July 16, 2005, with a new version of the *Trial of Davros*. This followed literally a month after the close of the first season of the relaunched Doctor Who under Christopher Ecclestone, and was produced with the express permission of both the BBC and the Terry Nation estate, making it semi-official, even pseudo-canonical.

Hey, it's the Time War, anything goes.

This new version was expanded in a number of ways. Kevin Taylor, now Chairman of Hyde Fundraiser, and Michael Wisher wrote additional scenes and dialogue, which in turn was expanded on by Terry Malloy.

Who was Terry Malloy? He was literally the third person to play Davros, and played the character through the three 1980s appearances - Revelation, Remembrance and Resurrection of the Daleks.

This time, it was Malloy rather than Wisher returning to play Davros.

Peter Miles though, was back, recreating his character of Nyder, for the third time on stage.

Also joining the cast were John Leeson, best known as the voice of K9, Brian Miller, a Doctor Who actor and husband of Liz Sladen,

A few more names are worth mentioning - Hylton Collins, from the Planet/Pacific UK/Ad-Lib collective is back; a new face appears in the form of Jeremy Bulloch, who has no previous Doctor Who connection, but did play Boba Fett in *Star Wars*; Andrew Wisher appears, he's the son of Michael Wisher; and finally Katarina Olson rounds out the cast.

Another key figure is Philip T. Robinson, who is not part of the cast. Robinson was originally part of the Timebase fan group that produced films like *Regenesis* and *Phase Four*. His forte is masks and costumes. He re-created Davros mask for the production, as well as a life-like face for the Delgado Master, and did Draconians, Exillons, Ogrons and other creature masks for video inserts. Robinson is just brilliant.

The story is much the same as the previous version, albeit expanded. The Time Lords decide to be officious jerks by kidnapping Davros from the beginning and putting him on trial for things he hadn't actually done yet. Davros puts up a good defense, and then in the final scenes turns it all around when he reveals it's all part of his plot to invade Gallifrey, or harvest Time Lord DNA, or steal the secrets of the Matrix… or something.

The Time Lords begin as jerks, finish as fools, and Davros is left cackling in victory, evil triumphant.

Now, the difference between this and the two previous stage productions is that this time we actually have a recording.

Not video, but an audio recording of the trial.

Okay, that's not perfect, but it's not bad. And seriously, this is a courtroom drama about a guy in an almost expressionless rubber mask, in a wheelchair, engaged in verbal fencing with his accusers. We're not here for the visual spectacle; this isn't *Seven Keys to Doomsday*. If you're going to have a stage production reduced to audio… this is the one to do it.

So what's it like?

The recording is a lot of fun. Malloy's in his element as Davros, and you can feel the malicious glee of the character, as he slowly drags the trial off the rails, meticulously dismantling proceedings. As he verbally fences with the Time Lord prosecutors, you can sense their frustration as things fail to go the way they'd planned, and this crippled being runs rings around them. Despite being the most evil man in the universe, you find yourself rooting for Davros, as he's confronted with a system so obviously rigged against him, and yet manages to steadily overcome it.

At the end, when he reveals it's all a ruse and he's played them, there's a wonderful sense of 'Oh crap!' among the Time Lords, and a genuine sinking feeling as the bad guys pull off their victory. Its genuine mixed emotions, as you can't help rooting for Davros pluck, while at the same time realizing that they're really awful and this isn't a good outcome.

The audio recording is hard to find.

On the other hand, this version of *Trial of Davros* really expanded the multi-media angle, and a half-hour's worth of mini-movies were filmed. I can understand why they did this – otherwise, it's just a long stage play about a bunch of people sitting around a courtroom, jousting with a paralyzed guy in a wheelchair. That's not really visually… anything, which is why an audio record works so well.

In order to liven up the proceedings, a series of shorts, three to six minutes each, were filmed showing the Daleks in action, which were then inserted through the play and shown to the audience and the cast as 'evidence' against Davros. Sprinkling the proceedings with actual exciting visual elements was really helpful to liven up proceedings and prepare the audience for when the Daleks marched onto the stage. It was probably appreciated by children who would otherwise be bored stiff by adults arguing with each other on stage.

That, and I think they just wanted to do it because it was fun.

These mini-movies are accessible on YouTube if you poke around a bit. They are:

Promo Trailer – About four minutes of footage, including scenes from the other short movies, accompanied by a driving beat. There's a couple of interesting things though. There are the shots of the Daleks moving through jungle, which suggests that they shot some footage based on *Planet of the Daleks*, I'm not sure what happened to that.

Dalek Invasion of Earth 2005 – What it says on the tin. A six minute short of a group of Daleks invading modern day London, and slaughtering the fleeing population. The Daleks here are the brightly coloured movie version, with claws rather than the usual suckers, making this essentially a prequel to the Peter Cushing film, *Dalek Invasion of Earth 2150*.

Space Year- Roughly four minutes. The representatives of some Galactic Federation are meeting to discuss these new Daleks who are tearing up their worlds. Among the delegates is a representative from Hyperon, which is mentioned in *Genesis of the Daleks*. Just as they get their act together, a Dalek shows up and starts killing them off. There are a lot of aliens and cyborgs. Prominent among them is an Ice Warrior, but he doesn't have any lines. I don't think I recognize any of the other aliens. It's a bit dull, despite the alien costumes; it's just bickering in a small auditorium.

Day of the Daleks – Roughly six minutes. This is inspired by the Pertwee serial that brought back the Daleks after a five year hiatus. The story is that in the future, the Daleks, with their apelike Ogron slaves, have conquered Earth. Freedom fighters are travelling back in time to stop this future by killing a politician at a peace conference who unwittingly set the disaster in motion. The Doctor travels back and forth trying to sort it out. In this mini-movie, the Daleks and their

Ogrons travel back into the past (our modern day), and a full scale battle breaks out with UNIT forces. I believe that the building and grounds may be the same one from the Pertwee serial. This production features five Daleks, more than Pertwee had to work with back then. The Ogron costumes are terrific, it's a shame they only had a few appearances in the Pertwee era.

The Ogrons, by the way, were an effort to get around a problem – the Daleks couldn't actually do much. They could wave their plungers and eyestalks and glide around, but that was it. For things like actually picking up stuff or doing pretty much any other action, they were pretty futile. So, in *Dalek Invasion Earth* Terry Nation decided to give them henchmen – Robomen, robotized humans. That was fine, but after the Cybermen came along, Robomen just seemed redundant, and new henchmen were needed. So along came the Ogrons, shambling ape-men. Planet of the Apes was big in the early seventies, so that was probably an influence.

Ogrons appeared in *Day of the Daleks, Frontier in Space* and make cameo appearances in *Carnival in Space*, and *Dimensions in Time*. As it turns out, henchmen were generally unnecessary for Daleks, and kind of obvious. It was a hat on a hat. So they were just abandoned. But it's nice to see them here.

In the end, UNIT gets their behinds righteously kicked, and the whole thing ends in an explosion. It's a terrific action sequence, depicting the Daleks ruthlessness, the Ogrons brutality and UNIT's desperation.

Frontier in Space: Roughly five minutes. Based on the Pertwee serial of the same name, and the next appearance of the Daleks in the Pertwee era. This serial was about the Doctor stopping a war between the Human and Draconian Empires. A war that was being engineered behind the scenes by the Master, the Daleks and their Ogron slaves. In this segment, Draconians travel to the barren Frontier world (a rock quarry) where they get ambushed by the Ogrons. Although they defeat the Ogrons, the Daleks show up and wipe them out.

The Master then appears with more Ogrons, but since the Daleks no longer need any of them, they wipe them out. The Master, being a Time Lord, barely survives the Dalek's guns, but their energy blasts have left him weakened and with his face melted into the skull like visage that will plague the 4th Doctor in the Deadly Assassin and Keeper of Traken. There's another deleted scene featuring the Master, that offers a little more background.

This segment explains how the Master ended up as a living corpse in the Baker era. In reality, of course, *Frontier in Space,* an inconclusive story was Roger Delgado's last appearance as the Master. Delgado was supposed to come back to reprise the character one more time, but he died on a shoot in Turkey. With his death, they just decided to lay the character to rest for a while. So the Master's 'arc' was never concluded.

And of course, we've got the Ogron and the Draconians. We've mentioned them elsewhere.

Overall, of the Trial of Davros segments, this is probably my favourite.

Death to the Daleks: A three minute segment, wherein the Daleks fail to blow up the Tardis but successfully enslave and kill a bunch of Exillons and then prepare their assault on the mysterious city. This was inspired by the final Pertwee Dalek serial, also of the same name.

The overall theme of all of these shorts is, of course, 'Daleks Conquer and Destroy!' They don't just say it; they do it, over and over, relentlessly and mercilessly. And of course, in addition to Daleks, we get Ogrons, Unit, Draconians, Exillons, the Master himself, Ice Warriors, an assortment of aliens, a couple of well-choreographed battle scenes, and assorted death and destruction. What's not to like?

There's hints a *Planet of the Daleks* jungle sequence was shot, but I don't know if it was ever finished or released.

Including the trailer and the 1993 video short, that about 30 minutes. The segments are so well done, that they could be slipped into the appropriate serials without anyone noticing too much.

CHAPTER 10, THE AGE OF BEDLAM

Review: Planet of Storms (1996)

The Scovell Doctor, Epic on a Shoestring

STORY: Earth and its colonies are at war with golden-skinned aliens known as the Pertinax. The Doctor stumbles into a secret Earth military project around Jupiter. Unfortunately, the Pertinax are also aware of the project and have plans to foil it. They have hired a mercenary... The Terrible Zodin!

REVIEW: *Planet of Storms* is an interesting hybrid. Technically, it's both a BBC licensed stage production and also a fan film.

So what's the story? Well, cast your mind back to the 1990s, to that peculiar period when Doctor Who was undead. Officially on hiatus, not quite cancelled, but not coming back. This was the period when fans had gotten tired and frustrated with waiting, and decided to go out and make their own - the time of the Rupert Booth Doctor, of *Downtime* and *Shakedown,* of the BBV and the *Stranger*, of *Devious* and *Resurrection of Evil*, and the *Trial of Davros*.

There's a young actor at the Portsmouth Art Centre Theatre named Nick Scovell. In 1996, a slot opens up in their schedule; they ask him if he wants it.

He says sure.

They ask him what he wants to do.

He says, Doctor Who! He then proceeds to write a Doctor Who play, *Planet of Storms*. He gets some actors together, rehearses for eight weeks, and puts it on in October. It's that simple.

Never mind that Doctor Who had been off the air for seven years by this time. Or that the anniversary had fizzled out three years ago. Somehow, for Scovell, the show was still alive and vital enough that he wanted to jump in. In that sense, *Planet of Storms* seems to be part of that creative wave of fan productions of the 1990s that refused to let the show go.

But I digress. The very cool thing about *Planet of Storms* is that Scovell actually had permission granted from the BBC, which meant that, on some level, he was doing an authorized, official Doctor.

Honestly, I can't imagine why the BBC would have done this, except for sheer negligence. The BBC, since 1985, had pretty much been dicks on the subject of Doctor Who.

There had been endless private efforts to license the series which had simply been spun in circles. They'd jerked around the Daltenreys Group's film project to the point that the frustrated producers sued them. The *Dark Dimensions* project had gone down in flames. The thirtieth anniversary had been a fiasco. The past seven years, had seen Doctor Who trapped in a passive-aggressive development hell.

Now, in 1996, with Fox about to air a television movie/backdoor pilot for an American Doctor Who series, there were genuine reasons not to give Nick Scovell a license to do his own Doctor Who. Why on earth would they license an obscure actor to do a stage play, when it seemed like Hollywood was actually going to do something with the property?

But there you go. I'm not sure why. Perhaps because Portsmouth's venue was a reputable local theatre? Perhaps because it was in some sweet spot, big enough to be respected and taken seriously, not big enough to make waves? Perhaps because the proceeds would go to charity? Perhaps because Nick Scovell was naive enough to simply ask nicely? Or maybe it was just too small a matter for them to get upset over.

But then, I suspect that a lot of the BBC's attitude towards fan productions of any kind, especially in the 1990s was based on neglect. To be blunt, they really didn't care about the show, and they were happy enough to let fans do whatever they wanted, so long as it didn't tread too heavily on their toes.

But anyway, Scovell apparently went and asked, and for some reason they said yes, and suddenly, Nick Scovell became that small group of actors, alongside Peter Cushing, Richard E. Grant, Rowan Atkinson and Trevor Martin to play an official, although non-canonical, version of the Doctor.

Scovell's *Planet of Storms* was an entirely new story, featuring gold covered aliens called the Pertinax, the Terrible Zodin and a plot to destroy the planet Jupiter. It ran three whole days at the Portsmouth Art Centre, October 24 through 26, 1996, and that was it.

Then in 2015, a long lost videotape of *Planet of Storms* showed up and was released to the internet. This record of the stage play, along with *Millennium Trap* and *Power of the Daleks: Reimagined*, forms the Nick Scovell trilogy. We actually get to watch it.

So... how is *Planet of Storms*?

Not bad at all.

To start with, it's very reminiscent of the recordings of *Ultimate Adventure*. Which is to say, you have a stationary camera of mid-level 1990s technology mounted from the audience section. The sound is fairly clear, the image is decent though limited - it's hard to make out faces or facial expressions. For instance, one of the lead villains wears two eye patches (one on top of the other, not over both eyes - that wouldn't have worked at all), and that detail is completely lost for us (You can see it in production photos though). Technically, it's a bit better than the *Ultimate Adventure*, likely a factor of the recording being deliberate and overt, and the technology having progressed a bit in the seven years between.

Fundamentally, the video is a recording of a stage play, and that's a limit you can't get around. The physical limitations of a stage and set pieces are there. There's just barely enough set to keep us going, lighting is used effectively, but it's a fairly Spartan production. The audience is visible and audible, which gives us a sense of what it was like to actually have been there. But there's a remoteness that's inescapable, particularly when we're used to the close ups and camera movements of film and video. Despite that, if you let it, it's still engaging and watchable.

It's also broad, which goes with stage plays. Zodin is flamboyant. The Pertinax shout and stomp about playing thugs and enjoying it immensely. Scovell's Doctor is charming and outgoing. In the *Millennium Trap* and *Power of the*

Daleks: Reimagined, Scovell plays his Doctor much more restrained, but you can afford to do that on film and video.

Here his Doctor is far broader and more physical, partly because he's developing the character for himself, but I think more importantly because that's the way you have to play to a stage audience, to the back row as well as the front row. In this recording, the camera seems to be well back, and that distance even if it handicaps us in terms of image quality, gives us an effective appreciation of the Scovell Doctor.

Apart from that, it's a good story. Better actually than either the *Seven Keys to Doomsday* or the *Ultimate Adventure.* In both of those, Terrance Dicks was hampered by a kitchen sink approach, a need to throw just about everything he could cram in there. *Planet of Storms* in contrast is much more focused.

Rather, Scovell simply concerns himself with telling a good Doctor Who story, with the result that he produces something that feels much more like the classic television productions than Dick's efforts.

One thing going for Scovell is that he allows himself to think big. The background story is set several hundred years in the future, when Earth has expanded into space and established colonies. It's also gotten into a deadly war with a race of gold skinned aliens called the Pertinax. Into this opening comes The Terrible Zodin, negotiating casually with faceless alien powers.

The Terrible Zodin is an ultimate in joke. Zodin first 'appears' in *The Five Doctors* when the Troughton Doctor reminisces about her to the Brigadier. She 'appears' again in *Attack of the Cybermen,* when the Colin Baker Doctor remarks that they don't make villains like her any more. After that, she's mentioned in comics, novels and audio stories. Mentioned, but never actually appearing. Zodin is always terrible, and always absent. She is the legendary great unseen villain.

What does this tell us? Back in 1996, Nick Scovell was a nerd, and proud of it. Zodin's the ultimate in-joke, and Nick has put her front and center as the lead villain.

Anyway, where was I? Thinking big: The central conceit is a project to accelerate Jupiter's age in a time field by two billion years, in order to blow it up... For some sort of very good (but completely unexplained) reason, at least according to the Earth forces. That's right, the good guys want to blow up Jupiter... because... reasons! The villains, however, have hijacked the project and plan to reverse the timestream back to the big bang, with will obliterate the entire solar system, earth included.

I like the chutzpah there. The production is taking place on an almost bare stage, but what you give to the audience is a struggle over the explosion of the biggest planet in the solar system. That's a nice sense of epic scale on a half dime.

Another thing is that Scovell manages to emulate the twisty complexity and surprises that was the classic series at its best. There are two separate major villains - Zodin and the Pertinax, both are flamboyant and over the top, neither is stupid. There's a genuine cliff hanger at the end of act one. There's interesting subplots - a base commander is initially a hidebound bureaucrat but comes over to the Doctors side as he realizes what's really going on; and a scientist from the fourth quadrant who has to wrestle with his conviction that it would be better for his colony if Earth loses its war. This stage play really does mimic the feel of the classic old serials.

The story keeps barreling forward, Scovell's Doctor keeps coping with adversaries who are almost as smart as him, and the arc keeps changing. It's funny in the right spots, but the humour isn't buffoonish. It has pace and smarts. You could have given this script to Tom Baker or John Pertwee, and they'd have done fine by it.

What more is there to say?

CAST: *Nick Scovell - The Doctor; Fiona Scovell - The Terrible Zodin; Becky Giddings - Jenna; David Head(?) - Security Commander Bouchier; Dan McCrohon - Brigadier Tyacke; Ian Wheeler - Captain Bernick; (Incomplete)*

CREW: *Nick Scovell - Producer/Director/Writer; Ian Wheeler - Video; Mark Humprhies - Preservationist; Rob Richards - Poster Design. Performed at Portsmouth Arts Centre; (Incomplete).*

Review: The Millennium Trap (1997)

Daleks and Thals in Black and White

STORY: Alien warriors steal a unique substance from a research compound, walking through a hail of gunfire. The Doctor is summoned to investigate. Arriving at the compound, he discovers that the scientists are working with other aliens, survivors of a crashed alien saucer. But who is really on what side, and what are the agendas of the alien forces warring with each other in the skies over Earth....

REVIEW: This isn't a stage play; this is actually a fan film. But its history ties in so intimately with stage plays and related films that I've chosen to include it here.

The Millennium Trap is deliberately retro, clearly inspired by fond memories of the black and white era of Troughton and by the swashbuckling years of Pertwee. It plays like a love letter to the classic Who of the Troughton era. There's something charmingly old fashioned to it, while still somehow being determinedly its own creature, with a unique Doctor.

Here's what happened. Nick Scovell's Doctor Who play, *Planet of Storms* ran for only three nights at the Portsmouth Arts Centre. But on one of those nights, a young man named Rob Thrush was there.

Thrush was already doing fan films, or trying to do them. All the way back in 1984, he wrote and produced his first Who film, *The Sigma Factor*, which he described as *"four episodes of bleurgh made by a team who knew nothing about film making,"* But they stuck with it, and year and some after a serious learning effort, came second in a BBC competition the next year. Over the next few years Thrush and his friends made a dozen or so non-Who films.

In 1989 and 1990 they do *The Metamorphosis Effect*, a three part serial, in which James Harper plays The Doctor. It also introduced the character of Major Harvey, who's in *Millennium Trap* and *Power of the Daleks – Reimagined*. This story was about a capsule landing on Earth filled with toxic alien waste, causing the local humans to mutate. It's basically lost now, VHS tapes are around, but in very bad shape.

They also made had a pair of unfinished projects with James Harper as the Doctor. The first featured the Master and set in a historical theme park with displaced historical characters slowly going mad. The other was a post-apocalyptic tale set in an almost abandoned city – row of brick houses scheduled for demolition. There were some other proposals and projects but nothing came together.

Then came *Millennium Trap*. Originally, it was developed with James Harper in mind, but he wasn't available. So it was serendipity that Rob Thrush ended up in that audience at *Planet of Storms*, for the birth of a new Doctor.

Millennium Trap has all the most recognizable elements of Classic Who - there's UNIT, scheming Daleks, carping scientists, alien invaders and time spanning plots, all given their head and wrapped up in a three episode serial that moves and feels like the original series.

The serial format was the hallmark of Classic Doctor Who. Anywhere from two to ten episodes strung together, to make it work you needed several subplots, each maturing at the end of a different episode, and successive climaxes for the end of each episode, each building onto the main story. Supporting characters often didn't just support, they needed to do things, to be actual characters, to have actual lives, in order to fill out the subplots. The main stories had to throwing in new twists to keep things going. This elaborate form of storytelling really was the secret to Doctor Who. It's a difficult format to master, but they've got it down pat here.

Beyond that the look and feel of the production are very reminiscent of old time Who. The black and white helps that a lot. It's evocative of the Hartnell and Troughton stories, and especially of the serials like the *Evil of the Daleks* and *Power of the Daleks*. It's not nearly as confined as the Troughton stories. *The Millennium Trap*, features cutaways to both Daleks and Thals, scenes set in space, a struggle inside a flying saucer, a visit to the Dalek homeworld, Skaro, and even the Dalek city. No base under siege here, or much less of one.

Despite the black and white, it's strongly reminiscent of Pertwee, particularly in his later, swashbuckling phase. It moves fast and confidently, with a pace reminiscent of the 70s. UNIT is a presence here, for instance, and although UNIT or its predecessors appear in Troughton's *Web of Fear* and *The Invasion*, the relationship seems much more like Pertwee's later years. Certainly there's a closeness between the Brigadier and the Doctor. The Thals are the ones from Pertwee's, *Planet of the Daleks*, space-faring human adversaries, rather than the primitives of Hartnell's original serial. In the end, it's kind of a hybrid of a Troughton and a Pertwee story.

Interestingly, the black and white format that makes it so distinctive is an accident. They were shooting with three different video cameras, they couldn't bet the colour balances to match up, so they were forced to go with black and white. That proved to be fortuitous, because it works very well for

Nick Scovell's version of the Doctor. His Doctor is a mile away from Troughton or Pertwee, or for that matter, any other Doctor we've seen. There's something profoundly old fashioned about the Scovell Doctor, he could well have stepped out of an English film or play from the forties or fifties. Black and white just works for the archaic quality of the character.

Scovell gives us one of the most restrained portraits of the Doctor. The performance is toned down from *Planet of Storms*, possibly way too much. This isn't the charming eccentric that we've come to love. Rather, this is a perfect English Gentleman, low key and polite to a fault. He's Sherlock Holmes without the neuroses or mania. Even when he's dying of radiation poisoning, he's utterly composed and dignified. It's a polished performance, Scovell is an accomplished actor, but personally, I find his Doctor here is almost too low key.

He clashes a bit with the flavour of the story. With the goings-ons as they are, you find yourself looking for someone with the energy or the presence of a Pertwee or a Troughton, someone outgoing. Instead, you find this glacial, remote, sort of introverted personality that almost seems more inclined to watch than act. In his opening appearance, he's reluctant to answer UNIT's call; he finds their constant badgering irritating. In the end, he answers because it's only slightly more interesting than playing chess with himself.

This remoteness might, in part, be due to the fact that Scovell's Doctor has no companion. He's like Sherlock Holmes without Watson. He has no confidant to talk to and bounce off of. Companions weren't just a convenient vehicle to let writers explain the plot to the audience, they also served to complete the Doctor's character, they allowed him to be human. Here, he's a solitary and aloof figure, keeping a chilly, if cordial, distance, from everyone. He's polite, even compassionate, and he completely lacks the arrogance of other Doctors, but there's a remote quality to him. The only hints of sentimental affection are with the Brigadier.

In the *Millennium Trap*, Scovell's Doctor is at his best when he's facing off against the Daleks. There it's a duel of cold alien intelligences, a chess game of icy wits. There's a scene where Scovell's Doctor pries a Thal prisoner out of the Dalek's clutches which is simply masterful. They have captured a Thal and are unwilling to give her up. They're lying to the humans about pretending to be benign, he knows they're lying, they know he knows they're lying, and he still manages to trap them in their own pretensions and free the prisoner.

Not that the Daleks are foiled for long. The Doctor's successful gambit opens the door for them to put a new scheme in play. And so it goes, move and countermove; with the stakes steadily climbing. It's an engaging exercise in meticulous plotting, and really, a textbook for anyone who wants to tell an effective story of dueling adversaries.

The Doctor and the Daleks don't just sit there, representing good and evil, they're both active, playing against each other, each ones actions drive the reactions of the other. It's compelling, because it's a genuine contest of wits and wills.

Which brings us back to the story, and the three-part serial structure, which is brilliantly realized. Scovell may be a restrained Doctor, but the story proceeds with its own energy and verve, and Scovell moves through it with unshakeable confidence.

Locations like the Submarine Museum and Fort Nelson base provide the usual extraordinary production value we see in the best of these films. The secret government research laboratory buildings and interiors have the right combination of bureaucratic stolidity, militarization and research - it feels authentic. A shoot in a quarry does the duty for Skaro. Spaceship or Skaro interiors are realized without either calling attention to themselves or disrupting the suspension of belief. There's an effective use of greenscreen and CGI effects, available in the 1990s, to expand the story in ways that hadn't been possible twenty five years before.

There's so much that evokes the stories of the 60s and 70s, and yet it isn't quite like any of them. Its pace is modern. Its Doctor is unique. *The Millennium Trap* is like distilled essence of Doctor Who. But somehow, it's its own thing.

Oh, and James Harper, remember him? He gets to come back as the Doctor, right at the end.

In 2009, Thrush and Scovell produced an upgraded edition of *The Millennium Trap*. Both versions are eminently watchable and can be found online.

CAST: The Doctor - Nick Scovell; The new Doctor - James Harper; Colonel Harvey - Vincent Adams; Khel - Nikki Wooldridge; Captain Williams - Zoe Millett; Commander Gavin - Kevin Jacks; Barton - Debs Sutton; Pilot - Rik Ker slake; Professor Stanton - David Head; Doctor Jeffries - James Harper; Corporal Lennox - Gary Rocky; Tremaine - John Blackwell; Scientist - Marian Korndorffer; Newscaster - Kevin Jacks; Pilot - Rob Thrush; Guards - Tony Walden, Rik Kerslake; UNIT Troopers - Tracy Vear, Rob Vear; Kevin Jacks, Rik Kerslake; Tony Walden, Rob Thrush; Dalek Operators - Deb Sitton, Daniel McCrohon, Phil Pennington, Gary Rockey, James Harper; Dalek Voices - Rob Thrush, Nick Scovell, Vincent Adams, Zoe Millett, Kevin Jacks, John Blackwell.

CREW: Bedlam Theatre Company, 1997; Writer/Producer/Director/VT Editor - Rob Thrush; Vision Mixers - David Tozer, Gary Rockey; Camera Operators - Gary Rockey, Kevin Jacks, Rob Thrush, David Tozer; Production Assistant - Marjan

Korndorffer; Clapper Loader - Simon Harper; Designers - Phil Pennington, Rob Thrush; Incidental Music Composer - Dudley Simpson; Performed by Heathcliff Blair; Thanks to Ashcroft Arts Centre, HM Submarine Museum, Royal Armouries Fort Nelson, Matt Philipson;

Review: The Dalek Masterplan and Others

Four Re-Imaginings of Classic Serials

The Millennium Trap was a success, as far as Doctor Who fan films went. I suppose success is a hard thing to measure in this milieu - fan films don't get audience or Nielson ratings, you can't chart box office. But it was completed, it achieved its goals, it looked and felt thoroughly professional, it received a couple of impressive reviews, and it established an enduring partnership.

Nevertheless, there was a maddening indirectness. Nick Scovell would never sit in an audience hall to watch a crowd of people watching the *Millennium Trap*. He wouldn't be standing on stage for a round of applause. *The Millennium Trap* would be passed and copied from hand to hand, from collectors to clubs to conventions, it might receive reviews in fanzines, might show in the video room at a convention, or in some library AV room a club screening. Watching or obtaining the *Millennium Trap* was an almost furtive exercise, it was an underground thing. I don't think you get a lot of feedback and affirmation, beyond the satisfaction of a job remarkably well done.

Nick Scovell was foremost a stage actor. His first performance as the Doctor had been a year before in a play he wrote called *Planet of Storms*. That had been licensed by the

BBC. With the *Millennium Trap*, Scovell had found a collaborator in Rob Thrush.

They returned to the stage.

Thrush and Scovell, over the next few years, collaborated on a series of four Doctor Who stage plays, made with the express permission of the BBC, Terry Nation, David Whittaker and others, including *The Web of Fear* (June 2000), *Fury From the Deep* (27–30 March 2002), *Evil of the Daleks* (25–28 October 2006) and *The Dalek Masterplan* (24–27 October 2007.)

Again, I'm at something of a loss as to how he got these rights from the BBC. This wasn't just the right to use the Doctor. This was a step further, recreating and revising actual BBC serials that had aired. I have to say, I'm fairly astonished.

Maybe I shouldn't be. Virgin Books had been publishing *New Doctor Who Adventures* for years. Although I suppose that this was just a continuation of the long established publishing tradition. Big Finish Productions had won the right to do audio productions of Doctor Who and steadily built its own universe from that. Big Finish arguably maintained a continuous relationship with the BBC.

But this was just two guys who kept going back to the BBC, and kept getting new licenses to produce his versions of their stories. Again, maybe it was because it was theatre. Maybe the Portsmouth Art Centre hit the sweet spot of being big enough to be respectable and small enough that the bureaucrats didn't get excited. Maybe it was because the proceeds went to charity each time. Maybe they just found someone in the BBC bureaucracy who liked them. Who knows?

It couldn't have been easy. On top of the BBC, they needed licenses from writer Victor Pemberton for *Fury from the Deep*.

Then with increasing apparent difficulty, from Henry Lincoln and Mervyn Haisman, who had had an epic falling out with the BBC. Lincoln and Haisman had written the *Abominable Snowman* and the *Web of Fear*, and created the Great Intelligence, the Yeti and even introduced the Brigadier and UNIT. Then they'd written *The Dominators*, which had created a toyetic race of robots called the quarks. Both the BBC and Lincoln and Haisman had seen commercial potential in the Quarks, and this had resulted in a nasty fight. It hadn't been pretty.

Then they'd had to get rights to use the Daleks from the notoriously difficult estate of Terry Nation, as well as the estates of Dennis Spooner and David Whittaker for the actual scripts for *Evil* and *Masterplan*.

Actually managing to obtain the rights was probably an odyssey in itself.

They also required massive adaptation. *Dalek's Masterplan* was 12 episodes, that's a 6 hour running time. *Evil of the Daleks* ran 7 episodes. The others were all 6 episodes. That's three hours apiece. All of which were designed for television, which allowed for a multitude of sets and locations. These plays were chopped down to an hour and a half, tops, and they were entirely stage bound.

There's some indication of clever stuff going on. For instance, in *Evil of the Daleks*, they apparently built a breakaway fireplace and chimney, behind which was built the Emperor Dalek. You can just imagine the emergence of the gigantic Dalek Emperor in a climactic moment. There are photographs and even a brief YouTube clip of the Emperor Dalek, if you look for them. Five regular Daleks were used in that production.

Unlike *Planet of Storms*, all of these productions are mostly lost to us. They're known to us from scripts and playbills, still photos, video clips, reviews and the reflections and recollections of the players and audience. Theatre is ephemeral.

Scovell himself notes that the terms of his BBC license precluded his videotaping these adaptations. That just wasn't on. No recording for posterity, this was three days only, all proceeds to charity, and that was that. Or maybe not?

Scovell was prohibited from recording these productions, and he respected those terms. But it's not as if he was going to be able to frisk every single audience member, or shake down every stage hand. Starting with 1984, camcorders had gotten better and better each year, better resolution, longer batteries, smaller, more compact. By the time you got to the late 1990s, you could carry a camcorder in a purse, or conceal it in a jacket, wield it with one hand. There's no way to control that.

In fact, a couple of years ago, someone had the stage version of *Fury from the Deep* up online. It was only for a few days, so I missed it. Believe me; I kicked myself when I realized I'd blown a chance to download it for my files. But it's out there, teasing us, waiting to be uploaded again someday, or played at a convention.

Elsewhere on YouTube, there's a snippet of *Evil of the Daleks,* there are a couple clips of the stage version of *Dalek Masterplan,* one of them almost fifteen minutes long. I'm willing to bet that complete video recordings of both of them are out there, perhaps residing on a Camcorder cassette, or downloaded into a hard drive. But they're all out there, somewhere.

In 2007, Scovell and Thrush mounted their final stage production: *The Dalek Masterplan,* October 24-27, to sold out crowds.

The Dalek Masterplan is the Hartnell epic. A twelve-episode serial spanning the universe from Ancient Egypt to the far future; with the Meddling Monk as a guest villain. I would have said it couldn't be translated to the stage at all, not without major revision. There's actually quite a lot of material out there on Scovell's *Dalek Masterplan*. The script is available, there's the fifteen minute clip, another short clip, a promo, three documentary segments. There's actually enough here to write a review.

To begin with, it's massively cut down – obviously it had to be. All the stuff in the original with the Meddling Monk, that's out the window. That was filler anyway. The original story is distilled very neatly.

Egotist and would be Dictator, Mavic Chen, throws in with the Daleks, thinking that he can use them in his plan to dominate the Universe. Chen is an arrogant buffoon, constantly hectoring the Daleks and anyone within earshot, unwilling to take responsibility, and blaming the Daleks for whatever goes wrong. He's such a jerk, and the Daleks are so patient with his nonsense that you almost cheer when they finally kill him.

Meanwhile, the Daleks attack planet Kembal, wiping out the population, except for three survivors – Brett, Katarina and Steven, who the Doctor rescues. Returning to Earth, the Doctor discovers the Daleks scheme to build a Time Destructor using Terranium. He steals the Terranium core from the Daleks. The Daleks send a robotic doppelganger who manages to kill Katarina. Mavic Chen sends Sara Kingdom, a double agent and old flame of Brett's to steal the Terranium back. But Sara has a change of heart when she's forced to kill Brett. The Time Destructor is designed to selectively wipe out species. The Doctor manages to jigger it so that it wipes out the Daleks, but a surviving Dalek initiates restart. The Doctor absorbs the energy, at the cost of his own life. Sara joins him.

The Doctor regenerates into the Nicholas Briggs Doctor. Who is the Nicholas Briggs Doctor? He's in the third volume, wait for it.

The play has a high body count! People are dying all the way through, and that gives the production a grim serious quality. The characters, except for the relentlessly obstinate Mavic Chen, are not playing around. Rather, there's an element of desperation and tragedy. Katarina mourns Marc Cory, who is killed at the beginning. She's then killed by a robot double of Marc. Sara Kingdom kills her brother Brett, in the course of duty, and it almost destroys her. Even Trantis, Mavic Chen's sidekick is distraught, increasingly aware that he's serving an out of touch lunatic. Good performances, the little that we see.

One thing that doesn't come across in the script, but is apparent in the video clip, is the brilliant use of the empty stage. Flats are moved around to establish locations. Lighting effects are used brilliantly. There are even pyrotechnics.

The Daleks are brilliant. There are six of them, and to give you some perspective, the original BBC story only built four. And they're terrific Daleks, shiny, well-constructed, professional looking. The Daleks of both *Masterplan* and *Evil* were actually borrowed, and refurbished and repainted, from another fan film project, *Devious*, which we'll talk about elsewhere.

To add further authenticity, Nicholas Briggs, the modern voice of the Daleks on the television series, does their voices here. Briggs was also active with the audio-visuals, with Big Finish, and with the *Auton trilogy*. On a flat stage, these Daleks are in their element, gliding about with smooth menace. Their swinging domes and eye stalks give them an amazing degree of expressiveness.

The quality of the main video clip is exemplary, the image is clear and pristine, the sound is good. It's a shame that we don't have the entire thing to enjoy.

That was it for the stage, though. The BBC was sitting up and taking notice. In 2005, Doctor Who was back on the air, but that was something of an experiment. The BBC could still be pretty casual about the property in 2005 and even 2006.

But by 2006-2007, Doctor Who was a runaway success on television, generating its own spin offs with Sarah Jane and Torchwood. The BBC was going into full corporate battle mode protecting a hot lucrative property. Getting the permissions to do the Daleks Masterplan had been an uphill battle for Scovell and Thrush.

Scovell and Thrush had a trilogy of Dalek plays in mind. Their next stage project was going to be *Power of the Daleks*. But after 2007, the door was firmly shut. They couldn't get the rights for another stage production. The long run was over.

Still, the end, this leaves Nick Scovell as perhaps the only man to have been permitted by the BBC to play the Doctor on stage five separate times. That's a respectable footnote in Who History.

Of course, that wouldn't be the end of it.

Review: Power of the Daleks Re-Imagined (2012)

Completing the Scovell Doctor Trilogy

STORY: Earth, present day. On a remote, volcanic Island in the south Atlantic, an isolated research station has discovered what appears to be a capsule of extraterrestrial origin containing dormant robot-like beings. Meanwhile, an investigator from UNIT has shown up, he calls himself 'the Doctor'....

REVIEW: Technically, I suppose, *Planet of Storms*, *Millennium Trap* and *Power of the Daleks: Reimagined* is not a trilogy. It's two films and a video of a stage play, but it works as a trilogy.

If you wanted to be a nit-picker, the Scovell Trilogy would be two major fan films, some minor fan films, five consecutive stage plays and some audio adventures, some of which, the stage plays, are extremely hard to obtain copies of. This would be technically an aggregate number greater than three.

But the thing was, these projects aren't just projects. They are labours of love. This is the secret to fan films. Ryan K. Johnson and Barbara Benedetti, Marq English and Mark Bennett, Paul Ferry and Rupert Booth, Luke Newman and all the others. They did it because they loved it.

It wasn't about money, there wasn't any. Scovell and Thrush simply really wanted to do Power of the Daleks, and if they couldn't do it one way, as a theatrical production, then they'd do it as a fan film. It's a genuine commitment.

Fifteen years after the *Millennium Trap*, Scovell and Thrush released another fan film: *Power of the Daleks: Reimagined*, effectively a sequel or prequel to *Millennium Trap*.

Power of the Daleks was originally a six part serial aired in 1966. It was Patrick Troughton's first real outing as the Doctor, following immediately after the Tenth Planet. The Doctor has just regenerated, his companions are suspicious, and the Tardis ends up on the Planet Vulcan, where the Doctor witnesses a murder and becomes embroiled in the local politics of the human colonists. At the same time, the Daleks have shown up, and pretending to be friendly, are using stealth and treachery to subvert the human population.

In terms of the show's history, *Power of the Daleks* is almost as important as the *Unearthly Child*, or The Daleks themselves. It was the bridging serial; it was Patrick Troughton proving to the production and to the audience, that he could step into the role of the Doctor.

We're used to changing Doctors now, we've seen a dozen. But back then it was a real risk. There had only ever been one Doctor: William Hartnell. It was by no means certain that the audience would accept a new Doctor, or that the show could survive the transition.

It's entirely possible that a lackluster serial could have proven the end for Doctor Who - Troughton would have been considered a failed Doctor, a hollow copy, some cheap and sleazy attempt to prolong the show past the departure of its star. The audience might have melted away, never to return, the show might have limped through its fourth season and then faded away forever.

That didn't happen. *Power of the Daleks* was a gripping serial, one which managed to give Troughton a platform to establish himself, one which brought back the Daleks with a new and menacing slant. The *Power of the Daleks* was a success. Troughton was a success. The rest is history.

Definitely history: *Power of the Daleks* is one of the lost serials. Today, through the efforts of fans and groups like *Loose Cannon*, you can watch a reconstructed version. Based on those Reconstructions, the BBC re-created the full serial as an animation.

Power of the Daleks: Reimagined, is not a remake of the Troughton serial, it's an adaptation. For one thing, Nick Scovell doesn't play Patrick Troughton's Doctor. He never did. The four stage plays after Millennium Trap were adaptations of Troughton or Hartnell serials, but Scovell never played the Troughton or Hartnell Doctor.

Scovell has always played his own Doctor, one born in *Planet of Storms* and developed in the *Millennium Trap*, and refined through five stage adaptations, short videos, and a series of audio adventures. This Doctor was calm and cold, courteous and caring. He was an imperturbable, almost glacial, somehow compassionate, intelligence. Scovell's Doctor is always obviously the smartest and most capable man in the room, but never a jerk about it.

This may be Scovell's best performance as his Doctor. One of the scenes available online is of his Doctor, in lock down, playing cards with another prisoner when an officious thug comes to get him, with no more than a raised finger he stills the thug and finishes his card game. It's a defining moment for the character. Cool, casual and incapable of being intimidated.

The stories may have been originally written for Hartnell or Troughton, but these were six or twelve part serials of 25 minute episodes, written for television, with the all the liberties that a television production provides. For the theatre, you had a story in a single night, divided into no more than two forty-five minute acts with an intermission, a single stage and limited space and lighting. So necessarily, there was always going to have to be some serious adaptations.

In *Evil of the Daleks*, for instance, Scovell emphasized the religious themes, and throws in the notion that the Daleks are from the far future. Together with the Supreme Dalek, these are the last five Daleks in existence. Instead of a standard fiendish plot, it's really about the desperate gamble of a dying evil race. That's a pretty radical re-conception.

For the *Dalek Masterplan*, running 12 episodes and 300 minutes, entire subplots were excised, backstory or location was rewritten. Scovell's and Thrush's plays have never been exact reproductions; rather, they have been reinterpretations or recreations, making adjustments or revisions. Often the revisions are simply to meet the demands of the stage or the reduced format. But it also incorporates ideas and concepts that make it interesting to Scovell.

So it is with Power of the Daleks: Reimagined. No longer stage bound in concept, Scovell and Thrush are free to make more use of sets and locations. But they don't have unlimited resources. Instead of six 25 minute episodes, they've boiled the story down to three episodes, substantially winnowing the story to its core.

It's no longer space opera. Gone is the planet Vulcan and its human colonists. Rather, it's set on Earth in the present day, on South McKinley Island, 400 miles east of the Falklands. The Vulcan Corporation has leased the Island and sent a Mining Survey Unit to refurbish an abandoned military base. The settings are recognizable and institutional: Walls are cinderblock, offices look functional, lights and light switches, stairs and doors and bulletin boards are all part of our familiar world.

The Second Pirates History, Page 110

The characters are modern everyday people in everyday wardrobe with modern sensibilities: Working stiffs, middle management, security, geologists and technicians and a radical environmental activist. For most of the characters, you get the feeling that they just want to do their job without too much headache and go home. There's a universal 'everyperson' vibe to them. They live in our world, even if they're away at a remote location.

The Doctor comes onto the scene as an investigator from Unit, having detected strange emissions. All that preliminary stuff about the regeneration and the Doctor finding the body of the assassinated investigator and taking his place is out the window. A subplot about a covert movement and rebellion on Vulcan is ditched. The story is cleaned up and simplified.

This change of set and setting makes a profound difference, leaving us with a production that feels more like John Carpenter's *The Thing*, or perhaps an *X-Files* episode. It's the modern day, modern world, and there's an immediacy to the situation as matters go slowly off the rails.

No surprise, the emissions turn out to be from an alien capsule. The alien capsule turns out, to the Doctor's horror, to contain Daleks. The Daleks are powered down, so they make nice, misleading the humans, playing on curiosity and greed, until they can get the upper hand. The Daleks are particularly scary looking, influenced by the modern versions, but a metallic grey. They're kind of a hybrid of the old and new, and look weathered, like battered, used war machines. The Daleks themselves are the only genuinely alien thing, and they're all the more alien because the world around them is so normal an d recognizable.

Meanwhile, London gets the message that there's a Dalek on Earth, and the Prime Minister and members of his Cabinet grimly gather around a holographic display, preparing to send warships and nuke the Island. The Vulcan Company Survey

The Second Pirates History, Page 111

Team doesn't know what they're dealing with. But the British government does and in cutaway scenes they're literally crapping their pants. This ramps up the tension.

Overall, it seems to play as a kind of sci fi political or espionage thriller. The clock is counting down, both for the Daleks and their accumulating menace, as well as for the British government and its nuclear weapons. Caught in between are the different personalities Vulcan team, oblivious, out of their depth and in increasing danger, with only the Doctor desperately trying to save them.

Power of the Daleks: Reimagined was completed and released to YouTube in 2012. Then, in 2014, the BBC had it taken down with a copyright notice. You can still see fragments, including the first episode, trailers and clips. If you search hard enough, you can find the whole thing.

The BBC's seemingly capricious action in 2014 after the thing was online for two years spurred a whole flurry of rumours that the original Power of the Daleks had somehow been recovered.

Two years later, the BBC released an animated re-creation, using the sound track of the original serial. Was that the cause? I suspect that we won't know the reason why. There seems to be very little pattern to the BBC's occasional objections and interventions.

Power of the Daleks: Reimagined is hard to find for now. These things have a habit of floating up to the surface. But in the meantime, we have the footprints - a Facebook page, teaser trailers, sneak peaks, making of segments, a handful of online reviews, at least one of the three episodes can still be found.

In the meantime, *I Can See You* is available.

CAST: *Nick Scovell - The Doctor; James George - Hensell; Suzy Needle - Janley; Phil Cottrill - Lesterson; Paul Denney - Bragen; Paul Butler - Quinn; David Bickerstaff - Valmar; Adrian Cranwell-Child;*

Kebble; Sarah Strange - Resno; Vincent Adams - Colonel Harvey; Tony Dart - Foreign Secretary; Mark Wakeman - Defence Secretary; Sean Ridley - Aide; Rod Cameron - Air Commodore; Mark Harold and Daryl Liebert - Security Guards; Dalek Operator - Stuart Currie; Guest Starring: Barnaby Edwards - Prime Minister; Lisa Bowerman - Admiral Cunningham;

CREW: Nick Scovell - Director and Script; David Whittaker - Original Script; Rob Thrush - Producer and Director of Photography; David C. Tozer - Technical Director; Mark MacKenzie - Gaffer; Hazel Kenyon - Grip; Steve Bull - Boomist; Steve Brassington and Jenny Vanderplank - Assistant Directors; Emma Shelley - Script Supervisor; Adrian Cranwell-Child - Art Director; Paul Butler - Art Assistant; Mark Harold - Standby Art; Martin Johnson - Composer and Sound Mixing; Rob Semenoff and Richard Brookes - CGI Artists; Daleks created by Terry Nation; Cameras - Chard House Media; Technical Services - Gemini Production Services; Studio and Post Production - TNT Films Ltd.; Audio Post Production - Everybody Else; With Special Thanks to: Rod Cameron; Ferneham Hall, Fareham; Steve Degon; HMS Sultan Engineering School; Pam Braddock; English Heritage, Fort Brockhurst;

Review: I Can See You (2019)

The Other Bedlam Doctor

Fan Films occupy a peculiar niche.

Most film or television, we judge on their own terms. They succeed or fail on their own devices and on their own merits. Sometimes we have to look past the limitation of a zero budget, or a b-movie sensibility. Sometimes we measure them according to genre conventions, or their ability to subvert genre conventions. But mostly, we're looking at the movies themselves.

There are some exceptions. Sequels, reboots and rip offs both exist in the context of something that has gone before, and are measured by their predecessors. Usually, it's hard to measure up. For every *Godfather II*, or *Star Trek: the Next Generation*, there's a lot of abysmal dreck out there. Same with reboots, once in a while we get a wonder - *Battlestar Galactica*, but mostly it's mediocre, *Ghostbusters*, or utter drivel like the *Total Recall* remake.

Rip Offs are a little easier, there's fewer expectations in some ways, more in others. But generally, it's risky business to tread a well-worn path. You're always going to be compared to your inspiration.

We don't watch movies or television that way normally. We don't watch the *Big Bang Theory* or *The Office* and measure them by how faithfully they recreate *Cheers* or *Friends*. We just watch them. We don't compare the *Avengers* to *James Bond*, and wait for a '*shaken not stirred*' martini. We just watch them.

And that's the challenge and strength of fan films in a nutshell. It's not necessarily the low budget, or sometimes nonexistent production values, amateur acting. Rather, these films exist in a kind of symbiotic relationship with their inspiration. They are created for their inspiration, they're watched for their inspiration, and they're judged on their fidelity to that inspiration.

That's how we watch fan films. When we watch a Doctor Who fan film, what we are looking for is Doctor Who. It stands or falls on its ability to get Doctor Who right, its ability to remind us of the real thing, whether by parody or emulation. Every single fan film has that target. It's not a rip off; it's not a reboot or a sequel, all of which are supposed to diverge. It has to hit the target exactly, and that's how we measure it. We judge them by how close they come and how they miss the mark.

The very best of them? The very best of them close that gap, they are Doctor Who. You can be a purist canon-whore all you like, but the truth is the BBC doesn't give a damn about canon and it never has, just legal rights. Frankly, I enjoy Doctor Who for being Doctor Who and not a piece of property.

Seriously, if I want to enjoy a property as property, I'll buy a cottage.

Which takes us to *"I Can See You."*

This is Doctor Who. It hits the mark perfectly. This isn't just an effort, this is Who. If you can sit down and love David Tennant, or Tom Baker, or Peter Capaldi, and if you can see all three as the same thing, then this is the same, and you can watch it with the same love and appreciation. It's so close to the real thing, that the difference isn't meaningful.

At the center of *I Can See You* is James Harper's angry irritable version of the Doctor. It is electrifying.

The Doctor is the hardest character to get a grip on, especially because he's been played so many times, in so many incarnations. You have your classic Doctors, your new Doctors, your miscellaneous Doctors like Cushing and Grant, and he's played in all sorts of ways. It can be hard to pin down what defines the Doctor - intelligence, eccentricity, a streak of humour, a slightly alien quality, a renegade streak. The Doctor is one of a kind. Not even all the actors who played the Doctor quite grasp the character.

James Harper is the Doctor. He's not a Doctor we've seen before. With his tousled mop of hair, and his angry eyes and perpetual scowl, this is a new interpretation. This is an angry Doctor, who kicks a fleeing woman out of his Tardis with a blunt *'call the police, it's not my problem.'* It's a Doctor with no patience for fools, or anybody else for that matter. It's a Doctor with one last nerve, and these humans are stepping on it.

But by God, he's definitely the Doctor, razor sharp, living by wits, never missing a trick, and he can't help getting involved when someone needs help. He's the Doctor because you can't stop watching him.

The story is flat out entertaining. A young woman gets caught up in a hunt by body snatching aliens. The premise isn't particularly novel. But then, they seldom are, there's just so many stories out there. It's what you do with it that makes it interesting.

In this case, it's craftily done. The story begins in media res with the woman running for her life into the Tardis. The aliens are a weird mix of amusing and terrifying, terrifying in that they kill people and seem unstoppable and omnipresent, and yet amusing in their awkward floundering handling of their stolen bodies, or their fixation on their target. It holds together though, as the Doctor figures out and explains what's going on, it all makes sense. And really, I don't want to say more than that.

The story is a chase of course. The Doctor always seems to be running, and it shifts through a number of locations - tunnel, park, clothing store, back of a taxi, cosmic void. The point is that it is always on the move, and that offers a fair bit of energy, it feels very modern. You can almost see David Tennant or Matt Smith in the story, running to escape the menace and solve the mystery. There are CGI effects, but they tend not to be flashy or intrusive. Mostly, they're subtle, supporting the story, and helping to keep things moving.

Another bright spot is the relationship between Harper's Doctor and Mary Stone's Jo Jo, a homeless woman in over her head. At first he doesn't want anything to do with her, but he responds to her desperation and her situation, and they slowly start to form an awkward careful bond. Harper's Doctor doesn't exactly lighten, but he softens and mellows just a bit, and she shows strength. The scene in a clothing store where they're trying to disguise themselves, or the one in the park where they're grabbing a bite, are both excellent - moving characters, relationship and plot forward seamlessly, exactly the way an excellent scene should do.

One weak spot is the resolution which follows on a genuinely emotional moment. It doesn't actually make any sense. It's pulled out of his butt. The Doctor just... wins. He explains it later, but the explanation is clearly such 'watered down for your chimpanzee intelligence' it doesn't hold up.

It reminds me of how the Tom Baker Doctor explained the Tardis' interior dimensions to Leela. You go, 'that's kind of clever and poetic' and then 'but that didn't actually make sense.' You just have to accept it.

At least they spared us the technobabble.

For what it's worth, *I Can See You* carries along so briskly, that it doesn't really matter. The Doctor always wins, that's what he does, just accept it, it's just fun to watch him Doctoring.

At twenty five minutes, the length of a single classic series episode, this is tight, economical storytelling and film making. There's literally not a wasted breath or dragging moment. And it's all done by volunteers working for free out of simple love, with less money than the catering budget of the real show.

Bottom line - terrific performance as the Doctor, by Harper, who is everything that a Doctor needs to be, and manages to do something new with the character, good relationships, good performances, an interesting story that works on different levels and is briskly told. Terrific.

The New Who series could watch this and take some notes on how it's done. Films like *I Can See You* are why we watch fan films in the first place, and why fans make the effort to learn the craft and create their own.

CHAPTER 12, A COPYRIGHT CONUNDRUM

Here's a shock. The BBC doesn't actually own all of Doctor Who. They own a lot of it. For instance, they own the Doctor. They own the Tardis both as a concept and as an iconic blue box, although they had to fight a lawsuit with the London police to get it. They own Gallifrey, the Time Lords, quite a few other bits and pieces.

But the Daleks? That's owned by a gentleman named Terry Nation, or his estate, at least. The Sontarans are owned by Robert Holmes, as are the Autons, and the character of Sarah Jane Smith. The Great Intelligence and the Yeti, the Quarks and the character of Alistair Lethbridge-Stuart are owned by two gentlemen named Mervyn Haisman and Henry Lincoln.

Other bits and pieces, characters, monsters, worlds, stories, are owned, or at least co-owned by other people.

Behind the scenes at least, the world of Doctor Who is a lot more complicated than we expected, a situation that lead to some unexpected developments in the 1990s.

Let's back it up a bit. How did this situation come about?

Way back at the beginning, when Doctor Who was starting up, television was still seen as an ephemeral commodity. In the 1950s and early 60s, when television started up, no one really knew how it was going to work. Because of this, the people who were working in television were inclined to treat the business and legal side in certain ways.

No one knew or thought about reruns, or syndication or long term ownership, or the rights issues. A lot of television was broadcast live - it was the equivalent of a live stage show or radio performance. Recording was possible but unwieldy.

Back in those early days videotape existed, but was almost impossible to edit – you literally spliced it like film.

Video formats differed from country to country. It was inconvenient and unwieldy. When the BBC wanted sell Doctor Who episodes overseas they would actually point a film camera at a television set and film the image.

Television in the 50s started out primarily as a licensing operation.

Television in England and America, when it started up, was not creating a lot of new content. That was risky and expensive. It cost money to produce a program, and no one was quite sure what was going to work, or not work. Everything that television put up amounted to taking a chance.

Rather, the custom was to buy a limited license, essentially, to rent, intellectual property – novels, plays, songs, etc., which were already owned by someone and already in use and already producing or potentially producing revenue. They went with work that was already known and had a track record. *Sherlock Holmes*, Orwell's *1984*, the *Beatles*... etc.

It was just a lot safer and easier to rent the rights to something that was proven, rather than to take a bigger risk in creating content.

The owners of these pre-existing properties were not prepared to sell the whole thing to television for a one-time fee, or even a royalty.

Rather, the custom was that they simply sold a 'license' a limited right to use the property in a television broadcast. But that was it. It was very limited, one time stuff, sometimes twice.

It wasn't open ended; the people making television didn't want to pay for more than they needed. No one was thinking of reruns then. They expected to broadcast something once or twice.

Who needed permanent rights in that situation?

It's important to understand this, because that establishes the playing field, it set the ground rules for people who came in later, and for other situations that evolved.

Because of this, the BBC basically had a policy of very limited rights and usage. You bought a script, you paid actors, but you weren't buying permanent rights to the script or the actors performances. You didn't need forever, and you weren't going to pay for indefinite rights. It was for a license of one or two uses. That was it.

That's what leads to the destruction of so much of the early seasons – it wasn't seen as valuable or reusable properties. It was just taking up space.

Doctor Who had already had its two showings. If they wanted more showings, they would have had to pay more. If they wanted all rights in perpetuity, they would have had to pay a lot more.

It was that policy of limited rights and usage that would come back to bite the show in the ass. Because the rights that were being bought and sold back then precluded re-runs, there didn't seem any use for old episodes. Eventually, the BBC began to clear the old serials out, resulting in the loss of about a hundred episodes of Doctor Who, and an incalculable volume of other television programs.

But we'll come back to that.

First some basics: Who is the owner of an artistic work? Under copyright law, the owner is the original creator – the artist, the writer, etc. That's the basic principle.

But in Copyright Law, there is this thing called 'Work for Hire' – that's how Corporations get to be copyright holders. A corporation or an employer hires someone on as an employee with the task of producing the work – that work and the copyright is owned by the corporation or the employer.

Now, apply this to the BBC. When the BBC puts on a production of Sherlock Holmes or 1984 it doesn't own the copyright in those works, it buys a license to use those works. The rights stay with the original owners.

But if the BBC as an employer or corporation creates a work 'in house' – i.e., its employees and underlings, its staff, producers, executives, technicians etc. create something – that's owned by the BBC: Doctor Who, the Tardis, Timelords, Gallifrey, Regeneration, the Master, and a few other things.

Here's the thing though – the BBC wasn't as huge as the American television studios or television networks. It couldn't maintain a huge staff, including in house writers for programs.

Instead, the BBC is hiring outside creative talent – actors, singers, music and musicians, artists, and of course writers.

They aren't employees. They're contractors. Contractors own their own copyright in their creation. So in contracting these people on, they don't own the rights, they licensed them. The ownership of Copyright remains with the contractor.

Apply that to a script – what it means is that the writer owns the script and has licensed his script to the BBC. This means that the writer outright owns all the unique elements and characters in a script.

For example, let's say Robert Holmes writes a serial, The *Time Warrior*, in which he invents the Sontarans. The BBC owns the Doctor and the Tardis in the script. But Holmes owns the script, and the characters and creatures he invents specially for the script. So Holmes ends up owning the Sontarans. You have this situation where the script represents divided rights – some owned outright by the BBC, some owned by the writer and licensed to the BBC.

It's true that Robert Holmes can't do much with his Doctor Who script, because the Doctor is in it, and the BBC owns the Doctor. But if Holmes revises the script to take out the Doctor and references to the other BBC owned properties like the Tardis, Gallifrey, the Master, then he can do whatever he wants with it. It's his script.

That actually happened a lot. Notably, Douglas Adams did it with his *Dirk Gently* novels, revising Doctor Who scripts without the Doctor. But there were other examples, unused Doctor Who scripts belonged to the writer, who could adapt them by removing the Doctor and replacing him with some other Doctor, and they could sell it, even to the BBC.

Why did they Brits do it in that peculiar cockeyed way? Were they stupid?

No.

Partly it was simply the way the television industry practice evolved in England.

As I said, television started out by licensing everything, they were working from previously owned or outside owned properties. And on top of that, British television evolved out of the traditions and conventions, including legal ones, of the British stage, and of British movies, which themselves evolved from the British theatre. That set the templates and industry standards that followed.

America had a different history, and rapidly developed different legal and intellectual rights practices, that eventually became the rule. But for a long while, the British had their own idiosyncratic way of doing things.

In a nutshell, American television came out of American film and out of Hollywood, where a film or movie was a long term property, and you wanted complete control of all the rights.

British television evolved from British theatre, and in the stage, there was always a limit to the run, and a limit to your use of the rights – you didn't need or want complete rights, just the rights for your run, and the artist or writer didn't want to give away complete rights for what would only be a theatrical run, particularly when they hoped to license those rights to other or future theatre companies for more runs.

Look at it from the point of view of the British artist or creator. Imagine you're a writer – you sell your short story or novel to the BBC, it's a license.

You deal with the BBC a year later, writing a script for a television program. Why would you agree to a worse contract, or give up more rights than you had to the last go round?

Industry standard, as I said. Writers were not cattle – they were unionized, there were standard contracts, rates, collective agreements, rules.

The other part was economics: Sure, the BBC could have bargained for and bought all rights, forever and ever and ever. If they wanted to pay for all that.

But in selling those rights, the writer would potentially forego revenue and opportunities. So if the BBC wanted to buy the whole enchilada, then you would have to pay whole enchilada rates. It was not going to be cheap.

If you were only going to broadcast a program twice then why bother? You had a budget to think of. That budget didn't include buying unnecessary lifetime rights worldwide or hiring a lot of unnecessary staff as "Work for Hire" just in case.

Let's take a quick look at the Daleks and Sontarans. They're owned by Terry Nation and Robert Holmes (technically, their estates) respectively. However, they're not completely owned.

The 'concept' of the Daleks, and some of the design elements are directly from the script by Nation. The physical design – the peppershaker look, those bumps, eye stalk, plunger - that was all in-house design by the BBC staff.

The same with the Sontarans – they are owned by Robert Holmes, but the look is owned by the BBC. That was why the Reeltime productions *Shakedown* a non-BBC production which licensed the Sontarans for use from Holmes estate, had to tweak the design a bit.

Similarly, as another example of the distinction between concept and design, while *Frankenstein* the novel and the character is in public domain, Karloff's particular flat headed-bolt necked look was owned by Universal Studios, so when Hammer Films did *Frankenstein*, they had to create a monster very different looking from Karloff's version.

Now, here's the thing with the Daleks: They were very hot! Hot! Hot! Hot!

Did I mention they were hot! The mid-60s had Dalekmania. It was a fad, a kind of weird public obsession. Suddenly, kids everywhere were running around with their arms outstretched warbling 'Exterminate!'

Dalek toys were selling like hotcakes. Two Peter Cushing Dalek Movies were made back to back. Nominally, they were Doctor Who movies, but they were really about the Daleks. But Doctor Who's name isn't even on the title to the second movie. It's called *Dalek Invasion Earth 2150*, the Doctor doesn't even get billing. There was a stage play *Curse of the Daleks*. On Doctor Who itself, Daleks appeared in eight serials and 46 episodes in the first four years. They appeared at supermarkets and on talk shows. There were Dalek cards. There was even a song, *'Christmas With a Dalek'* on the radio (I am not making this up).

Daleks were viral before there was such a thing as viral.

Daleks had been the make or break for the first season – transforming a mildly interesting show to a full-fledged phenomenon. After the first appearance of the Daleks, the BBC was crazy desperate to use them again and again.

Do you know what that is?

That's leverage!

Terry Nation, and his agent, had unprecedented leverage in bargaining with the BBC. He had them by the balls. They wanted the Daleks… all he had to do was say *'No, I don't think so.'* They'd say *'Well, what do you want?'* He could say *'I want to do a stage play!'* Or *'I want to try and sell it in the United States, not your show, my Daleks.'* Or *'I want a solid gold toilet!'*

And they'd say *'Done!'*

The runaway popularity of Daleks meant that Terry Nation got to drive a fairly hard bargain on the BBC.

The basic underlying rules remained in place for a long time. Even after the the classic series, independent writers still owned their properties.

At the 1994 Worldcon I got to talk to a fellow who had had a script that was cut from *Trial of a Time Lord*. Nice guy. I've long since forgotten his name, and can't guess at who he was. He owned the rights to the script. The BBC paid him a kill fee for his work, but he owned it. He could have taken it and sold it to Target Books as a Doctor Who novel, and he may well have done so.

Or he could have stripped out all the BBC elements and resold his story to another television series. Or he could have published it as an independent novel without the Doctor in it. It was his property.

In fact, you could insert your own previously created characters into a Doctor Who story. Eric Saward had done some radio drama featuring an Elizabethan actor and swashbuckler named Richard Mace, and later had him guest star in the Peter Davison serial, the *Visitation*.

Robert Holmes, as I said, owned the Sontarans, the Rutans, the Autons and Sarah Jane Smith. The BBC paid him and licensed them every time they brought them back. They didn't do it often, but it happened now and then.

Malcolm Hulke owned the Sea Devils, the Silurians and the Draconians. A couple of guys named Lincoln and Haisman owned the rights to the Dominators, the Quarks, the Yeti and the Great Intelligence. And so on…

It was important for the writers, and they weren't going to surrender rights easily. For one thing, everyone was on the lookout for the next Dalek-mania, the next runaway viral monster to strike gold for both the BBC and the writers. Particularly during the Troughton era, there were a series of potential 'new Daleks' put forward – Cybermen, Ice Warriors, Yeti, Quarks, Autons, etc. Usually the BBC would give them a couple of serials, to see if they caught on.

Of all of them, the one that came closest to the Dalek's success was the robot companion, K9 owned by Bob Baker and Pat Martin, who spun off into a series of children's books, audio adventures, eventually his own twenty-six episode Australian television series 2009-2010, and came back to both new Who and the Sarah Jane Adventures.

But that didn't stop people from trying to create the next big robot or monster or character, or writers from being possessive.

There were disputes. Back in the 60s, Lincoln and Haisman, a pair of promising writers who had a major fight with the BBC over who owned licensing rights for a particularly toyetic robot, the Quarks. They parted company with the BBC, which then buried their creations for a long, long time.

Chris Boucher had a dispute with the BBC over the ownership of the character of the Tom Baker companion, Leela.

Robert Holmes passed away in early 1986, but his estate retained these rights to monsters and characters. So, when fan groups approached seeking a license to use the Sontarans, or the Autons, or Sarah Jane Smith... Well, look at it this way, it's not like Holmes was worried about jeopardizing future writing assignments for the BBC.

This was a loophole for Fans to legally work and play in the Doctor Who universe; to have Doctor Who, albeit without the Doctor.

The first to exploit the loophole was Reeltime Pictures. In the 1980s, they'd produced a series of videos featuring interviews with cast and crew members from Doctor Who, called *Myth Makers*.

Documentaries which can be legally sold, because reporting and journalism are legitimate infringements specifically allowed for in law. Copyright law makes an exception for reporting and journalism.

In 1987, Reeltime tried their hand with *Wartime*. This was a half hour story involving the Pertwee era character, Sargent Benton, with permission of the BBC, played by the original actor, John Levene, encountering the ghosts of his past while on a mission. It wasn't great, and it didn't make much of an impact.

Then in 1991, after the cancellation of the series, a fan named Bill Bags came up with the idea of bringing back Colin Baker as The Doctor in everything but name - the character known as *The Stranger*.

This was not technically exploiting the loophole in the BBC's copyright. It was just using the same actors to play essentially the same character in the same sorts of situations and adventures, without using the name. Think of it as being similar to William Shatner playing a heroic and somewhat lusty starship Captain, with Leonard Nimoy as his unemotional sidekick, cruising around the galaxy in the 25th century, but not actually naming their characters Kirk and Spock, and not calling the series *Star Trek*.

And if you think that's thin ice, yes it is. People do get sued over stuff like that. *Star Wars* sued *Battlestar Galactica*, *Superman* sued *Captain Marvel* and later sued *Greatest American Hero*. For every case some shtick like this sneaks past, there's another where it ends up in court. And many cases where it lost in court.

But Colin Baker was a free agent; he could do whatever he liked; act for anyone he wanted, including playing a nameless character who was, who was essentially the Doctor without his Tardis. Nicola Bryant, who played Perpugilian Brown, the 6th Doctor's companion, signed up to play a character named Ms Brown, on the basis that Brown is a pretty common name. It's not as if they were jumping in and out of a Police Box. Whatever machine they use to get through time and space is not onscreen or even mentioned by name.

The Second Pirates History, Page 129

The first film from 1991 was called *Summoned by Shadows*, the second in 1992, was *More than a Messiah*, the third was in 1993, *In Memory Alone*.

They featured appearances by recognizable stalwarts from the series. Michael Wisher, who had played Davros; Louise Jameson, who played Leela; and Sophie Aldred who had been Ace; had guest starring roles. They didn't come back as analogues to their Who characters. But fans knew who the actors were, and there was the familiarity of recognition.

The three stranger videos were short, averaging about 40 minutes. They were cheaply made. Baggs didn't have anything near a BBC budget, and the shoestring nature of the productions show through. They contained all sorts of oblique references and comments that seemed to allude back to Doctor Who.

Basically, they were low budget Doctor Who adventures, everyone knew it. It was a little too obvious for comfort and the BBC was not happy. Lawyer noises were made. For the next three Stranger videos, Baggs took the character away from The Doctor, giving him a new name and a backstory.

But it did well enough that Baggs, through his company, the BBV, went on to hire Caroline Johns who had played Doctor Liz Shaw, the first companion of the Pertwee era. Somehow, Baggs obtained a letter of permission from the BBC to use the character, or at least the name.

Caroline John's played a Doctor Liz Shaw who was now head of an *X-Files* type paranormal investigation agency for a quartet of adventures known as *PROBE*, which was actually an acronym for something or other. There was 25 years distance between the BBC's Liz Shaw and the BBV's Liz Shaw; the two characters were fairly different. But in the first *PROBE* adventure, there were a handful of oblique references back to suggest it was the same character.

Another selling point for *PROBE* was the return of several actors through the series who had either played the Doctor or Companions.

Spearheaded by Nicholas Briggs, the Autons were brought back in the late 90s for a trilogy of UNIT stories. Even the Zygons came back in 2008.

The BBV also did audio productions, including further adventures of K9, the Rani and other Who characters and monsters. But more on those in the next volume.

In 1994, *Dreamwatch Bulletin*, a fanzine which had managed to go professional and had then branched out into running conventions, decided to get into movie making, with *Shakedown: Return of the Sontarans* (and the Rutans), featuring Doctor Who and *Blake's 7* actors in new roles.

Around the same time, Reeltime Pictures followed up its 1987 video *Wartime,* with *Downtime.* This production brought back the Great Intelligence and the Yeti, but no less than four companions, Doctor Who actors playing their original characters, notably the Brigadier, Sarah Jane Smith, Victoria Waterfield and Jack Waterfield.

Reeltime followed up with *Mindgame, Mindgame Trilogy,* using a Draconian, a Sontaran and an unidentified human who might have been Ace.

The Pertwee serial, the Daemons inspired Reeltime to recycle those monsters for *Daemos Rising,* and the setting for *White Witch of Devil's End.*

Reeltime's recently *Sil and the Devil Seeds of Arodor,* featuring the villainous slug from the Colin Baker serials *Vengeance on Varos* and *Mindwarp.*

Add them all up: Sontarans, Rutans, Yeti, Draconians, Autons, Daemons, the Great Intelligence, Sil, the Brigadier, Liz Shaw, UNIT, Sarah Jane, Victoria, K9…

That's a lot of chunks of the Doctor Who universe running free.

To give you an idea of how bizarre this is, it's as if, after *Star Trek* went off the air, some completely unrelated group managed to get a portion of the rights from the writers of episodes, and began making movies about Harry Mudd or Uhura or the Klingon Empire, without the permission of Roddenberry or Paramount.

As a group these 'loophole productions' are a mixed bag.

Some are slow moving and talky, and several of them veer from the look and feel of Doctor Who. On their own, some just don't stand up very well, and really need the forgiveness and tolerance of fans desperate for a Who fix. I'm not going to bother reviewing those.

The budgets were low, often impossibly low, which leads to visibly cheap production value, and non-standard running times.

But some, the best and most interesting, yeah, I'll talk about those.

Although technically legal and commercially available productions, none of these didn't really get mass market penetration - they tended to be sold to and among fans. You'd buy them at conventions, or specialty shops and comic stores, or through mail order. I've always wondered about the viability of the business model.

But hey, through the 90s Doctor Who was cancelled indefinitely. So if the BBC wasn't doing it, why shouldn't the fans go ahead?

Reviews: The Stranger (1991-1996)

Summoned by Shadows (1991)

STORY: Summoned by Shadows - the Stranger seeks a hermit-like existence, to the frustration of Ms Brown, his companion. But the alien Conjurer has other plans....

REVIEW: In 1991, former Doctor, Colin Baker, and former companion, Nicola Bryant, starred in the first Stranger video - Summoned By Shadows.

Who or what was the Stranger? Here's what Colin Baker had to say in 1992, at the Visions Convention, *"'Stranger' films, that's a trilogy. Or a multi-gy, we hope, lots and lots of them. The BBC owns 'Doctor Who' so no-one else can make that. But Bill Baggs is a resourceful fellow and he's written a series about a man called the Stranger, who travels through time and space with a lady called Ms. Brown, played by Nicola Bryant! And we battle evil people who happen not to be Daleks or Cybermen. It's a very neat way of continuing without…"*

Later in the same panel, asked if the BBC might consider picking up the Stranger, Baker says, *"I think there'd be absolutely no point the BBC bringing back 'The Stranger', because if they're going to do that, they might as well bring back 'Doctor Who'. Whatever fiction we all put together for the purposes of avoiding litigation, the similarities are so close that they might as well use the property they've got."*

The Second Pirates History, Page 133

There you have it. If Colin Baker says that the Stranger and Miss Brown, is just the Doctor and Peri Brown with the serial numbers painted over, that's pretty much all she wrote. The BBC tended to agree, which was why Bill Baggs was eventually forced to take the Stranger in different directions after the first three.

Summoned by Shadows opens with the Stranger, dressed in a dour gray overcoat, sitting in a tent in the middle of nowhere, as a visibly frustrated and exhausted Ms Brown tries to push him out of his funk.

This actually seems to be a callback to Colin Baker's first Doctor Who serial, the *Twin Dilemma*. Near the beginning of that story, shortly after regeneration, Colin Baker's Doctor is a bit insane. At one point, he tries to strangle Peri Brown. Horrified by his actions, Baker's Doctor snaps out of it, and vows to become a hermit, retreating out to some barren desert planet, with poor Peri dragged along unwillingly.

Then plot happens, the hermit thing is forgotten instantly. *The Twin Dilemma* goes on be one of the most reviled serials in Doctor Who history. To be honest, it was a misstep on just about every level. John Nathan-Turner elected to introduce his new Doctor in the final serial of the Peter Davison era. His idea was that Davison's audience would carry on over to the new Doctor that season. The trouble is that all the money and resources had been used up, so there wasn't much to work with. Then on top of that, there was Baker's hideous costume, a choice that Baker himself hated but had to live with, not fatal. But not a good start.

There was the idea for a greater character arc - Baker's Doctor would be like Mr. Darcy in *Pride and Prejudice*, he would start out appearing cold and unlikeable, and warm as the audience got to know him. Well, that guarantees a bad first impression, and quite often in media, you live or die by that first impression.

The Second Pirates History, Page 134

Also, let's face it, the story stank on ice: Homicidal mania and an altogether too realistic episode of domestic violence? That made an unforgettable and unforgiveable impression. As an example of the terrible writing that characterized the *Twin Dilemma*, the horrific incident is forgotten a few scenes later, dropped and never referred to again. As was so common with television characters, the Doctor never really has an emotional arc; everything is forgotten by the next serial. But this was inside an episode, so it was pretty egregious.

I've always thought that *Summoned by Shadows* sprang from that early moment in *The Twin Dilemma*. The Doctor, horrified at strangling Peri in his moment of madness, deciding to renounce his name, renounce his colourful cloak, and going off to become a hermit.

Which is basically where we find the Stranger, sitting in a tent, all sackcloth and ashes, feeling sorry for himself, with his companion, Ms Brown, unwillingly dragged along.

It plays that way. The Stranger is rather more dour than Bakers Doctor. The character is chastened and reflective. His wardrobe is the Doctor's colourful overcoat reduced to gray plaid, with a monk-like rope for a belt. For me, The Stranger is the redemptive arc that Baker's Doctor never went through.

(Note – this isn't necessarily the way the creators of the Stranger saw it. Their idea was more far in the future, after many adventures, the Colin Baker Doctor gets depressed and burned out. Take your pick – I like mine better.)

It's not an exciting choice. The Stranger is too depressed. He's not really fun to watch. But I think that he is emotionally authentic in a way that Baker's Doctor wasn't allowed to be. In a fit of madness, he almost murdered a companion. He needed to come to grips with that, and here he does so. I can see why this would have appealed to Colin

Baker. He had been so badly mistreated as the Doctor, I think he just wanted a chance to go back and set a few things right.

Ms Brown eventually gets fed up with the Stranger's self-absorbed mopery, and wanders off in search of a party. She finds it - wandering into an aristocratic garden party, led by an aristocratic master of ceremonies. Elsewhere there's a sort of perpetual carnival in which a painted trickster seduces people, and sends them hunting through ruins for mysterious artifacts.

The master of ceremonies and the painted trickster turn out to be extensions of the Conjurer, played by Michael Wisher. Wisher is famous in Doctor Who circles for being the first actor to play Davros, in *Genesis of the Daleks*. The Conjurer is an alien who has gotten trapped on this world. His spaceship is up in orbit, but he can't get to it. So he's psychically enslaving the population to find the trinkets needed to repair to repair his teleport so he can get back to his spaceship and go home.

Next thing you know, the Stranger is dragged out of his sulk by a mute boy looking for his girlfriend. He gets captured by the Conjurer, and with Ms Brown as a hostage, he's forced to help solve the problem. The scenes with the Stranger and the Conjurer are the best parts of the video. Colin Baker's character steadily reverts back to his Doctor self, and Wisher plays an engaging bad guy. The two actors know how to bounce off each other.

It's not bad. Not necessarily great, though. The production is only thirty-five minutes long, so it falls a bit into that uncanny valley of feeling too short and too long at the same time. The editing, particularly early on, is choppy. The musical scoring is heavy handed. The plot is straightforward. It lacks that twisty feel, the subplots and cliff-hangers that made Doctor Who serials so charming. Admittedly, the BBC show has that feel because it's a serial, and this is only a half hour. But Ryan K.

The Second Pirates History, Page 136

Johnson pulled off that authentic twisty feel in *Wrath of Eukor* and *Visions of Utomu*, and they were half hours. That said, the production design and costumes, particularly the carnival and garden party, are better than the budget would allow.

One fun and peculiar fact: The spaceship model seen at the beginning and end of *Summoned by Shadows* would reappear as the Rani's Tardis in 1993's *Dimensions in Time*, a peculiarity for which I have no good explanation. Of course, *Dimensions in Time* also includes Zog from *The Ultimate Adventure* stage play, so why not?

As I've said, it's a bit of a downer. There's a dourness to the proceedings that never quite goes away, so it's not as much fun as Doctor Who, but I can live with that. I can even like it as more emotionally authentic than the Twin Dilemma ever allowed Colin Baker to be.

Summoned by Shadows was written by Christian Darkin and produced and directed by Bill Baggs on a shoestring budget. Apparently, it was co-produced or co-funded by something called the BBC Film Club. I'm not sure what that was, or how it related to the BBC itself. From there, Baggs went on to form the BBV and produce a series of video and audio productions.

CAST:: *Colin Baker - The Stranger; Nicola Bryant - Ms Brown; Michael Wisher - The Conjurer/Trickster/Host; Jon Wadmore - Dane/Mute; Jon Sayers - Interpreter; Heather Tracy - Tanya; Helen Hewlett - Escaping Woman.*

CREW: *Bill Baggs - Producer/Director; Christian Darkin - Writer; Dick Kursa - Camera/Lighting; Paul Lunn and Evelyn Prior - Costumes; Penny Bowers - Make up; Tess Weightman - Production Manager; Duncan Chave - Sound; Derek Handley, Mark Readman, Bryan Sharpe, Mike Tucker, Crawford Wilson - Special Effects; Julian Boote, David Lines, Steve Mezullanik - Grip; Jill Hallowell, Clair Sairfield - Stage Manager.*

MORE THAN A MESSIAH (1992)

STORY: Relaxing on a vacation planet, he Stranger encounters a feral woman with supernatural powers who becomes obsessed with him....

REVIEW: In 1992, came the follow up. It was actually an adaptation of a Doctor Who audio story, written by Nigel Fairs, and originally produced by a fan group called the Audio-Visuals. Bill Baggs had been one of the founders of the Audio Visuals, but had moved on after a few years. The Audio Visuals, in turn, eventually went pro, evolving into the now famous Big Finish Productions. Nicholas Briggs, another Audio-Visuals alumni, would also become important, both to the BBV and to Big Finish.

More than a Messiah is a bit lighter in tone than Summoned by Shadows. The Stranger is still dour, but he is coming out of it. There is more of a cast of performers, they have more to do, and there is a genuine mystery at work.

The Stranger and Ms Brown travel to the world of Majus 17, which seems to be a vacation colony. This doesn't quite sell to the audience. Majus 17 is a bit too homey and cottage country in look and feel. It's hard to get your head around the notion that this is another world, much less a vacation world. Apparently, it's a vacation world for really boring aliens.

And actually, the aliens that we see come across as really boring humans. And very human identical aliens, there's no makeup, no prosthetic forehead, nose or ear appliances. Not even space costumes.

On the other hand, there was a design to that. Baggs is at pains to present a normal world which we recognize as our own, but which steadily goes off kilter with ape men, mysterious feral women and exotic references to alien societies. The story slowly unveils both a strange world and a hidden mystery which the Stranger must solve.

It doesn't quite come off. But you can see where they were going, and what they were trying to do. They do come closer to pulling it off than you would think.

Once again, the Stranger is having a rest, and once again Ms Brown is frustrated with him and goes off on her own. She ends up having an adventure with the other vacationers. This is similar to *Summoned by Shadows*. The Stranger and Ms Brown start out together, they have a spat, and then she goes off on her own for much of the episode.

The Stranger encounters a feral woman, played by Sophie Aldred, who has some sort of supernatural or spiritual powers, and leads him on a mystical journey. She gets a little too infatuated, and a little too godlike. Once again, Colin Baker's character starts off slow and kind of dour, but becomes very much the Doctor. Interestingly, there's a subtle evolution of the character - the Stranger foregoes his previous gray coat and rope belt, for a black coat and bright red trousers.

Aldred's mysterious character becomes obsessed with the Stranger. The next thing you know, she morphs into Nicola Bryant, giving the actress an opportunity to play two roles - as Ms Brown, and as a shapeshifted, obsessed, alien temptress.

More than a Messiah is a more ambitious production than *Summoned by Shadows*. The cast is larger, and they have more to do. There's a subplot, there's more sets and locations. The editing and directing is more polished. The music is still heavy handed, and as I've said, the production design doesn't quite carry off its ideas of rustic English cottage country doubling for an alien 'back to nature' spa. It's still only about 43 minutes but this seems to be more tolerable length.

CAST:: *Colin Baker - The Stranger; Nicola Bryant - Ms Brown; Sophie Aldred - The Spirit; Julian Boote- The Ape; Peter Miles - Bernard Darton; Barbara Shelley - Charlotte Darton; Nigel Fairs - Nick; Mark Trotman - Mark.*

CREW: *Helen Hewlestt - Executive Producer; Bill Baggs - Producer & Director; Nigel Fairs - Script; Dick Kursa - Lighting and Cameraman; Alistair Lock - Music; Penny Bowers - Make up; Julian Boote - Assistant Director; Robert Hill - Sound Recording; Susan Moore- Special Effects; Robin Johnson - Gaffer; Gary Penman - Costume Dresser; Phil Baxter - Speedboat Sequence; Roger Clark, Derek Handley and David Miller - Production Assistants.*

IN MEMORY ALONE (1993)

STORY: In 1993 came *In Memory Alone*, an adaptation of an Audio-Visuals story called *Conglomeration*. The Stranger and Miss Brown find themselves trapped in a mysterious old fashioned train station, stripped of their memories, confronting a robot and dealing with peculiar holographic traveler.

REVIEW: Almost entirely shot on a few simple sets, it actually works better that way, the artificiality of the sets doesn't conflict with sci fi premises the way that natural locations sometimes do.

A lot of the baggage of the two previous episodes is stripped away. The Stranger isn't soul searching this time out. He can't mope because he can't remember. Instead, he simply sets about trying to sort out what's going on, throwing himself into the mystery. It's much more engaging without the heavy subtext. It's as if the Doctor has worked his way through his issue, shaken his angst, and is on the verge of being himself again.

Unlike the previous episodes, Ms Brown isn't frustrated and walking away from the Stranger. Instead, they start out separated and amnesiac, confront pieces of the puzzle, and gradually come together to pool their resources and information. Bryant's character actually has a substantial role this time as she confronts and eventually subverts the robot. She's clever and inventive. For once, they work as a team with real chemistry.

Particular impressive is the effects work. There's a floating robot, the hologram man, and eventually a robotic war-suit on a tear. It's not really high end, but it works and it feels comfortably BBC.

From one episode to the next, Bill Baggs grows more confident and polished as a director. The camera work is more assured, the editing is more coherent. Summoned by Shadows is a bit messy with choppy editing and direction, salvaged mostly by Colin Baker and Michael Wisher's interplay. *More than a Messiah* works better. But with *In Memory Alone*, we really have a story that fully evokes the feel of the original show, not a low budget clone. It was becoming something you could slip into a Sixth Doctor DVD collection and without feeling out of place.

By this time, they were actually starting to actually approach the production value of the classic series... That might have been a bit much for the BBC.

The next three *Stranger videos*, in 1994 and 1995, broke away from Doctor Who. Instead, the Stranger turns out to be from a race of Dimension travelers. The Dimension lords are engaged in a civil war. The dominant faction is the Protectorate. Their opponents, the Preceptors, carry out covert operations, hit and run and terrorist actions. The Stranger's name is Solomon, he's actually a Preceptor captured by the Protectorate. His previous adventures are Protectorate rehabilitation exercises, or something. It seems to have worked, because Solomon's had a change of heart about the whole civil war. He's not really a fan of the Protectorate; he just wants no part of the war and the killing.

Nicola Bryant's Ms Brown turns out to have been a Protectorate Agent. She vanishes after the third episode. The next three episodes feature two Preceptor Agents, Saul played by Jon Wadmore, and Egan, played by David Troughton (the son of Patrick Troughton). They try and rope an unwilling

Solomon back into their cause in the fourth. They get trapped on Earth, and end up looking for a way out through the final two episodes. It's a definite retcon. You can go back and look at the first three episodes, and it's not quite meshing with the backstory presented. Still, the final three are well done, the acting is polished, the characters are vividly drawn and work well together, the stories intrigue and the whole thing holds together. The series achieves and maintains professional levels of quality.

The Stranger stories were the first commercial attempt to spin off the Doctor Who universe out from under the BBC since the cancellation. Before that, there had been John Levene's *Recall Unit: The Great Tea Bag Mystery*, a fringe festival stage play, and Reeltime Pictures *Wartime,* from 1984 and 1987.

But the Stranger wasn't a supporting character from some forgotten corner of the franchise. The Stranger was Colin Baker's Doctor, caught at a critical moment in his life, accompanied by Peri/Ms Brown. Whatever the strengths or weaknesses of the production, this was new Doctor Who, without the BBC, two years after the show was cancelled.

It's hard to describe just how ground-breaking that was, or what a void it had stepped into. Fans were still waiting for the show to come back in any form; the rumour mill was constantly churning. But there was nothing out there really, except old episodes on VHS tape, and a few fan films traded hand to hand.

The Stranger established that the Doctor Who fans were sticking around as a coherent group that would support productions. It established that the fans would watch stories on the basis of the show's beloved actors, even if those actors were playing different roles or characters. Although it didn't trade on subsidiary copyrights, in its effort to skirt the BBC it inspired subsequent productions to do so.

Starting with the Stranger series, BBV productions went on to produce a number of video and audio productions connected to Doctor Who in some ways. Sometimes it was a thinly veiled tread upon Doctor Who: Sylvester McCoy and Sophie Aldred had an audio series where they played the 'Professor and Ace' - the BBC made lawyer noses about that too, and it was retitled as the 'Dominie and Alice.'

Sometimes loophole licenses were used, as in the *Auton Trilogy*, the *PROBE* series, a K9 Audio series, and audio dramas featuring the Rani, Zygons, Krynoids, Sontarans and others. Sometimes, as with the *Airzone Solution*, they simply used Doctor Who actors in unrelated roles.

The Stranger series broke ground. Following in its footsteps came *Downtime* and *Shakedown* and a host of unlicensed fan productions, *Resurrection of Evil, Alliance, Phase Four, Millennium Trap* and so on. I can't say for sure that they were all inspired by the Stranger. I think that's putting a little much on it. Each of the subsequent productions has its own history, its own inspirations. But I think that the Stranger opened a door that hadn't been opened before. If not for the Stranger, other productions, other groups might have opened that same door. But the Stranger having done it, made it easier to walk through.

CAST:: Colin Baker - The Stranger; Nicola Bryant - Ms Brown; Nicholas Briggs - Hologram Miner;

CREW: Bill Baggs - Producer/Director; Nicholas Briggs - Writer; Dick Kursa - Camera/Lighting; Julian Boote - Assistant Director; Paul Lunn and Evelyn Prior - Costumes; Penny Bowers - Make up; Robert Hill - Sound Recording; Crawford Wilson - Special Effects; Derek Handley - Model Work; David Miller - Model Work; Robin Johnson - Gaffer; Ben Smithard - Assistant Camera; Harvey Summers - Music; Mary Ewen - Musician.

Review: Shakedown (1994)

Return of the Sontarans

STORY: Captain Lisa Deranne is a spacer just trying to make a living. Hired on to pilot a spaceship through a solar sail race by a consortium of wealthy dilettantes; her ship, full of passengers, is suddenly boarded by troops from a Sontaran battlecruiser. The Sontarans are searching for a Rutan spy who may have boarded the ship. The Sontarans promise to depart once they've found their spy; but secretly, they intend to leave no one alive. Meanwhile, the Rutan is simply intent on killing anyone in its path. Who will survive?

REVIEW: I have to say, I didn't particularly like this on first viewing. I found it clumsy, humourless, paint by numbers and peculiarly slow paced. It's grown on me after repeated viewings. I'm rather fond of it these days.

I was surprised to learn that this wasn't a project of either the BBV or Reeltime Pictures, although Reeltime distributed it. Rather, it was a Dreamwatch Production.

Let's back it up a bit. Back in 1983, a fellow named Gary Levy, or Gary Leigh, started publishing his own fanzine: *Doctor Who Bulletin*. It got popular over the years. For one thing, it was always willing to take the piss on John-Nathan Turner, the showrunner of Doctor Who during those years. This was the time period when Nathan-Turner's star started falling. It was the period when the show was in trouble, both in creative and production terms, ratings were falling and the fan base was angry. So a non-official source willing to take a hard run at Nathan-Turner was popular. It was able to scoop the official sources. It provided an alternative, and at times, angry and controversial alternative to the establishment publications: Doctor Who Magazine as well as the zine of the Official Doctor Who club.

Confrontation sells. We have an entire American Talk Radio industry to demonstrate that – guys like the late unlamented Rush Limbaugh, Bill O'Reilly, Ann Coulter; they make their bread railing at the 'establishment.' Same thing here. Doctor Who Bulletin became quite popular, embarrassing blunders aside. As its popularity grew, the production values went up. It became quite a nice looking publication. Magazine quality.

Come 1989, they hit a snag. Doctor Who was over. It didn't make a lot of sense to keep publishing Doctor Who Bulletin when the show was cancelled. But by that time, the magazine had a dedicated readership. Gary decided to keep the initials and rename it *DreamWatch Bulletin*. They broadened out into covering all sorts of science fiction, British and American.

I suppose that the end of the show produced a vacuum in the establishment publications. Doctor Who Magazine fell on hard times given that the show was no longer produced. The Doctor Who Appreciation Society didn't have much to do. Strategically, it was one of those situations where you grow or you wither, there's no standing still. Dreamwatch grew, keeping its audience, encroaching on the now bereft readerships of former rivals, and expanding its mandate. Readership kept on going up. In 1994, they went to full news stand distribution. This seems to have been their high-water mark.

Around this time, Dreamwatch was sponsoring or organizing its own science fiction conventions. The conventions were a major step up – a major financial venture, organizing large staffs, hotels, guests, wrangling hundreds or thousands of people.

It was also at this time, 1993 or 1994, that Gary and his Dreamwatch crew decided to get into actually producing their own Doctor Who adventure, or as close as they could legally get.

Now, for the next part, I'm going to quote liberally from Simon Guerrier and his blog:

"Keith Barnfather had been offering [the convention] Downtime,' says (Jason) Haigh-Ellery.

The script for this was by Marc Platt, and reunited several of the Doctor's companions – a major selling point for fans. 'But it just wasn't ever going to get off the ground,' Haigh-Ellery remembers. 'That was nothing to do with rights but the availability of the actors. Kevin Davies heard about this, and said, "I've got this idea for a Sontarans story."'

Again, my thanks to Simon Guerrier, whose blog I have quoted and to whom I give full attribution, but whose permission I have not sought. *(I did communicate with him later, and he was actually pretty flattered. But as a general rule, kids – don't do this at home)* All of the quotes in this section are from Simon, by the way. I will happily recommend Simon Guerrier's writings and blog to anyone interested. He is insightful, intelligent, talented and prolific.

The improbably named Keith Barnfather was another fan who headed up something called Reeltime Productions. Reeltime's main thing was doing documentary interviews called *Mythmakers* (named after a lost Hartnell serial set in the Trojan War) with members of the cast and crew of Doctor Who. Basically, these were DVD Extras before DVD Extras existed.

Back in 1987, they'd dipped their toe in with *Wartime*, a ghost story about UNIT's Sargent Benton. Now, in the wake of

The Stranger, Barnfather and his company were trying to do their own Who sidequel - *Downtime*. We'll come back to that.

Simon's tale offers a fascinating window into what was going on at the time. Reading between the lines, *Shakedown* seems to have been both inspired and in competition with *Downtime*. Given that Reeltime would end up doing distribution for both, it seems that the competition was pretty friendly.

But consider the context. Doctor Who had gone off the air in 1989. Not cancelled, the BBC refused to say that it was cancelled, rather, just taking a rest. Well, okay, in 1990, fans might accept that. In 1991, they're wondering. 1992, they're getting a bit antsy.

1993 comes along, it's the 30th Anniversary, and suddenly it's back! John Pertwee does his two radio serials. There's the documentary *Thirty Years in The Tardis*. There's all this talk and hoopla of the *Dark Dimension*, the return of Tom Baker, a multi-Doctor extravaganza, that's going to be the biggest thing since sliced bread. And then it's over! *Dark Dimension* fizzles, and instead we get the twelve minute *Dimensions in Time*. All the excitement leads to … nothing much. No future. That must have been so disappointing. There must have been this huge fan base and audience, just… waiting, wanting.

It's around this time that groups like the Projection Room and Timebase Productions started trying to do their own fan videos. Not surprisingly, it's also the time of *Downtime* and *Shakedown*.

This is when Keith Barnfather and Reeltime Pictures got their brilliant idea. So of course, Barnfather gets out there, trying to sell it, trying to put the deal together. Everyone's interested. Really, it's one of the only games in town. The BBC has gone back to sleep, so what else is there to talk about? So of course, his struggles are showcased officially and unofficially at the Dreamwatch Convention.

The Second Pirates History, Page 148

It seems to have fallen into a sweet spot around that time. Look at it this way – if Keith Barnfather had been crashing and burning spectacularly, then Gary Leigh would not have wanted anything to do with production. Barnfather would have been this giant, flaming cautionary tale: Don't try this!

On the other hand, if Barnfather's project had been a runaway success, everything coming together and falling into place, that would have occupied the field. Success would have been too dominant. Gary Leigh would have looked, gone *'I can't compete with that!'* And stayed home.

Instead, it was struggling, it was a good idea, it looked feasible, it was having trouble getting off the ground. It was exactly the sort of thing that people would look at and go "Okay, that's doable, I have a better idea though..."

"The Sontarans would be just one way of drawing the fans to Shakedown, as the project was christened. The script would be by veteran Doctor Who writer Terrance Dicks and the production could also use 'name' actors when casting its several human characters. Because these were new roles, actor availability was no longer a problem – if one former Doctor Who star could not make the proposed shooting dates, they could go to another...." Guerrier wrote.

Basically, Gary Leigh could think "Yeah, I can make this work." This could be the landmark production. As is so often the case with these things, enthusiasm trumped common sense, and a group of happy go lucky amateurs set out to make history or at least a footnote in history.

Now, let's take a breath for a second. Before we go further, let's canvas the resume of this production. I know, it's tedious and it pumps up the word count, but really, these are unique historical artifacts in that while they're essentially jumped-up fan films, part of their claim to history is their resume – the people involved and the connections to Who. There's no avoiding it, Sorry.

The Second Pirates History, Page 149

First up – the Sontarans: They'd originally appeared in the *Time Warrior* with Jon Pertwee. From there, they returned for the Tom Baker serials, the *Sontaran Experiment* and the *Invasion of Time*. They skipped over Peter Davison. But then came back to menace Colin Baker and Peter Troughton in The *Two Doctors*. They also featured in what is arguably the first ever minisode *A Fix With the Sontarans*.

They were the creations of Robert Holmes, one of the best writers to grace Doctor Who. He did eighteen Who scripts, from Troughton to Colin Baker, including some of the finest stories in its classic history. He had passed away in 1986. His estate wasn't really worried about stepping on the toes of the BBC, and was willing to cash a modest cheque, or simply extend his legacy, by licensing the right to the Sontarans. During this period they would go on to appear in Reeltime Productions *Mindgame* and *Mindgame Trilogy*, as well as in the BBV Production *Do You Have A License to Save This Planet,*' and some BBV audios. They got around. In the modern era, they've made the jump to the new series of Doctor Who and even the *Sarah Jane Adventures*.

The Sontarans are the distant fourths, as far as enemies of the Doctor go. The big three, grouped closely, are the Daleks, the Cybermen and the Master. Then there's a very big gap, and you get the Sontarans, at least by weight of numbers, then after that the Yeti and the Great Intelligence as a sort of fan favourite, then the Ice Warriors, the Monk, the Rani, Omega…. It thins out fast.

According to Holmes backstory, the Sontarans were at war with the Rutans. The Rutans had appeared, sans Sontarans, in *Horror of Fang Rock*, written by Terrance Dicks. So the Holmes estate, and possibly Dicks, threw them in too, which was nice of them. They weren't as well drawn out, being basically green glowing shapeshifting jellyfish with homicidal tendencies.

Not a lot of inner life going on with the Rutans, but then again, most of the Doctor Who monsters didn't express much of an inner life, come to think of it.

Not much inner life for the Sontarans either, now that we think of it. They were all pretty one dimensional. They were about what they were about, and that was good enough – nuance was for inferior species apparently. Basically, they were militarists and warmongers.

I liked their first appearance in the Pertwee serial *The Time Warrior*, where, really, being on Earth was an accident, the Sontaran didn't want to be bothered at all. He didn't want to conquer Earth, didn't even like the place, he just wanted to go back to his war.

Monomania is a tricky thing – it makes the Daleks scary, but it seems to have caused the Sontarans to descend to comic relief.

On the positive side, the Sontarans have much better than average mobility and expressiveness – they can actually see out of their costumes (when not wearing those stupid helmets). There's clear view for eyes and mouth, they have humanoid forms, simple costumes, but are still visually quite distinct. You can see how they beat out the Yeti and the Ice Warriors, both of whose costumes were pretty tough sledding for stuntmen. On the other hand, they never quite latched onto that scary/crazy vibe that catapulted the big three to greatness.

The script fell to Holmes friend and colleague Terrance Dicks. Dicks was a long-time Doctor Who veteran. He'd started off co-writing *Seeds of Death* and the *War Games* way back in the Troughton era. He'd been script editor through the Pertwee Years. During the Tom Baker years, he'd written *Robot, Brain of Morbius, Horror of Fang Rock* and *State of Decay*. *Fang Rock* by the way was the first screen appearance of the

Rutans. He also wrote two Doctor Who stage plays – *Doctor Who and the Daleks in Seven Keys to Doomsday*, and *Doctor Who: The Ultimate Adventure*. He was also involved with *Death Takes a Holiday*, reviewed in this series. And he's written an incredible number of Doctor Who books, extending all the way up to 2008.

My impression of Dicks is that he's one of these journeyman writers. Very competent, knows his stuff, knows how to craft and pace a story. Not necessarily brilliant, but technically skilled and hard working. He is entirely worthy of respect. Given that our friend Mr. Guerrier reveals that Kevin Davies had the original idea for a Sontaran story, it's not clear how much of the story or plot are Dicks, and how much of it is him creating the story or simply filling in the dialogue.

Kevin Davies was the director. My impression is that he was and is a hard-core Who Fan, though I think his bent is for Sci Fi in general, and that British flavour in particular. He was involved in some of the earliest known fan films, *Doctor Hoo* and *Oceans in the Sky*. At this time, his credentials were thin. He'd just had some success with the documentary *30 Years in the Tardis*, so he was riding high at this time. But prior to that, his professional credits were a couple of short films – the *Corridor Sketch* and a *UNIT Recruiting Ad*.

'The project got moving quickly. 'Within a couple of weeks,' says Haigh-Ellery, 'everything was signed, sealed and delivered. It was that fast.' Gary Leigh was executive producer, with director Kevin Davies and composer Mark Ayres also producing. How did Haigh-Ellery get involved? 'I'd done productions, I was really keen to do it and also I'm a businessman. I'd worked with Gary on his magazine so he trusted me. He said, "Can you help me out?" So I came in as associate producer.' Again quoted from Simon's blog.

If we look at the rest of the crew list on IMDB, a lot of them connect back to Kevin Davies – mostly *30 Years in the Tardis*, but also the *Corridor Sketch*. That explains how it came together so fast. One of the things that takes time with these productions is just basic organization, recruiting people, getting them into the right positions, getting them working together. All that had pretty much come together with *30 Years in the Tardis*. All Davies had to do for *Shakedown* was give his rolodex a shake and everyone fell into place.

After *Shakedown*, Davies directed *Dalekmania*, and another documentary on the making of *Hitchhikers Guide to the Galaxy*. He had a couple of regular directing credits for *Space Island One*, something called *Archangel Thunderbird*, and he did another fan film called *The Few Doctors*. But almost all of his subsequent credits are video documentary shorts, the stuff you stick on DVD's. It's a respectable living.

For *Shakedown*, I found the directing to be a bit flat. Staid at many points, workman-like generally. The whole thing could have been tightened a bit. There were some poor choices, where he needed a close up and went long, or where he needed to pull more of a performance from a cast member. It is what it is. Could just be the limitations of budget and circumstance. On the other hand, there were some very nicely framed images and shots. He does have a good eye, something that was apparent in *30 Years in the Tardis*.

We've already met Gary Leigh, of Dreamwatch. Jason Haight-Ellery is one of the founding members of Big Finish., In fact, he's the one who registered the '*Big Finish Productions*' corporation after *Shakedown*. He's credited with producing or directing over 300 audio or radio productions. *Shakedown* is the earliest credit he's got on the IMDB.

Mark Ayres is listed as producer, but he's also responsible for the sound edit and the musical composition. He goes back to the fan film *Oceans in the Sky*, through the semi-professional productions, *PROBE* and even *Curse of Fatal Death*, and did musical composition in the McCoy era, and sound work the new series.

To be honest, I didn't particularly like his work here. I didn't particularly like it on Sylvester McCoy's stuff. Generally, with music and soundscapes, less is more. It's a very subtle thing, you need to make your point, but not be noticed making it. Ayres tends to be brassy and intrusive, his soundscape, his music, calls attention to itself and not in a good way. It's too loud, and he doesn't seem to know when to quit, or how to do quiet – he gives us dramatic music for Sontarans climbing a ladder for gods sakes. Climbing a ladder should not need dramatic music.

I dunno, you do have to keep in mind, that he's a professional, and he's managed to get regularly paid for this stuff. I'm just a snarky guy writing a review. It may be that this sort of thing was in fashion in that era, and we're just looking at it from a different era's sensibilities. Or it may be as simple a thing as idiosyncratic tastes. My advice – watch it yourself, listen to it, and be the judge.

There you have it – a strange mix of the professional, the semi-professional and the enthusiastic fans, the few and the proud, the mad and the bad, united by love of Who, fond memories, the desire to revisit past glories or the insane dream of new glories, stepping stones to bigger and better things, or just cashing a cheque. Just enough naivety to think they could pull it off, and just enough competence to actually manage it, if they could just keep it together and not murder each other…

"What is the role of an associate producer? 'As I discovered on that shoot, it was to stop the executive producer from killing the director! It was quite fraught, as we were all very honest about in the Making of Shakedown video. I think the film is great, don't get me wrong. We were doing a Terrance Dicks Doctor Who script by any other name!' quoted again from Simon's blog.

Oh, and not enough money. Dreamwatch may have become a big fish in its little pond, but film and television production, even quite modest film and television production, is an insanely expensive proposition. I suspect no one was working for free on this; a lot of people may have been working cheap, but cheap is not the same as free. As Simon reveals, Gary Leigh blew his budget, and Jason Haight-Ellery had to reach into his own pockets.

"The production went over budget, but by this point Haigh-Ellery had got the family business into much healthier shape. 'I was able to say to Gary Leigh, "Don't worry, I'll cover it." It was good I had the money to do that.'

Even so, the production feels pretty shoestring.

How successful was Shakedown? *'It made its money back and it's still earning money today,'* says Haigh-Ellery.

That perhaps tells us a little bit more about how shoestring the project was. This wasn't television broadcast. It wasn't theatrical release. It wasn't even really typical Direct to Video fare like Charles Band's *Full Moon* productions.

Rather, it was straight up a specialty item – comic stores, gaming stores, collectibles, convention sales, mail order. That's a specialized and quite marginal market. I don't know enough about the marketplace back then to guess at what their realistic budget might have been, or what their prospective sales were, but if they came out of it with their shirts, I'm guessing it was a near thing.

I think that it's significant it was never repeated. Gary Leigh certainly had no stomach for it. But I think if it had been really successful, he might have gone back in, or Kevin Davies would have found another patron. They'd given themselves room for a sequel.

"He (Jason Haight Ellery) was keen to start work on a follow-up project, but others did not share his enthusiasm. 'Gary Leigh will say himself that he found Shakedown quite difficult,' he continues. 'We

talked about Shakedown 2, and Gary was like, "Yeah, but I'm not doing it now."

I think that's why the Audio Doctor Who universe emerged, both in terms of the fan audios and of Big Finish. Not only was it less of a technical challenge, and definitely less expensive, the economics just worked better. We'll touch on this in the next volume. There's probably a very interesting book waiting to be written to explore that Audio universe, both inside and out. I'm not the one to write it, but I'd happily read it.

But anyway, I've kind of gone down the rabbit hole. Let's back it up, shall we? *Downtime* and *Shakedown* represented the pinnacles of this genre. Almost everything else was downhill in terms of cast sizes, crew sizes, effects, production quality, etc. These were marginal productions, getting more marginal with every iteration, trying to find a budget supported by a very tenuous economic model.

On the front of the camera, we had some very familiar faces: There was Brian Croucher; recognizable from *Blake's 7* where he played the mad-dog Commander Travis. This role, he was much more restrained, and actually, he played the male lead, a member of the group of dilettantes who have commissioned a space yacht for a race. It takes a bit for his character to actually break out. The direction doesn't particularly serve his character well. On first viewing, I considered him fairly bland. On a repeat viewing, I came to like his reserved pragmatism and competence; he plays the part with a sort of low key Sean Connery vibe. His performance was an emerging pleasure.

Also up front is Jan Chappelle, also recognizable from *Blake's 7* where she played the Spock role – as the telepath Calley. She lasted three seasons and managed to distinguish herself in that. She's a thin woman with an angular face, and as designated star of this production, a lot of the weight falls on her slender shoulders. Her character is Captain Lisa Deranne, of the Tiger Moth, making ends meet by hiring on as a Yacht for a bunch of poofters she can barely stand.

Michael Wisher is one of her crewmen. No worries about him. He dies pretty fast. Then he gets better. Then he dies again, and gets better. Wisher is best known as Davros from *Genesis of the Daleks*, but he's done a lot of stuff in and out of Doctor Who.

The rest of the rich poofters include Carole Ann Ford, better known as the Doctor's granddaughter, Susan way way way back in the first years of Doctor Who. She plays a rich, somewhat arrogant dowager. Then there's Sophie Aldred, the final companion of the McCoy era. She plays a rich, somewhat arrogant playgirl, who has cast member Rory O'Donnell, as her plaything. Rory O'Donnell doesn't seem to have any significant credits, but then he doesn't have much of a role here. It is nice to see Aldred and Ford, familiar faces and all that, but really, there isn't much to their roles – they're playing rich, mildly unpleasant people who die on cue.

The Sontarans are played mostly by non-actors or unknowns. One the one hand, you know how it is; they're a band of thugs. That shouldn't take much in the way of chops. But the key Sontaran players, Commander Steg and Lieutenant Vorn, really needed people who had some idea of how to get a performance out from under all those latex prosthetics. As it is, they kind of force their delivery as a sort of monotone growl without any pacing or rhythm.

Of course, Sontarans are aliens. Who knows what they talk like? So that approach works well enough, or at least, it's justifiable. It's no worse than some of the Sontaran performances we've seen in the original series.

The nice thing about the Sontarans is that there are quite a lot of them, the internet movie database lists seven, and they're appropriately stompy and mean. Really, what more can we ask for? If you're going to have hostile, militaristic, stompy aliens, it's good to have a lot of them to fill up a screen.

By the way, Toby Aspin, who played the Sontaran Commander Steg, also played a Sontaran, Commander Steg, in Reeltime's *Mindgame* in 1999.

As is often pointed out, the Sontarans look a bit different than they do in Doctor Who proper. That was for copyright reasons. Not that the Sontarans were terribly consistent from one BBC appearance to the next. Holmes may have owned the Sontarans, but the BBC had some claim to the details of look, so they had to tweak it. No big deal. Any dedicated nerd could come up with twenty reasons in five minutes why these guys look the way they do. Maybe Sontaran clones just look like that when they get old. Maybe their ship suffered a radiation leak and they're a bit poisoned. Maybe they're a special lineage of clones. See? Easy.

In any event, the BBC themselves couldn't keep the look of the Sontarans straight from one appearance to the next anyway, which was peculiar, given that they were supposed to be a race of clone warriors. The Beeb never really seemed to have a good grasp of them.

With *Fire and Ice*, and the Ice Warriors, *Phase Four* and the Cybermen, and *Downtime* and the Yeti, we had the paradoxical situation of fans handling the monsters better than the BBC. Shakedown handled its Sontarans at least as well as the BBC, and better than some of their outings.

The production took place on the HMS Belfast, a British naval frigate that had been permanently docked in London as an Imperial War museum. Once again continuing the fan tradition of great production values through often astonishing locations. No worries about shooting over the top or past the edges of the sets, all those bulkheads and stair ladders, pipes and big metal things are pretty authentic, both retro and futuristic, and utilitarian. Ridley Scott might have improved on things by grunging it up, but I don't think the Imperial War Museum people would go for that.

Apart from that, the production values and effects are a bit hit and miss. The model work for the Sontaran Battle cruiser is nice enough. The various optical effects as ray guns are shot or the Rutan oozes around are passable.

There's a Virtual Reality, or VR, sequence which is just painful. VR used to be a big thing in the 1990s, I'm not sure why. I remember being talked into wearing a VR set at a mall once back then. This was in the days before liquid crystal and flatscreen. The VR set I wore was a fifteen pound helmet with a cathode ray television set bolted to the front of it. While that slowly crushed your cervical vertebrae you interacted with a 'reality' that was a very low resolution, super grainy, CGI image beamed at your eyes in oversaturated colour, while a computer tried to adjust your head and hand movements to the image in a manner contrived to induce epilepsy. Luckily, seizures never happened possibly because the neck strain and nausea were too distracting. I have no idea why it didn't catch on.

Anyway, they tried to do a VR scene here, keeping up with the cyberpunks, I suppose, and I kind of wish they hadn't. Trust me; it's just hard to watch, even if you don't have painful memories of a fifteen pound television set bolted to your forehead.

What's that you say? Am I ever going to get around to the actual review? I thought that's what I've been doing all along.

Okay, here's the good and the bad.

The good: Lots of provenance – recognizable names behind the camera, in the form of Dicks and Holmes, and familiar faces in front of the camera including Croucher, Chappel, Wisher, Aldred, Ford, although not playing the same characters. Croucher is very good, with a restrained and subtle performance that grows on you, Chappel holds her own, Wisher, Aldred and Ford are basically just showing up, but give decent performances.

If you're the sort of fan who is thrilled by the thought of Carol Ann Ford and Sophie Aldred in the same scene then this one's for you. But, even if you're not that sort of person, which would be a good thing, it's actually nicely watchable.

The story is serviceable – with plenty of scope for drama. There's that 'ten little Indians' thing going on, as everyone gets killed off one by one, the mutual suspicion and treachery of the Humans and Sontarans, the by-play among the Humans. There's actually more complexity and plot than they needed, and it clutters things a bit. But generally, I'm in favour of complexity over excessive simplicity.

The direction is a little slack, so that it seems undeveloped and draggy, but not in an intolerable way. The direction and cinematography is serviceable but needed to be a little tighter. The editing could have been sharper. I can't blame the Director, Kevin Davies too much, he had his limits, but he was also the essential person on this production. Without him and his rolodex, it just wouldn't have happened. And as I said, he did have a good eye for images.

It moves along, there's a nice sense of danger and menace, plenty of twists even given the straightforward premise. Production values are good, Sontarans are nicely realized. It's entertaining. I'm not looking at my watch as it plays, and honestly, sometimes I look at my watch a lot in movie theatres watching hundred million dollar blockbusters from Hollywood. So that says something very positive.

It's a shoestring production, but it's got some heart to it, and heart counts for a lot with me. There's nothing in here that I can't readily forgive, and a lot to enjoy.

Back in the day, in the wilds of Canada, I'd read about this in the tattered copies of Dreamwatch that made it out to the tundra. I'll give it to them, they were big on self-promotion. I was always curious and somewhat skeptical about the whole thing. Honestly, this sort of spin off just seemed a doomed venture conceptually. But I never thought I'd actually get to see it. So here we are years later, and it's on YouTube and a few other places, and I finally got to watch it.

My first thoughts were on the impossibility of ever truly divorcing a work from its context. I guess that applies to everything when you think of it. But it really came home here. I was watching something which was essentially a bastard child, so clearly an offspring, but so carefully distant from its parent. Something that had all this history and provenance, both self-evident and in all that old promotion. It was impossible to watch it as a fresh thing. I think maybe that's why I found it disappointing, it was perpetually in the shadow of Doctor Who. If anything, learning more about it, and it's strange sibling relationship and rivalry with *Downtime* intensified that shadow.

Strangely enough, on repeat viewing, it got fresher for me. I liked it more. Isn't that peculiar? Watching it again, I was able to see past the shadows and the provenance and the baggage it dragged around, and just appreciate it for what it was at heart – a modest, imperfect, but quite engaging little space opera. It doesn't need to be more than that. That's just fine.

Strip out the Doctor Who elements, and it could stand as a perfectly fine low budget VHS or DVD rental item in the 90s marketplace, not top flight studio fare, but more than acceptable as a B-movie, and better than quite a lot out there at the time.

Interestingly, after *Shakedown* came out, there was some effort put into treating it as a pilot, and seeing if some television station or network (other than the BBC) wouldn't be interested in picking it up as a series around Chappell and Croucher. It didn't happen, but it's intriguing to think about. Sometimes a "Yes" is a matter of luck and circumstance, or just knocking on the right door at the right time. The project had been brutal enough that the producers weren't going to keep on doing it on their own, this way more demanding than Baggs stranger. But if things had shaken out just a bit differently and it had been picked up, it might have made a legitimate spin off series.

Regardless, I'd recommend it, if not as a professional film, then as a labour of love by fans. And if you can't divorce it from its baggage, well, at least it's interesting baggage.

CAST: Jan Chappell - Lisa Deranne; Brian Croucher - Kurt; Carol Ann Ford - Zorelle; Sophie Aldred - Mari; Toby Aspin - Commander Steg; Tom Finnis - Lieutenant Vorn; Rory O'Donnell - Nikes; First Sontaran Trooper - Jonathan Saville; Sontaran Troopers - Keith Dunne, Derek Handley, Julian Jones, Stephen Mansfield; Michael Wisher - Robar;

CREW: Gary Leigh - Executive Producer; Mark Ayres and Kevin Davies - Producers; Jason Haigh-Ellery - Associate Producer; Kevin Davies - Director; Terrance Dicks - Screenplay; Dave Hicks - Director of Photography; David Rowston - Assistant Director; Tony Clark - Production Designer; Paul Vanezis - Editor; Mark Ayres - Music and Sound Design; Kelly McGrother - Costumes; Paige Bell - Make-up Supervisor; Helen Coltart and Margaret Aston - Make-up Assistants; Ian Scoones - Special Effects and Pyrotechnics; Derek Handley, Stephen Mansfield, David Miller and Susan Moore - Sontaran Masks and Helmets designed and build; Dave Brian - Spacecraft Design and Build; John Priest - Robar's Toolkit; Mat Irvine - Medical Kit; Dan Maier - Mari's Dress; Derek Handley; Studio & TV Hire and The Trading Post - Additional Props; Tony Clark - Additional Models & FX Animation; Kevin Davies - FX Animation; Gary Wales - Graphics; Keith Dunne - Set Dresser; Peter Gilman - Production Assistant; Daniel Cohen, Roger Dilley, Rob Francis, Stuart Hutcheson, Tony

Pulham - Floor Assistants; James Haviland - Runner; Robin Prichard - Stills; Eileen Handley - Transport; Jason Haigh-Ellery and Jonathan Saville - Stunts; James Mastorianni and Simon Cohen - Camera Assistants; Lisa Newsome - Sound Mixer; Jim Ireland, Tony Clark and Alistair Lock - Boom Operators; Mark Ayres - Dubbing Mixer; Paul Vanezis - Video Effects/Editing; Sontarans Created by Robert Holmes; Filmed at Pinewood Studios and on Location at HMS Belfast; Special Thanks to Patricia Holmes, John Wenzel and Commander Ron Fisher of HMS Belfast, Neil and Cliff Culley of Westbury Design - Pinewood Studios; Shirley O'Mara and Pip Cooper of BBC Post Production, Robert Allsop, Bill Baggs, Gateway Audio Visual, Andy Grant of World Leisure Corp, Passion Pictures, Ace Editing, The Moving Picture Company; BBC Pebble Mill - Video Post Production; Dreamwatch Magazine; Dreamwatch Media Ltd, copyright 1994.

Review: Downtime (1995)

Old Friends and Ancient Enemies

STORY: The Second Doctor's former Companion, Victoria Waterhouse, travels to Tibet, summoned by what she believes is her father. There she meets Professor Travers, secretly the Great Intelligence. Fast forward to London, a decade later, Victoria is the head of New World University, scientology-like cult with a secret agenda. Sarah Jane Smith, the Brigadier and his daughter are all drawn into a web of intrigue as the Great Intelligence plots world domination....

REVIEW: So.... Downtime. What's to say? I suspect that some might argue over whether it is a fan film. But then again, I'm not sure that it could properly be considered anything else. To tell you the truth, I don't even really know how or why it exists, much less where to fit it in.

In economic terms, these semi-official, loophole projects seemed to make no sense whatsoever. Designed for a self-limited market, sold in mail order and at conventions.

It's possible that *Downtime* played on television or showed up in video stores in England, but I'd honestly be surprised. They'd get coverage in *Starburst* or *Starlog*, show up at conventions. But in terms of revenue generation, it's hard to imagine them breaking even, even with minuscule poverty row budgets.

Of the bunch, I mark *Downtime* as the most ambitious, the most enjoyable, and one of the closest to being in the spirit of Who. Basically what we got here – was the equivalent of an archeological field trip through Doctor Who. Let me take you through it,

The main villain is the Great Intelligence and its operatives the Yeti – actually robots designed to look like actual Yeti in hopes of being inconspicuous. That's right, I said it. The Great Intelligence disguised his robots as Yeti so that they would be inconspicuous. Great Intelligence? I'm sorry, I don't think you should call yourself that if you have the same plot as a *Scooby Doo* villain.

Nevertheless, they appeared in two seminal Troughton adventures – *The Abominable Snowmen*, which actually was set in Tibet, which makes the Yeti thing merely stupid and ludicrous, and the recently rediscovered *Web of Fear*, where they invaded the London underground. Apparently because Yeti are inconspicuous... in England.

Even in *Downtime*, that little inspiration is lampshaded when the Brigadier explains his prior confrontation with the Yeti, another character asks if it happened in Tibet, and the Brigadier, utterly deadpan, responds *"London subway."*

The Great Intelligence and the Yeti were second tier Doctor Who villains – they were well remembered and well liked, and they'd had a couple of innings. But they'd been on the bench for almost thirty years, apart with a couple of cameos for the Yeti in *War Games* and the *Five Doctors*.

Their two outings against Patrick Troughton's Doctor were their only significant appearances, but they seemed to have a bit of cachet to them. For a while, there were hopes that they were going to be the next great Doctor Who monster – the next Daleks or Cybermen. This was back when the BBC were retiring the Daleks, but they were still hoping to find something to repeat Dalekmania. They were actually planned to come back for a third Troughton outing, The Laird of McCrimmon which fell by the wayside.

They were created and owned by Mervyn Haisman and Henry Lincoln, who had also created the character of Colonel Alistair Lethbridge-Stuart, who first appeared in Web of Fear and was soon to be elevated to the rank of Brigadier. They'd also created the Quarks and Dominators, another pair of candidates for 'next Daleks.' The dispute over toy rights to the Quarks lead to a fairly nasty falling out with the BBC, and while Lethbridge-Stuart would go on to be a Doctor Who icon, the Great Intelligence, the Yeti, the Quarks and Dominators all fell by the wayside. Strangely, the Yeti remained in the popular imagination as a classic Doctor Who monster.

Although their only subsequent appearance was a cameo in the Five Doctors in 1983, they had managed to get a leg up way back in 1970, when Jon Pertwee, freshly minted as the new Doctor, appeared in a famous series of publicity photos clowning around with the Yeti. They also featured prominently in a documentary that was frequently run, where Jon Pertwee remarked that nothing was as frightening as a 'Yeti on your loo in Toting Bec.'

Honest to god, I have no idea what that means. Loo is a bathroom, right? A toilet? Toting Bec? A place? Do the Brits have some primal fear of monsters abusing their plumbing?

Although Pertwee never actually had a Yeti story, his publicity photos and that pithy quote somehow kept them alive.

Basically with Doctor Who, you have the big three: The Daleks, the Cybermen and the Master, with the Sontarans coming in as a distant fourth. You can count on the fingers of one hand the enemies and aliens that were successful enough to rate a second go round. The Yeti were probably the most famous and recognizable of the bunch.

So…. we have a classic, well remembered Doctor Who monster and villain, associated with Troughton and Pertwee.

Then we had the Brigadier, played by Nicholas Courtney. I'm not going to waste a lot of time – the Brigadier's tenure in the classic series extended from the Second Doctor to the Seventh. Brigadier Lethbridge-Stuart appeared twice in Troughton adventures was a staple of the Pertwee era, showed up in Tom Baker, Davison and McCoy stories. He appeared in the *Three Doctors*, the *Five Doctors, Dimensions in Time, Death Takes a Holiday, the Sarah Jane Adventures*, probably a lot of Audio stories, and he was referred to several times in new Who. Well, he's in this one, and this time he's the star of the show – the action and the emotional centre of the story revolve around him.

Sarah Jane Smith, played Liz Sladen, was Jon Pertwee's last companion and Tom Baker's first and most popular companion. She came back to reprise her role in the *Five Doctors*, had her own pilot in *K9 and Company*, showed up in Dimensions in Time. In the new series, she came back to meet David Tennant, proving conclusively that the new series was a continuation, not a reboot of the old series, and quickly spun off into her own series, the *Sarah Jane Adventures*.

Victoria Waterfield, played by Deborah Watling, is more obscure. She was a Troughton era companion who travelled with the Doctor beginning in *Evil of the Daleks*, through *Tomb of the Cybermen*, through both the *Abominable Snowman* and *Web of Fear*, finally leaving in *Fury From the Deep*. Many of the serials that she played in are now lost to us. There was a reference to her in the Tom Baker era, in a quick little throwaway scene where Sarah Jane tried on one of her old dresses. She was also referenced, but not seen in *The Two*

Doctors. Finally, she had a quick appearance in *Dimensions in Time*.

Professor Edward Traverse is played by Jack Watling, Deborah Watling's real life father. He also guest starred in both the *Abominable Snowman* and the *Web of Fear*. The character was planned to return for the *Invasion*, but Jack Watling's schedule did not allow it, and so Traverse was referred to in the story – the Doctor and Jamie are looking for him, fail to find him, and the plot happens.

Then there's John Leeson as the disk jockey – Leeson is better known as the voice of K9. Geoffrey Beevers appears in *Downtime* as Harrods, who becomes the Brigadiers sidekick – previously he appeared in *Ambassadors of Death*, and more critically, he guest starred as the Master in *Keeper of Traken*. James Bree who has a small role as the Llama had shown up in *Trial of a Time Lord* as the Keeper of the matrix, in *Full Circle* as Nefred and in the *War Games* as the Security Chief. You can see where this is going. It's like a Doctor Who reunion party.

The script was by Marc Platt, the writer of *Ghost Light*, which is simultaneously the best and the worst serial of the McCoy era. *Ghost Light* is surreal, disturbing, intriguing and unpredictable, the production values are terrific, the performances spot on.

On the other hand, you have to watch it six times, listen to the commentary, read the novelization and play the DVD documentary features several to have a chance of understanding it. A flow chart helps. Platt's known for the Doctor Who novel *Lungbarrow*, which was seen as the culmination of the Cartmel Masterplan. He's also known for a Big Finish audio story - *Spare Parts*, which inspired or was adapted for the Tenant episodes *Rise of the Cybermen and Age of Steel*.

As a writer, I'm not really sold on Platt as a plot guy. Or maybe it's the opposite. Maybe he's got too much plot going on, elaborate machinations and threads breaking down into minutiae. His handle on dialogue is hit and miss. Sometimes his stuff sings, as when the Brigadier is jousting with Cavendish, one of UNIT's new blood or raining thunder down on the Great Intelligence, and sometimes it thuds as when the Brigadier is trying for a tender moment with his daughter.

Where Platt really excels as a writer is dishing out the strange. He's not so much a science fiction writer as a surreal writer, and he's very good at serving up haunting imagery, setting moods, and delivering something compelling. Here he indulges this penchant effectively, slipping the Brigadier into dreams and hallucinations, offering up mystical experiences and building tension effectively.

Meanwhile Chris Barry shares a directing credit with Keith Barnfather. Barry directed several episodes of the original *Daleks* serial, as well as the *Romans,* the *Rescue,* and the *Savages* for the Hartnell period. *Power of the Daleks* for Troughton. *Daemons* and *Mutants* for Pertwee. And for Baker – *Robot, Brain of Morbius,* and *Creature From the Pit.* His last work on Doctor Who had been 1979, and he'd pretty much been consigned to the wilderness in the John Nathan Turner era. But on the whole, by no means a hack, rather, a highly competent, perhaps above average Director and one with credentials across 16 years of the series and four different Doctors.

Keith Barnfather, on the other hand, was much more of a fan. Nevertheless, he produced and directed the *Myth Makers* video series, featuring extensive video interviews with stars and cast members of Doctor Who and documentaries about the show. Years later, he'd go on to do an effective job directing *Daemos Rising,* the sequel to *Downtime.*

Finally, we come to Ian Levine, who is listed as both producer and sound. Levine was arguably the ultimate Doctor Who fan, and as such personalities often are, flamboyant, controversial, and as much hated as loved. Levine is one of those people who, whatever their sterling qualities, can't help but provoke fury. I'm not here to praise or bury him, but it's worth listing a few of his contributions. First, he was one of the key people responsible for stopping the destruction of Doctor Who's old tapes by the BBC. A lot was lost, but without him a lot more would be gone forever. He was responsible for the return or recovery of a number of lost episodes. During the 1980s, he was an uncredited continuity consultant for the series. He also has a controversial claim for the story development on Colin Baker's *Attack of the Cybermen*. He provided the music for *K9 and Company*. In the modern era, he's occupied himself with 'fan films' Reconstructing *Shada* and a number of the lost or unmade serials.

All of this goes to give *Downtime* an astonishing provenance – it's got one of the great classic monsters, no less than four companions played by the original actors, including two of the most famous ones, a writer, director and producer all intimately associated, not just with the series, but with particular highlights of the series. No other production, with the possible exceptions of *Shakedown* and *Death Takes a Holiday* returned so many familiar faces in front of and behind the screen. Just in terms of these credentials alone, it's a must see.

So… is it any good?

Yeah, well, if it was eyeball gouging bad, I wouldn't be writing this, would I? Trust me, I wouldn't do that to you.

As with all Doctor Who fan films, you have to approach it with a certain amount of forgiveness. For me, the tough part are the Chillies – with their yellow duckbill caps and green sweaters. There are a lot of them, and they're used as best as they can be. But you know, they're supposed to be a slightly disturbing, vaguely menacing cult, like the Mormons or the Scientologists…. and the wardrobe just kills that. It's hard to take them seriously, and they need to be taken seriously. It's not as bad as the Elton John zombies in *Frankenstein Island*, or the army of alien Andy Warhol robots in *Cosmos 1999* (or whatever they called it on the DVD compilation you watched). But it's still a major misstep, and one that could have been easily avoided.

It also falls into that 'Uncanny Valley' at 68 minutes, where it's much too long to be an acceptable television hour, and much too short to be a film length, and so we're vaguely uncomfortable because the beats and rhythms feel wrong for us. It feels too slow and too fast at once, stretched into an uncomfortable position. It gives us this paradox of simultaneously feeling dragged out and undeveloped.

A lot of the BBV and Reeltime productions also seemed to make the mistake of falling into that awkward space – PROBE, the *Auton Trilogy*, *Cyberon*, etc. What really hurts is that most of these productions were shot on a shoestring, no real money, and so landing in uncanny valley, in this awkward length really exposes the paucity of the production.

Downtime, at least, manages to overcome this with a certain amount of lushness. There are some very impressive shots – there's a fake crane shot of a series of above ground walkways with Chillies strolling around, like some futuristic expressionist ant farm. There are some intriguing shots of ziggurat like buildings. The Brigadier wanders through a black and white tidal flat. His daughter lives on a converted canal barge. There are an astonishing number of extras in the Chillies and Unit Troops.

No matter what, this must have been a fairly marginal production, financially. In a documentary segment on YouTube, there's a reference by one of the actors to being lucky if they could do two takes, so I'm thinking that a lot of this is poverty row. I don't know how much money they had to spend, but they managed to get a remarkable amount of production value in there. I'm baffled by how they could afford the licenses for the Yeti, or actors like Liz Sladen and Nicholas Courtney, or a fraction of the usually impressive costumes and effects that are in use. No matter how cheap people worked, this must still have been, for the people involved, an expensive production. I'd love to know what the budget was. I suspect Ian Levine of having a fairly crucial role in personally funding and fundraising.

For the most part, they use what must have been very limited money well. Only rarely does what must have been the threadbare nature of the production show through. Once in a while, it does show – look, if you don't have money, then you don't have the time or the resources to do multiple takes or camera set ups to make a scene look good. You shoot your page and get it in the can and move on. You get the shot you get, not necessarily the good looking shot you wanted. You see some of that, but not nearly as much as you think. This is a movie that manages to make a hundred grand look like a million onscreen, and that's not a small accomplishment.

With all that said, when you come to any Doctor Who, you have to ask "How's the Monster?" Which brings us back, again, to the Yeti.

Before I saw this, I never saw the Yeti as scary. I mean, I'd seen pictures, a clip or two from the documentary featuring a Yeti running in slow motion, all of which had been massively underwhelming in the terror department. I knew that the Yeti's roar was a slowed down toilet flush. This didn't inspire fear or horror. And Pertwee's quote about a Yeti on the loo? Well, maybe that would be terrifying if you were the next person to use that loo. But come on. Even Pertwee couldn't keep a straight face when posing with them. They were just too big and round to be really scary.

But watching *Downtime*, the Yeti really are scary. Their secret is that they're huge. The Yeti are creatures of terrifying mass – they have this animalistic bulk, like a grizzly bear. They're best when they're up close against their victims, when their sheer mass is just overwhelming. Suddenly, they're not cute and rolly-polly, they're a solid wall of muscle looming over you that are more than able to tear you limb from limb.

A Yeti a long way off? Well, no monster is terrifying a long way off. But a Yeti right there in front of you? That's unnerving.

There's another subtle aspect that makes them terrifying here. They're faceless, almost featureless. Except for two glowing eyes, the Yeti are simply this shaggy brown mass. That's disturbing. The thing is, as people we have expectations. We expect faces – the Doctor may confront an alien monster, but it usually has eyes, a nose, a mouth, a jaw, all in the right places, it has arms and legs in proportion. We rely on this. Give us a monster that doesn't have recognizable features, or that subverts them, and we're creeped.

Interestingly, previous versions of the Yeti did have at least vague muppet-like facial features. Here, the Yeti's faces are nothing more than glowing eyes. It's a good choice. That, I think, was part of the success of the Daleks, they were non-human. But the Daleks were hyper stylized with their bumps and ridges, plates and plungers, stalk and dome. The Yeti are just a glowering, shapeless, featureless, faceless, hairy mass. A big heaping pile of darkness with two glowing spots staring at you. Think about waking up in the middle of the night with that in your bedroom, this huge almost shapeless, solid mass reaching almost to the ceiling, filling the space, with almost nothing recognizable in that bulk except two staring, glowing red eyes.

The Second Pirates History, Page 173

So yes: The Yeti are scary. They're also handled very well. They are talked about, but barely appear at all in the first half, except for a couple of quick shots. It isn't until later that one shows up and is an actual threat, and they don't come into full monster until the end. Their use is well played.

The Great Intelligence is properly menacing and scheming. There's not a lot of nuance to the Great Intelligence. Bad guy? Check. Wants to take over the world? Check. That's about it.

If the Great Intelligence has any trace of personality, it's about frustration. You can tell he's just fed up. You can tell he's just seething. It's all been dragging on and dragging on and there are all these stupid little obstacles and people getting in the way and having to be nice to them. You can just tell he's climbing the walls; he's just so desperate to finally get on with it.

Jack Watling plays the role with a large slice of ham, and to be fair, he brings the physical presence to carry it off. That's an underrated skill, not everyone can get away with it.

Credit where credit is due, the Great Intelligence's plot to take over the world this time is actually fairly innovative and rather techno-thrillerish.

Of course, the problem with Techno-thrillers is that they often date badly. When a story hinges on the Evil Villain chortling over his plans to rule the world with 640k and green screen cathode ray monitors…. well, maybe if we wait long enough, it'll have a retro charm. But we're going to have to wait. Years ago, I remember watching a cyberpunk thriller where a major plot point hinged on a five and a half inch floppy disk – you know, back when disks were actually floppy. I felt embarrassed for all concerned. So yes, not quite so bad, but this is something you'll have to make an effort to overlook.

Beyond this, the strengths of *Downtime* lie in two things: First, in the dead on performances of Nicholas Courtney, Liz Sladen, Geoffrey Beever and Victoria Kressman as people caught up in a web of strangeness and danger as alien machinations unfold around them. They and their established and developing relationships is really the emotional core of the movie. Deborah and Jack Watling are both serviceable in their roles as servants of the antagonist. Unfortunately, Mark Trotman, who plays a pivotal character, Daniel Linton, is a bit of a weak link. But overall, it's well done.

The other strength is the accumulating strangeness, the surrealism of the piece, as established by Platt's script. The most haunting moments are the Brigadier going in and out of fugue states, with hallucinations showing up at odd moments. This is something you couldn't really have seen in Doctor Who, and so in a sense, it goes beyond its source material.

Platt ably captures the 'matter of fact' bizarreness of dreams, the sense of portents and meanings just beyond grasp, and the tendency to take strange turns with equanimity. The Brigadier is the perfect character to be at the center of this because no matter how strange it gets he never loses his cool. For him, it's all in a day's work. A lifetime of working with the Doctor will get you that.

The direction and writing are wildly inconsistent. I attribute the first to the divided directorial responsibilities of Chris Barry, who as a pro knew exactly what he was doing and carries it off. Chris Barry is more than competent at bringing Platt's surreality to life. He knows his job. At the same time, he's quite straightforward. I found myself wondering what someone more in tune with say a David Lynch sensibility might have done with this material. But that's just me. Keith Barnfather, on the other hand, seems to have come in a video documentarian with little dramatic experience, so whether it's fair or not, I tend to attribute the rougher spots to him. As for the inconsistency of the script, the highs and lows are both traceable to Marc Platt, who I'll count as a talented but undisciplined writer.

Let's take the opening scene – Basically what happens is Victoria Waterhouse wanders through a Tibetan Monastery, called by a mysterious voice, encounters a Lama and has an ambiguous conversation. This scene is informed by a whole series of bad choices.

The set or setting of the Monastery is impressive, with vaulted arches receding into the shadowy background. The Lama sits in shadow; his costume a match with the decor, a part of the scene but completely unnoticed until he moves. Nice effect.

And thus endeth the good part of the scene.

As to what goes wrong – the initial image is terrific, a blurry constellation which resolves into hanging lights. But then it pans over to a bas relief face. Okay, so we've moved from one inert structure to another, that's not really an effective transition, and doesn't actually add anything. Then it pans over to the passageway of vaulted arches and Victoria Waterhouse stumbling forward. That pan to the stone face is just unnecessary, it's inert.

Victoria shows up, the Lama who has been sitting unnoticed all along, comes alive – a nice touch as I said. Then the conversation happens, and it's a mess. This is where it falls apart. It's basically a static long shot of two characters mumbling desperately at each other. The direction is pedestrian to be kind, there are few if any cuts to close ups. There's no sense of visual punctuation, of real action or reaction, there's no flow. I have no idea who shot what, but I'm inclined not to blame Chris Barry for this.

The dialogue is vacuous, Victoria and the Lama are very urgent, but they can't seem to focus. There are gaps in the information which makes it very hard to have any idea what this is about. That's on Platt, I think. He's good with mood, but not so good actually conveying specific information to the audience, and that's a critical skill. This is what they decided to open with. Ouch! It's a teaser, but it frustrates more than it teases.

We get the same kind of writing again when the narrative introduces Sarah Jane Smith. Apparently she's doing some sort of work for New World University, but we never quite figure out what that is. They dance around the subject. Then Victoria shows Sarah a big silver ball and Sarah goes 'you had it all along!' The audience is going 'whaaaat?' The effect is sort of like listening to someone talking on the phone, you get half the conversation. Except in this case, the missing half of the conversation is in Marc Platt's head. It's like a struggle for the man to write functional dialogue – by which I mean 'fill in background details so we know what's going on' expository stuff.

Now, contrast this with a scene later on where the Brigadier meets his successor in UNIT, a fellow named Cavendish. Just two guys sitting casually across from each other in a nondescript room talking. But it's riveting. They're explicitly not talking about what they're there for, they're tap dancing around the subject, sparring, each trying to learn what the other knows, without revealing too much themselves. The camera knows exactly where to be, picking up verbal sallies and reaction shots. Deftly written, and full credit to Platt who is now brilliantly in his element, and deftly directed, which I'll give to Barry.

Of course, there's no way to really tell who directed what. I'm just guessing.

The Brigadier's dream sequences, particularly his dream encounters with Linton, are spot on. The images and dialogue are haunting. The personality of the Brigadier ring through authentically. This is where the Linton character appears to best effect. In other places, he's almost a cipher, but in these scenes, there's a personality, an identity.

My impression is that as the movie proceeds, the production seems to gain more and more confidence. As the plot gears up, the villain's machinations proceed and matters approach a crisis. It becomes increasingly impressive.

The climax outright rocks. The skies are darkening, effects-lightning is arcing across the sky, and the Great Intelligences black webs are spreading across the planet. Meanwhile the Brigadier is captured, the Great Intelligence gloats, and an army of Chillies are gathered in the University Commons which now takes on the aspect of some Aztec temple complex. It is chilling and damned near apocalyptic. I'll take that back. It's chilling and outright apocalyptic. Not the bargain basement apocalypse of a shoestring production with a limited cast and barely enough money for two take. No, this is *Ghostbusters* level, end of the world, apocalyptic with hordes of extras, over the top villainy and just all kinds of hell breaking loose.

So, between all this – solid performances, a better than average alien invasion story livened up by a surrealist sensibility, a good monster well realized, more on and off screen Doctor Who references than you can count, and a production that, despite its wobbles, improves dramatically as it goes along, I'd recommend *Downtime* as a 'must see.'

True, it's far from perfect. Given the limitations, there's no way it could be. But you know, watching these things, I find myself appreciating the potential. A bit more time, a bit more money, perhaps something as simple as making a better choice in costume or editing at a pivotal moment. I see in these things the shape of much better movies, the shadows of brilliance barely missed, and oddly, it makes me forgiving.

The Second Pirates History, Page 178

Am I trying to talk you into liking these things? I don't think that's actually possible. It's about the gut. You'll either like it or dislike it, and there's nothing much I can do about that. But maybe I can talk you into a more forgiving mood.

Look, the thing is, these film makers, even in a case like this where the on screen and off screen talent is astonishing, they're working without deep bench of skills and resources. They don't have the advantage of a full crew of technicians, entire departments and staffs of people with years and decades of experience and the time and the money to do it right. Marc Platt didn't have the benefit of a real script editor to winnow the incoherencies out of his script. There's no wardrobe designer to actually come up with a sufficiently cult-ish outfit for the Chillies. Chris Barry doesn't have the luxury of multiple takes, the time for set ups, the staff of 1st AD, 2nd AD, grips, director of photography, focus puller, all the way back up the line. What you have is talent and love and maybe one take to get it right.

Compare this to the Wachowski Siblings *with Jupiter Ascending*, or Lucas with the *Phantom Menace* – these guys had the resources of whole countries, entire armies of honed professionals to put to their vision. So they have no excuses, they stand or fall, and can easily fall. When they fall, they have no other excuses but themselves.

For something like *Downtime*, you can admit that they blow it on some point or other, but you can also see where they were going, you can appreciate how close they came, and you can appreciate what they got right. It's like a talented amateur coming out onto Ripley field and taking a swing, and maybe they didn't hit it out of the park, but godallmighty, that was a hell of a swing.

Watching it, I was struck by the fact that it didn't actually have to be a Doctor Who vehicle at all. The basic concept of the villain and its plot was portable. It would have worked as a straight direct to video, or even a limited theatrical release sci fi thriller. The Yeti could have been replaced by some equivalent looming shapeless bulk. They could have filed all the Doctor Who references off completely. They might have actually been more successful that way – disposing of the Doctor Who references might have given them more opportunities to push the envelope in certain other directions, and they might have accessed a much wider market and audience, gotten a little more dangerous.

As it is, this is targeted exclusively to Doctor Who fans and I can't see that as anything but a self-limited market. But then again, it' a targetable niche. So who knows? Perhaps the strategy of going straight Doctor Who made financial sense. Still, I don't have any impression that anyone got rich off of this or launched a glorious career.

Nevertheless, I think it says something about the production that, had they gone in that direction, they could have stood on their own as a successful Sci Fi thriller. Thinking it over, I'd say that's probably the highest compliment I can pay it: That it could have succeeded without Who.

Bottom line – there's more than enough to make it worth the watching for any number of reasons.

Downtime is unique in having the tide flow the other way. Kate Lethbridge-Stuart, played here by Victoria Kressman, as the daughter of the Brigadier, actually migrated into Doctor Who canon. The character, as played by Kressman, reappeared in a second Reeltime Production, *Daemos Rising*, in 2004. From there, Kate Lethbridge-Stuart, now played by Jemma Redgrave with a blonde dye job, made the jump to Doctor Who itself, following her father's footsteps, as Scientific Advisor to UNIT in *The Power of Three* in 2012, *Day of the Doctor* in 2013, *Death in Heaven* in 2014, and returned again for the *Zygon* episodes in 2015, and some *Flux* episodes in 2021.

So far as I know, this is the only time a fan creation has actually been incorporated officially into BBC continuity. Does this mean that *Downtime* and *Daemos Rising* are retroactively canonized? Who knows?

But if an official production like *Scream of the Shalka* can be retroactively de-canonized, then anything is possible.

CAST: *Nicholas Courtney - Brigadier Lethbridge-Stewart; Elizabeth Sladen - Sarah Jane Smith; Deborah Watling - Victoria Waterfield; Jack Watling - Professor Travers; Beverly Kressman - Kate Lethbridge-Stewart; Mark Trotman - Daniel Hinton; Geoffrey Beevers - Harrods; Peter Silverleaf - Christopher Rice; John Leeson - Anthony; Miles Richardson - Captain Cavendish; James Bree - Lama; Kathy Coulter - Receptionist; Alexander Landen - Gordon Lethbridge-Stewart; Jonathan Clarkson - Chilly 1; Miles Cherry - Chilly 2; Richard Landen - Lead Yeti; David Howe, Tony Clark and Conrad Turner - Yeti; Stephen Bradshaw, Keith Brooks, Mark Moore, Gabriel Mykaj and John Reddington - UNIT Soldiers; Caroline Adlem, Bernardo Allen, Daniel Beagles, Patrick Barker, Daisy Beevers, Tom Beevers, Helen Bibby, Will Bird, Hannah Boutton, Michelle Brady, Sally Burrell, Chris Challis, Paul Coslett, Simon Cox, Myoko Costello, Neil Currant, Rebecca Colley, Emma Butt, Louise Bullock; Neil Currant, Nina Dobson, Anita Frank, Pasquale Frewer, Louise Gray, Helen Greenwood, Lisa Grigg, Ian Hayllar, Joe Hickey, Alex Izzo, Derek Johnson, Marina Johnston, Richard Jones, Robin Lindsay, Charles Marenghi, Ben Marion, Gabriella Mauch, Scott Miller, Dave Owens, Sonia Paternosta, Emma Penruddock, Matthew Radford, Simon Raisey, Peter Robinson, Sergio Rosendo, Andrew Savory, Heike Schroder, Steven Shaw, Eli Silverman, Ben Shepherd, Lucy Smith, Zeb Soanes, Romek Sczczesniak, Posy Walton, Kelly Westlake, Richard Wood, MatthewWest, Nina Terlinden and Andrew Stitt - Chillies.*

CREW: *Keith Barnfather - Producer; Chris Barry - Director; Marc Platt - Original Story and Screenplay; Ian Levine, Paul Cuthbert-Brown, Andrew Beech - Associate Producers; David Rowston - First*

Assistant Director; Ben Hicklin - Second Assistant Director; Edward Strickland - Second Unit Director/Line Producer; Alistair Lock - Additional Visual Effects; Geraldine Landen - Set Decorator; Robert Moubert - Assistant Cameraman; Robin Lee - Second UnitLighting Cameraman; Sara Dickenson - Second Unit Make-up; Robin Prichard - Stills Photographer; Terrance Dicks and Mervyn Haisman - Script Advisors; Gabriel Mykaj - Stunt Co-ordinator; Robin Lee - Stunt Double; Mark Stammers - "New World" Graphics; Gary Fenton - Satellite Animation; Lena McKenzie - Production Accountant; Edward Strickland - Off-Line Editor; Caroline Lees - Production Assistant; Andrew Savory and Simon Litton - Runners; Julian Vince - Yeti Designed and Created; BBC Visual Effects Department - Visual Effects; Mike Tucker and Alan 'Rocky' Marshall - Visual Effects Supervisors; Ian Levine, Nigel Stock and Erwin Keiles - Theme and Incidental Music; Troicana Studio's London - Music Recorded at; Tim Eames - Music Recording Engineer; Dan Harrison - Music Recording Assistant; Richard Landen and Andrew Beech - Production Designers; Zoe Randall - Make-up; Steve Picco - Location Sound; Dubbing Editor - Michael Daniels; Admusic Shepperton Studios - Sound Re-Recording; Buster Field - Dubbing Mixer; Lighting Cameraman - Keith Watts; Anita Ladd, BBC Costume Department - Supervising and Main Costume Designer; Clive Burgess, Angels & Bermans - Brigadier's Uniform; Roy D. Bell - Lama's Robes; Limelight Ltd. - Location Facilities Supplied; Robert Moubert - Computer Displays; Frame Store - Animation and Digital Effects by; Tony Almond - Graphics Designer; Jason Bartholomew - Animation Supervisor; Paul Vanezis at BBC Pebble Mill - Editor; Non-Linear Editing - Porst Production Sound Facilities; Roger Stevens - Post Production Sound Supervissor; Alistair Lock - Special Sound and Radio Jingles; Land Rover Ltd. - Range Rover Supplied; With Thanks To: The University of East Anglia, Livewire, Nexus University Television, Mark Abis, The London Dungeon, Forte Crest Hotel Regent's Park London, English Nature, British Waterways, General Cemetery Company, Holkham Estate, Sainsbury's, Sharon Reed, Roger Moffat. By Reeltime Pictures Production; Tropicana Holdings Production; Dominitemporal Services Production

The Second Pirates History, Page 182

Review: The Auton Trilogy (1997-1999)

Invasion from the Uncanny Valley

As I have searched out and watched these fan films, one of the things that's struck me is how well they've done Doctor Who's monsters.

The Cybermen in *Phase Four, Deconstruction, the Experiment, Trident, Gene Genius* and *Flight of the Daleks* are used as effectively as the classic series ever managed. Then there's *Fire and Ice* and the *Holly Terror*, which manage to do justice for the Ice Warriors, *Downtime*, which does a terrific job with the Great Intelligence and the Yeti. The Sontarans come off very well in *Shakedown, Mindgame, Mindgame Trilogy* and the *Churchtown Incident*. The Daleks in the *Millennium Trap* and *Power, Reimagined*.

Why is that, I wondered? I think that part of it might reflect a level of commitment. You don't get these things at the corner store. A Cyberman or a Dalek, an Ice Warrior or a Yeti, they represent a serious and painstaking effort to build a really elaborate prop or costume. It's not done overnight, it can't be. It takes time and care.

And I think that there's a lot more personal investment in the series and its lore. It's not a question of just dragging out whatever is available for marketing, or rummaging through the mythology for another monster. If you're doing a Fan Film and sticking the Ice Warriors in it.... You really really want Ice Warriors.

Typically, these things are done on a shoestring, so if you're going to the effort of doing something like that, that's a huge commitment. You're inclined to think about it, to work hard at it, and to take it seriously.

This brings us to Autons, a surprisingly popular monster. They showed up twice in the seventies, lead serials for Jon Pertwee's first two seasons: *Spearhead From Space* and *Terror of the Autons*. They almost came back with Colin Baker for *Yellow Fever*, and of course, they were the lead monster for *Rose*.

They are also a surprisingly popular fan film monster. There's *'Plastic Treachery'*, there's Westlake Film's *'Auton Diaries'* (created as a DVD extra for the Auton Series), Planet Productions *'Unit-Revival'* of course, there's a little Cameo in Chris Hoyle's *Masterplan*, and of course, there's the BBV's *'Auton Trilogy'*

So what is it about the Autons that works? I think it's because they live in uncanny valley. Humans tend to see human faces everywhere, in smiley faces buttons, on Mars, cartoon animals, you name it. But roboticists when they were trying to make robots with human faces discovered something.... People were creeped out. The robot faces were too close to human, but not close enough. The effect was called 'uncanny valley' that place between the completely human, and the vaguely human but comfortably nonhuman.

There is something genuinely creepy and off putting about Autons blandly handsome, immobile, blank features. There's an indifference to them. You see an Auton coming at you, and you know that it could walk on by, or simply feed you into a wood-chipper, and do either with complete indifference.

Is a blank mask really scary? Sure. Look at the mask of Michael Myers from the Halloween series; it has that same effect, bland, blank, dangerous indifference. To a lesser degree, there's also Jason Voorhees iconic hockey mask, and all the rest of the slashers with their bags over their faces. No dripping fangs, no snarls, no furrowed muzzles, wild eyes or shaggy brows. Just.... bland indifference. No expression. Simply relentless steady malignance. Come to think of it, the Cybermen share that bland, expressionless quality.

There's also an engaging simplicity to the Autons. Black suit, blank mask, and there you go. By comparison, just about any other alien – Cybermen, Sontarans, is a costumer's nightmare. But Autons can be chugged out in a flash. Never underestimate simplicity.

The easier it is on the actors and costumers, the better its chances of being effective. Crazily elaborate and complicated costumes tend not to hold up to scrutiny and often are difficult to move in, and therefore difficult to shoot.

For whatever reason, they've ended up a surprisingly popular Doctor Who monster. You'd almost think that if they'd have showed up in the 60s, when the producers were desperate to find the 'Next Daleks' they might have been pushed much harder.

Auton 1, or perhaps just '*Auton*' – I'm skeptical that a trilogy was the hard plan, is actually quite watchable. It's a limited production, a handful of speaking parts, what looks like a single or limited set of locations.

Apparently, what UNIT has been doing, is that following all those Alien Invasions, Subterranean Eruptions, Dimensional Hijinks and Mad Scientists, once the smoke clears, they gather up all the leftovers, stick it in crates and then send it off to some top secret warehouse.... Where they promptly forget about it.

The Second Pirates History, Page 185

That actually makes sense. Not the forgetting about it part, that's daft. But the notion that someone's got to take care of all those leftovers and put them somewhere. Anyway, in this case, it appears that UNIT has some low level research division puttering around the thingy's, and one of the scientists, played by Bryonie Pritchard, triggers one of the things that should have been left alone, activating the Autons once again.

At this point, Lockwood, played by Michael Wade, and his clean-up crew are summoned. The game begins as they try to figure out what got out and how to catch it and kill it before it escapes the building. It turns into a classic bug hunt, as soldiers and protagonists play cat and mouse with the monster, handicapped by not knowing what the monster is, or who exactly is the cat and who is the mouse.

Now, we have to swallow the idea that UNIT is so badly managed and its bureaucracy is so incompetent that they can't properly keep track of or even maintain proper documentation of their alien remains. Ideally, all Lockwood should have had to do was look up a couple of serial numbers, and he'd know what got out. Hell, if the lab rats had been able to look up serial numbers, they'd have known what they were messing with. That's a pretty big pill.

But if you can swallow it, what's left is quite an effective little thriller. The direction is tight, the performances are competent. It's a bug hunt, as I've said, but it makes maximum use of its assets – claustrophobic settings, the characters uncertainty as to what they're dealing with, and the nature of that adversary when it acts, the whole 'enemy within' vibe. It's modest but entirely competent and well done.

It's all taking place inside a UNIT Warehouse/Research Lab. Everything is indoors. There are no external shots, no wide angle stuff, no 'vistas' or glorious scenes. Instead, it looks like a warehouse, the walls are gray, everything is functional and utilitarian, the living quarters and research lab are drab. There's a consistency to the look and feel which helps to sell the production.

The standout, however, is the character of Michael Wade's Lockwood. He's everyone's scary old schoolmaster, the voice of sarcastic authority, merciless, pitiless, and judging. Everyone's run across someone like that. The teacher, the supervisor, the investigator who coldly asks uncomfortable questions and has a sarcastic remark at your answer. Wade plays that part to perfection, probing, dissecting, questing.

But Lockwood is imbued with just enough humanity to make him compelling. He shows enough kindness, enough appreciation and humility, that we like him under his frosty exterior, and he exhibits enough vulnerability that we can sympathize with him. He is an appealing creation, and he steals the show

Bottom line? *Auton* is a modest but genuine pleasure. It's nowhere near the budget or the ambition of *Downtime* or *Shakedown*, but it knows its limits and it works effectively within them.

Auton 2: Sentinel, is the sequel to *Auton*. It seems that the lump of Nestene Goo from the last movie managed to escape. Engineering a hijacking, the Autons reactivate and march off, homing in on their next location, an Island containing the village of Sentinel. UNIT calls Lockwood in and the chase is on, but it soon becomes apparent that he has some sort of connection to the Nestene? Can they really trust Lockwood? Can he trust himself?

This is a much larger production than the first *Auton* movie. It's not restricted to a single indoor studio. Instead, there's all sorts of outdoor and location scenes. The principal cast is larger, Michael Wade is back as Lockwood, with the addition of Jo Castleton as a telepath, Bryonie Pritchard is there in a reduced role, and there are a number of new actors playing UNIT or Villagers on the Island.

The outdoor locations, on the boat, the church, the truck, village streets are all visually rich. There are some genuinely iconic scenes. In one the Autons are striding through the field, when they come upon what seems to be a village idiot who crouches down grinning, most of the Autons simply stride past him without even looking, except for one who stops and looks down. Then a little later, the Autons stride into a village, and the handful of villagers who witness it, stop and applaud as the Autons walk past them. Those images are as disturbing as they are unforgettable.

It seems that the Nestene goo, taking the form of Winslet, the caretaker from the first Auton, has made its way to the village on the Island and set itself up as Vicar, hypnotizing the population, and using their collective psychic energy to activate a full sized Nestene Entity which has been buried beneath the Church.

UNIT shows up, they get into a firefight with the Autons. Lockwood and the telepath race to confront the Vicar, and at the climax, a whale sized Nestene Entity, rendered with CGI, full of tentacles erupts from beneath the floor and makes its way to the roof of the Church, where it emits a 'Dinner Time!' signal to the rest of the Nestene out in space. It's a smashing climax.

Then it, and the signal, disappears. Just like that. Vanishes, without a trace, as if someone just turned off the CGI.

The Telepath announces that Lockwood has done it. Although we have no idea what "it" he's done, or how, or if it's a good thing, or part of the evil plot, or whatever. Even Lockwood doesn't seem to have a clue.

Anyway, that's it. Nothing to do for it but to have a nice cup of tea on the boat ride to the mainland.

So yeah, problem with the non-ending here. I'm not actually giving away much, since this is very clearly a cliffhanger intended to set up and take us into the next movie.

Unfortunately, the ghost ex machina style ending kind of throws it for us. Listen, if you're going to go to all the trouble to CGI up a glowing bean-shaped thing with tentacles and have it climb up on top of a church and go all screechy sending a signal to its bros…. You can't just have it disappear. And especially not for a nebulous reason.

The end result is a lack of coherent resolution. Which is a shame because most of the rest of the film is brimming with interesting characters, dialogue, imagery and ideas.

Auton 3, sadly, turns into something of a mess. Perhaps this has something to do with changes behind the scene. Nicholas Briggs wrote and directed the first two, but there seems to be a falling out. He wrote the third, but instead chose to be credited as Arthur Wallis. Not a good sign when the writer takes his name off the project. He shares his writing credit with someone named Paul Ebbs. Bill Baggs and Patricia Merrick share directing credit – nothing wrong with them, but Briggs directed the first two, so it's probably not a good sign that he stepped down on the third one.

Plot! The Nestene consciousness captures Lockwood, and it and the Autons retreat to yet another small town, where they throw a force field over the whole place. The various UNIT staff trapped within flounder around ineffectually fighting Autons and trying to link up, until finally the Autons round them up and bring them all together. The key, it turns out, has been Lockwood all along, who has been waging a terrific psychic struggle to contain the Auton broadcast signal within himself.

The Second Pirates History, Page 189

There you have the problem. The central character for the story is Lockwood, again played by Michael Wade, as he's been for the previous installments. But this time, Lockwood doesn't actually have anything to do. He lies in a hospital bed, occasionally mumbling vague nonsense, while all the other characters talk and ineffective actions are taking place elsewhere.

Now, according to the script, he's engaged in a ferocious life and death psychic struggle with the Autons. Okay. But the trouble is that he does this by lying in a hospital bed and making the odd pointless remark.

It's not visually interesting or effective. Admittedly, internal struggles are always difficult to portray visually in film. For this reason, film and television tend to stay away from that kind of conflict, or at least to minimize its screen time. Wrestling with a conscience may be terrific for writing on a page, but its death on a screen. It's a visual medium, and you need to portray things visually. When your action revolves around a guy lying in a bed… time to go home.

There's also the fact that he's a prisoner the whole time. So essentially, the real fight is over and done, the good guys are in check. It's as if Luke Skywalker opened *Revenge of the Jedi* by being captured by Darth Vader and spending the rest of the movie in Vader's dungeon. It's a tough choice and it kills the movie.

Now, given these two central issues – the fact that the core conflict of the movie is all about Lockwood's psychic struggle, and the fact that Lockwood is already a prisoner – that literally screws every other character in the movie. Almost nothing that the rest of them do is meaningful, they run around, they shoot at Autons, they try to communicate with each other, they wonder if they've been compromised, but nothing much comes out of any of it. The whole bunch of them could have spent the movie playing checkers, until the climax rolled around and the Autons herded them into Lockwood's hospital room.

It's a disappointing conclusion, particularly when the first two movies were quite well done.

Perhaps Briggs wrote in some means of dramatizing Lockwood's psychic struggle, and it was unwisely abandoned either because it was too costly, too difficult or made no sense. Any of those three would be a good reason to jettison something, but I say 'unwisely abandoned' because they didn't actually replace it with anything. Maybe Brigg's original version actually addressed some of the issues I'd highlighted, maybe the other characters were effectual, maybe Lockwood was running around loose. Who knows?

So that's the *Auton Trilogy:* A terrific, low budget B-movie opening with an interesting central character; a very good second entry with some really arresting images and visuals, strong characters and an unsatisfactory conclusion; and a lackluster third which barely resolves the cliff hanger, but seems to have lost its mojo.

A major standout is Michael Wade's character of Lockwood. He's not necessarily likeable, but he is formidable and fascinating, and he very nearly singlehandedly salvages the third story. There's also a strong supporting cast, although not necessarily handled well. Bryonie Pritchard is rock solid in the first, Jo Castleton in the second, and then they both kind of get lost in the third. The villain, Auton-Winslett is solid. There are no bad performances.

The production values and direction are quite good. The first is a bug hunt through a warehouse, that's handled well. The second is much more ambitious, and has some great visuals. Even the very minimal CGI construct is okay for the time. The problem with the third episode has less to do with production value and acting – its crippling flaws are built into the story structure, and it would be hard to direct your way out of it, but they don't try.

I'd happily recommend the first two as worthwhile watches. Pretty meh about recommending the third. But hey, you got to complete the set, am I right? Two out of three is not bad. The *Terminator* franchise is running what... Two out of six?

Originally, the first movie was going to be a vehicle for Nicholas Courtney playing his Classic Who character, the Brigadier. Unluckily, Courtney wasn't available for the project, word was he suffered from clinical depression and just pulled out, so it was rewritten to center around the newly created Unit Operative, Lockwood. It was a good move, Lockwood is very compelling.

Then there's the dynamics of the stories – the first story is quite self-contained, and it ends with Moore's Lockwood inviting Bryonie Pritchard's character into an effective partnership. Certainly there were a few loose threads hanging about, but that seemed to be where things were going – a sort of Mulder & Scully ghostbusting duo.

That isn't where the series went. Pritchard is relegated to a peripheral character in the second movie, and while she plays a role in the third, it's far from central.

Instead, things jump in a different direction, focusing on the Autons and their fiendish plot. It's not necessarily a bad decision, and certainly the seeds were planted in the first movie. But it seems like a swerve.

All this leads me to suspect that the Trilogy is more a post-facto thing. The BBV started with Auton, when that was a success, they followed up. There may have been some talk of something more, some ideas, but I don't think that there was anything resembling a concrete plan.

Review: Do You Have A License To Save This Planet? (2001)

Look, It's Just Funny, That's All

STORY: Earth is under assault from a series of ruthless alien conquerors, the Sontarans, the Autons and the Cyberons. Arriving to save the day is the Chiropodist, aka the Foot Doctor, played by Sylvester McCoy. But can he defeat his greatest enemy?

REVIEW: There have been a number of Pseudo-Who licensed productions. *But Do You Have a License to Save this Planet* stands out as the BBV's crowning work, even more than their early *Stranger* videos or their *Auton* series.

Why? Three reasons: 1) It has Sylvester McCoy playing the role of the Chiropodist or Foot Doctor, a character and performance indistinguishable from his BBC Doctor; 2) It's a manifesto, a 'take that' to the BBC who had spent an entire decade as the dog in the manger, treating their property with appalling shabbiness and condescension, as well as the BBV's fuzzy embrace of the fundamental ridiculousness of the property; 3) It's funny as hell. Really, that's it. It's simply funny.

The BBV had spent most of a decade straddling very fine lines to messing about with the Doctor Who universe.

Sometimes they would simply to come as close to infringing on BBC's copyrights as they could, without actually tripping over the line - we see that in the *Stranger* series, where for the first three adventures, Colin Baker is playing the Doctor but no one ever actually calls him that, and he's travelling through time and space, but the Police Box is never shown.

This approach was repeated again with *Cyberon*... they couldn't get the rights to Cybermen so they tweaked the name and the look just enough to avoid lawsuits. *The Airzone Solution* featured four of the living Doctors, Pertwee, Davison, Baker and McCoy, all playing non-Doctor roles in a rather goofy no-budget environmental thriller. Nominally a straight science fiction feature, unconnected to Who, it really sold on the basis of the various actors' prior history playing the Doctors.

Their other line of attack was simply to obtain licenses for specific characters or monsters. Liz Shaw, the Jon Pertwee Doctor's first companion (and the actor who played her) came back twenty three years after her last appearance with the Doctor, to play an *X-Files* style investigator through four adventures in *PROBE*. Guest starring were actors and actresses who had played Doctors or Companions, albeit in different roles, but readily apparent to the viewer.

The Autons and UNIT were both licensed for a trilogy where they battled it out without the Doctor. Nicholas Courtney was originally to return as the Brigadier, but had to bow out due to illness. Even the Zygons got a movie to themselves in 2008, with a rather creepy serial killer mystery featuring explicit nudity.

The BBV output was full of familiar faces from Doctor Who, sometimes reprising their roles, sometimes doing something different. That familiarity is the key selling point for the BBV output. BBV stories even created some of their own recurring characters, such as the UNIT operative, Lockwood, in the Auton series. The productions had real talent involved. Mark

Gatiss, for example, who would go on to mainstream success with Sherlock, started out writing the *PROBE* series. Nicholas Briggs, now a Doctor Who institution was also involved with the *Auton trilogy*. Lance Parkin, Kate Orman, Pip and Jane Baker, all contributed scripts for video or audio productions.

On the downside, they often had no money and it shows. So instead of things happening, you end up with long stretches of people talking and killing time. The stories are sometimes lacking, with a meandering pacing, and shot with fairly dull camera set ups. The videos are almost all of non-standard length which must have made them difficult to sell in the mainstream.

There are high points. Some of it is surprisingly well done. But sometimes the BBV's output is more intriguing than accomplished. It can lack the panache of the BBC series, or even the more enthusiastic fan productions. Mostly, it feels sincere, but a little dull.

Ultimately, like Reeltime and Dreamwatch, the BBV's productions traded on nostalgia for Doctor Who. Traded? Hell, they existed for that purpose. This often lead to them being caught in a no-win situation, with enthusiasm, without resources or training, trying to appeal to nostalgia while still trying to do something new with the material.

Maybe I'm being too hard on them. They produced steadily through the 1990s into the 2000s, and that needs to be respected. Dreamwatch ultimately produced a single film, Reeltime a handful, the BBV was in it hard core.

So why is *Do You Have a License to Save this Planet* such a standout? Because here they go all out on both approaches. Because here they throw in the kitchen sink. Because this feels like Bill and Helen just woke up one morning and said, *'To hell with the BBC! We're just going to do what we want! Go for broke!'*

The Second Pirates History, Page 195

It was actually their tenth anniversary production, so that might actually be it. I imagine that ten years of carefully skirting the BBC, occasionally fighting them, and watching their combination of bureaucratic obfuscation and proprietary aggression.... Well, there are things you just want to get off your chest.

On the other hand, they were also clearly inspired by the BBC charity special *'Doctor Who and the Curse of Fatal Death'* which featured Rowan Atkinson (and for brief moments, Hugh Grant, Steven E. Grant, Jim Broadbent and Joanna Lumley) as the Doctor.

The result was a grab bag - Sontarans, Autons, Cyberons, even a Krynoid. All of them, for once, with lives of their own apart from their struggles with the Doctor. The Autons are out to conquer, the Cyberons just want to blend in and take over. There's a goofy subplot of a Cyberon-Auton romance, and another subplot of next door neighbors valiantly trying to welcome the interlopers into the community. A Sontaran shows up and is frustrated to discover that the planet he's come to conquer is already multiply invaded and he's at the end of the line - his last scene is calling UNIT to complain about all these alien invasions, and being put on hold. But the true nemesis is the Licensed Reality Corporation and its increasingly camp and utterly soulless chief executive.

Sylvester McCoy, a gifted comic actor long before he ever became the Doctor, gets a perfect foil in Mark Donovan, an Oliver Hardy style sidekick. Together, they're a classic comedy team: Laurel and Hardy, Abbot and Costello, Martin and Lewis rather than a Doctor and Companion per se.

It's genuinely smart and funny. In some ways, it reminds me of the *Airplane* movies, the gags keep on coming, and eventually you're just overwhelmed. If something doesn't work, just wait a second, and something completely different will come along. There's a lot of in jokes and referentiality, but I'm actually good with that. This is aWho spoof, by all means, take the piss.

But unlike the *Airplane* movies, there's a lot more diversity. Here, we get everything from *Benny Hill*, to *Carry On*, to *Monty Python*, broad clowning, to clever satire, 1920s silent comedy, to sitcoms, pratfalls, wordplay, you just never know what's coming next. A metafictional gag comes out of nowhere as a circle appears around a bad costume sleeve announcing budget cuts. An attack by aliens is defeated with spoons and turns into an impromptu dance number, which in turn leads to extraterrestrial romance. There are animated sequences, action, the production continually shifts point of view from the Foot Doctor, to the various aliens, so you never know what's coming next.

At times, Sylvester McCoy mugs like a clown at a circus, and then in the next minute, he'll toss off something so casual and sublime it feels like it came from a Pinter play. There will be a joke which plays directly on the series, such as a regeneration scene, followed by a fourth wall breaking throwaway out of a Hope and Crosby movie, and then a bit of shtick straight from the Three Stooges. It's all good hearted and there's nothing truly malicious.

It's a shame, since Doctor Who has always been known for its wit, but I've never noticed a lot of humour or comedy in BBV stuff before this. Their work always came across as dead on straight, sober and po-faced to a fault. Perhaps that was a reaction to their delicate situation licensing and nibbling around the edges of BBC ownership with threadbare productions. Maybe they just felt they couldn't afford to be light. If so, that's a shame, because it turns out, they were really good at comedy, and that's not an easy thing.

In terms of notables involved, Sylvester McCoy needs no introduction. Mark Donovan, who plays his sidekick is a working actor with a decent list of credits, but no particular affiliation to Who or its spin offs.

Sharp eyed observers, however, will spot Nigel Peever in the credits. Nigel was one of the key people involved in the Planet Video/Pacific UK/Ad-Lib groups, and you'll find his name on the credits of a great many fan films. The other notables are Rupert Booth and Philip T. Robinson from Timebase productions who play the various aliens. The Sontaran costume, by the way, is probably from Timebase's legendary unfinished production, the *Churchton Incident*.

Most of the rest of the cast and crew seem to be known chiefly from prior BBV productions, with Nigel Fairs and Jo Castleton standing out as BBV repertory players.

Interestingly, at least in some jurisdictions, *Do You Have a License to Save This Planet* might have an additional legal defense. Copyright Acts across the world contain exceptions and allowances for public purposes – it's called "Fair Use" in the United States and "Fair Dealing" in England.

American copyright law expressly allows for works of parody and satire. Parody and Satire in the United States being extremely broadly defined, as we see with 'Porn Parodies.' (Yes, Virginia, there are Porn Parodies of Doctor Who, quite a few of them, some of them not bad at all) (No, Virginia, we are not going to cover them, not in the second edition, anyway). So this, along with much of the work of the old Federation fan group, like *Save WHO'* and *Reign of Turner*, would be perfectly fine.

British copyright law is rather more restricted, but there is some basis for Fair Dealing claims.

Regardless, bottom line is that *Do You Have a License to Save This Planet* is probably pretty tough going if you're not a knowledgeable Who fan. Even a casual Who viewer would end up going 'What?'

But the better you know the show, and particularly its classic history, both on screen and off, the more rewarding and hilarious it will be. But that's the thing with jokes, you need the context.

CAST:: *The Foot Doctor/Chiropodist - Sylvester McCoy; The Salesman - Mark Donovan; Geoff/The Licensor - Nigel Fairs; Gloria - Jo Castleton; Rassilon - Nigel Peever; Delivery Man - Gareth Preston; Sontaran - Rupert Booth; Autons - Rupert Booth, Philip T. Robinson, Paul Griggs; Cyberons - Gareth Preston, Paul Griggs, Philip T. Robinson; Cyberon Voices - Paul Ebbs, Steve Johnson*

CREW: *Directed and Produced by Bill Baggs; Script - Paul Ebbs and Gareth Preston; Cyberons designed by Terry Cooper; Sontaran/Auton costumes - Philip T. Robinson; Sound Recordist/Sound Effects/Incidental Music - Mike Neilson; Main Theme - Steve Johnson; Editor - Bill Baggs; CGI/Video Effects - Steve Johnson; Production Assistants - Rob Neilson and Paul Griggs; Special Thanks to David Elms, Rob Shearman, Zoe McAden, Helen Baggs, Sherry Howell, Steve Butler; Props - Helen Gazely*

Review: Daemos Rising (2004)

Return of the Brigadier's Daughter

STORY: Following the events of *Downtime*, UNIT Operative Douglas Cavendish has a breakdown and flees to an isolated house in the country. Troubled by paranormal incidents, Cavendish summons Kate Lethbridge-Stuart for help. Together, they confront a mysterious statue, ghosts, deal with visions of hooded cultists and face the return of a Daemon.

REVIEW: *Daemos Rising*, from 2004, is the sequel to 1995's impressive *Downtime*, picking up on the stories of Kate Lethbridge-Stuart, the Brigadier's daughter, and former UNIT commander, Douglas Cavendish. It's also a sequel to the Pertwee serial, *The Daemons*, from 1971.

Sequels are often tough sells. The original always has the virtue of novelty.

To replace that, most successful sequels need to go bigger. Bigger scope, bigger cast, bigger effects, bigger stakes. The audience knows what the bang is, so you need to make a bigger bang. So I had some trepidation about *Daemos Rising*.

Downtime was an epic - the Brigadier, Sarah Jane, Victoria Waterfield, the Great Intelligence and the Yeti, fate of the world at stake, a huge cast, lots of extras, locations, you name it. Normally, you would follow that up with something grander.

In contrast, *Daemos Rising* is basically a two-hander, set in and around a house in the countryside and is basically a ghost story. Gone are the cast of familiar characters like the Brigadier and Sarah Jane, no rampaging monsters, no apocalyptic fate of the world shtick. That didn't seem like it was really going to set things on fire for me.

I was wrong. It turned out to be a pleasant surprise. Keith Barnfather's direction is assured. Beverly Kressman and Miles Richardson turn in solid engaging performances. The script works. The visuals are engaging. This was a compelling, economical, but very effective story. Its only real problem is that it stands in the shadow of *Downtime*.

The plot is fairly straightforward. As we've said, it's a ghost story. Douglas Cavendish, a former UNIT Operative, last seen jousting with the Brigadier in *Downtime*, seems to have had some kind of breakdown.

The things he's seen has unhinged him and left him unhealthily obsessed. He's stolen a handful of paranormal trophies and retreated back to a house in the countryside. Unfortunately, the paranormal isn't finished with him. He's troubled by strange apparitions and visions.

And he seems to be prone to sitting in a pentagram casting spells and reading from some ancient book. That's never a good sign. So, weird reclusive guy, creepy old house in the country, and paranormal incidents. Yep, it's a ghost story.

Cavendish summons Kate Lethbridge-Stuart for help. I'm not sure why. They don't seem to have any significant history, and Cavendish seems to be hiding out from UNIT, so his motivations are a bit obscure.

I gather that he had a breakdown following the incident with the Great Intelligence and the Yeti, and Kate was nice to him. He's become a bit infatuated with her, so he calls her for help.

Which leads to the opening scene: Kate shows up and the path takes her to a clearing with a strange demonic statue in the center. She stops, notes its ugly as hell, and goes on her way, returning back to the clearing.

After that, no matter which way she goes, to her increasing frustration, every path leads back to the clearing. She's being toyed with by paranormal forces. Angry, she touches the statue, and is struck down by visions of chanting robed figures.

Perfectly done. No special effects, no big flamboyant moment. Just a quiet ordinary scene, that smoothly and steadily drifts away from normality, becoming comic, then creepy and finally frightening. It won me over, it's a wonderful example of how to draw an audience in and build suspense.

Cavendish shows up to break the spell, and Kate follows him home. I have to say, at this point, I'd have gotten the hell out of Dodge. But Kate is made of sterner stuff.

There are all sorts of nicely mysterious bits - the strangely alien statue that never seems to be in the right place, the visions of the cultists, the door that can't be opened, the disturbing things in the shed.

There's a continuing juxtaposition of the normal and the unearthly that works very well. Everything looks fine, until you look more deeply.

The house is an excellent example, it's prosaic and homey. But then there's a door that Cavendish is afraid to open, and when Kate unlocks it, it leads to a subterranean hellscape -

actually Kent's Caverns. Beneath the facade of the house, there is literally a subterranean abyss.

Speaking of the shed, they can't tread on Doctor Who copyrights, but the script and props go out of their way to allude to the Doctor Who universe. As he rambles about his UNIT experiences, Cavendish talks about a warehouse filled with department store mannequins, clearly Autons, and a tip of the hat to the BBV's *Auton trilogy*. He talks about dead aliens in glass jars, about 'bits of flesh and tentacles' which we'll recognize as the mutants inside the Dalek casings.

It's all nice Who stuff. But even if you don't recognize it, it's still surreal and almost Lovecraftian.

Cavendish takes Kate to the shed where he keeps his stolen trophies. His big prize is a giant maggot in a jar of green liquid, clearly from the Green Death. Again, nice choice, because, more than anything else, it maximizes the unearthly creepiness factor. If we watch carefully, there's a Cyberman breastplate, a jar of Jelly Babies, the gun arm of a Dalek, something that looks like the demon doll from *Terror of the Autons*, and what might be an Auton head itself.

Anyway, about half way through, the ghost shows up and it gets all *Scooby Doo* on us. In the sense that it's not the supernatural going on, but rather sci fi - bastards from the future messing with us. The ghost isn't really a ghost, though technically, he's dead and a shade of himself. The robed cultists aren't Satanists, just a power mad clique. The supernatural trappings are replaced with science trappings.

In the end, Kate comes through for the win. A Daemon materializes, coming through as a crude CGI construct which probably was tolerable for its day, but Kate talks it into submission.

Well, that's not entirely fair, she argues her point of view forcefully and fearlessly and the Daemon grudgingly comes around.

Is this too much plot? I don't think so. This isn't really a story about story. There are other things going on here. It's really about setting a mood, creating and amplifying a feeling of strangeness. Beneath the ordinary world is an abyss of dark and mysterious forces.

It's also an engaging character study. Watching this, I realized, that this is the Kate Lethbridge-Stuart who makes it into the new Who series. It's here that the character really comes into her own and becomes defined and established.

In *Downtime*, Kate Lethbridge-Stuart was a subplot and a supporting character in a much larger story. Here, it's Kate's story from start to finish. What we get is a Kate Lethbridge-Stuart who is utterly indomitable. She's fearless, practical, hard-headed. The stuff that drove Cavendish out of his mind she takes with a shrug. She has conversations with ghostlike entities out of time, confronts her own doppelganger and eventually gives what for to a Daemon; all of it with unflappable pragmatism. The rest of us would be gasping to get our heads around, or screaming, or attacking, full on flight or fight reflex in play. Kate just looks a Daemon in the eye and asks it what it wants.

In contrast, the character of Cavendish is so weak he's literally disintegrating as we watch him. He bleats. He blathers. He hears voices, he's afraid. He wanted power, or the taste of power, but he's found he's become a pawn instead. The stuff that Kate somehow manages to take in stride has broken him. It gets a little much; you want to give him a slap.

But the thing is that where Kate's the central personality of the story, Cavendish is little more than a plot tool - he's there to amp up and emphasize the creepy factor. He's the guy that looks like a leading man, but the fact that he's gone to pieces brings home to the audience that things have gone seriously dark and weird. Richardson plays the part of a man in free fall well. He's unshaven, fearful, his voice quavers, his eyes are a little too wide, too liquid. His disintegration is obvious with at a glance.

Initially, I expected some sort of romance arc, or at least some interpersonal relationship stuff. That would have been a little too obvious. Richardson and Kressman are married after all, although their marriage was breaking up around this time. But they avoid that. If anything, she mothers him a little, seeing a man who can fall to pieces at any moment, and doing her best to handle him gently.

This is the thing with ghost stories - two people in a haunted house? Usually, there's nothing to do but develop their relationship and wait for the ghost to show up. Wisely, the script steers clear of cliche.

Michael Wisher, more famous for playing Davros, here shows up as the ghost. His character is basically there for exposition, but he plays against type. Wisher's ghost is calm, conservative and businesslike.

In the end, it's clearly a more modest production than Downtime. But it's one that hits its marks perfectly. They knew what they were trying to do, and the production values, location work direction and editing line up nicely. Philip T. Robinson's demonic statue is nicely disturbing and the location work in Kent's cavern is perfect. In particular the performance of Kressman and the writing for her character stand out. Kate Lethbridge-Stuart was someone we needed to see more of.

Postscript: Sometime after writing this, I became aware of Chris Chibnall's claim that when he wrote his blonde, fearlessly pragmatic, daughter of the Brigadier who just happened to be named Kate, he had no idea of the existence of the Kate Lethbridge-Stewart of *Downtime* and *Daemos Rising*. Believe it if you want, I don't buy it for a second.

CAST: *Kate Lethbridge-Stuart - Beverly Kressman; Douglas Cavendish - Miles Richardson; the Ghost - Andrew Wisher; Time Sensitive - Amanda Evans; Hooded Priests - Andy Delafield, Christian James, Stefano Rossini, Bevis Taylor; Daemon Voice - Alistair Lock; Narrator - Ian Richardson;*

CREW: *Produced and Directed by Keith Barnfather; Written by David J. Howe; Lighting Cameraman - Neil Oseman; Sound - Luis G. Garibay; Location Manager - Colin Campbell; Production Assistants - Rosemary Howe, Robin Prichard; Costumes - Academy Costumes, Torquay Flame; Statue Design and Props - Philip T Robinson; Additional props - This Planet Earth Ltd.; the Book created by Bob Covington; Daemon and Computer SFX - Christopher Gregory and Kevin Gregory; Edited by Anastasia Stylianou; Sound Treatment - Mark Ayres; Music & Sound Design - Alistair Lock; With thanks to Nick Powe, James Hull and all the staff at Kents Cavern, Torquay; based on characters and concepts created by Barry Letts & Robert Sloman; some concepts and characters based on the TIME HUNTER books from Telos Publishing Ltd., Script Consultants - Marc Platt and Barry Letts. Copyright Reeltime Pictures Ltd. 2004.*

Review: Zygon, When Being You Just Isn't enough (2003-2008)

Love, Sex and Shapeshifting

STORY: Robert Kirkwood, mild-mannered electrician, is plagued by dreams of being a shapeshifting monster called a Zygon. He goes to see a psychiatrist, Dr. Lauren Anderson, who is intrigued by his dreams and attracted to him. Shortly afterwards, the Doctor Anderson is accosted by a very creepy guy who is interested in Kirkwood. When she goes to the police, she discovers its Bob Calhoun, a serial killer. Despite criticism and enforced time off at work, a romance with Kirkwood blossoms. Then Bob Calhoun appears unexpectedly, and things get weird. Those dreams aren't really dreams...

REVIEW: The opening of *Zygon* is pretty off putting. Within the first minute or so we get a slow pan of a thoroughly unremarkable young man, nude, fully frontal and flaccid. I'll repeat: Unimposing graphic full frontal, anatomically correct, genitally displayed male nudity.

It's a strange choice, and I have no idea why director Bill Baggs made it, or what he was thinking.

I think possibly this opening contributes a lot to the undeservedly poor reputation. After all, male nudity just isn't nearly as appealing or photogenic as female nudity for most people. That's just a fact of life, full frontal male nudity just doesn't work for most people, it doesn't play on television or on movie screens, it's just not popular.

And while it might appeal to a certain part of the population, the people who would appreciate it probably wouldn't really appreciate this particular guy or his tackle. Not that he's terrible. He's... average, not remarkable, not particularly handsome or appealing. It's just a regular shlub of a guy who happens to be nude.

As I said, strange choice, and a bit off putting.

Zygon has a fairly negative reputation of being the Doctor Who soft core porno. It's not. And frankly, it would be pointless if it were. Since 2005, there have been real hard core Doctor Who porn parodies, some of them rather impressive. There are hard core Dalek porn parodies.

Soft core doesn't really exist anymore at all. Its heyday was the 50s through the 70s, and by the 80s and 90s, it was getting pointless. Nowadays? Gone. Time has passed it by.

What Zygon does have is both male and female nudity and an acknowledgment of sexuality as part of human identity. There are naked men, there are naked women, there's cheesecake, there's a few scenes of people making love. It's not the be-all and end all though. Quite often, the nudity isn't especially sexy or flattering, it's just there, a consequence of the story.

Instead, what it is, amounts to a claustrophobic little cat and mouse tale of identity and transformation. And it's a surprisingly good one, with a nice *Outer Limits/Twilight Zone* feel.

First, a bit of background: The Zygons are some of the most memorable Doctor Who monsters. First appearing in 1971,

Tom Baker's *Terror of the Zygons*, written by Robert Banks Stewart, they're bright orange-red, shaped like exotic dildos, festooned with suckers and ridges, and quite unforgettable... Oh, and they've got a human face right in the middle. Their technology matches, being visibly organic, full of cups and fronds, like some coral reef terrarium. It's some of the most inspired design work of 70s Doctor Who.

Doing a monster is hard. All too often, it looks like a guy in a costume and mask. Or, you can go off the deep end, and produce something that's just ridiculous gobs of latex, like some of the later monsters in the Sylvester McCoy era.

The Zygons, despite a glowering human face, somehow manage to thread the needle and come off looking both organic and alien.

In *Terror of the Zygons*, they crash landed here centuries ago and are just trying to get back home. They're not predators; rather, they subsist on the milk of some Loch Ness monster style creature.

Ultimately, they're jerks. But they're not homicidal loons like the Daleks or the Cybermen or even the Sontarans. You get the feeling that in their own environment, they'd be quite tolerable; you could have a nice cup of tea with them at the bottom of the sea.

The downside of a costume like that is it's really hard to move around in it, or to make a story work around. One of those critters gets spotted walking down the street of a Scottish village, and they'd be calling the constabulary.

For plot convenience, they needed to be able to pass as human. This is achieved by the device of kidnapping regular humans, and then using their technology to imprint or morph into the person they're imitating, conveniently with clothes, speech, memories etc. It's really hard to have a story that involves bright orange human-sized dildos walking down the street and carrying out dastardly plans.

This isn't really unusual in the Doctor Who universe; lots of races pull this kind of crap - the Faceless Ones, the Autons, the Rutans, etc. A lot of the time, the aliens are either disguising themselves as humans, wearing human suits, or using human agents. Shapeshifting and disguising as humans is usually necessary for story and budget purposes.

It's just that the Zygons are so weird looking; they picked up the reputation as the shapeshifters of the Doctor Who universe.

It's not really clear whether their shapeshifting is an innate biological thing, or whether it's a function of their technology, which may be biological. Can only Zygons do it? Or can anyone plugged into their technology do it? What is clear is that to copy a person, they need a template, the person, and they need to keep that person alive.

Anyway, the Zygons made a big return in the rebooted series, in 2013, as the lead monster in *Day of the Doctor*, the anniversary show that featured John Hurt, Matt Smith and David Tennant. Then a few years later, they returned in the Capaldi era, in a two-parter, The *Zygon Invasion/The Zygon Inversion*, in 2015. They were mentioned in the spin off, *Class*, in 2016. They've also shown up in audio adventures with both Big Finish and the BBV and in novels and comics. The Zygons are doing fine.

But back to *Zygon: When Being You Just Isn't Enough*, from 2008. Here's our backstory for this video: About twenty or so years ago, two Zygons, Kritakh and Torlakh, crash-landed on Earth (apparently, Zygons can't drive very well) on a mission to terraform the place (or Zygon-form the place). Nothing too aggressive, just help global warming along, pump some extra greenhouse gas into the atmosphere. Then in a hundred years or so, when the Zygon fleet arrives, they'll find Earth a pretty hospitable place. Humans? Not so much. But the Zygons will like it just fine.

But then, something goes wrong. The Commander, Kritakh, has spent too long pretending to be human, he gets hit on the head and forgets he's a Zygon. He thinks he's human, except that he keeps having these terrible nightmares where he dreams of being a monster. Troubled by these dreams, he goes to see a psychiatrist. She's not nearly as horrified by his dreams, you get the impression her life kind of sucks, and the idea of being able to shapeshift, to have power, is kind of appealing. He's not nearly as enthusiastic, and is pretty horrified by them. Attracted by his vulnerability, she starts to fall in love with him...

The complication is that she's buying two for the price of one. Hell, she's buying a whole crowd. You see, the second Zygon, Torlakh, is still around, and he'd really like his Kritakh to stop screwing around, remember who he is, and get back on the job of terraforming Earth. The only way to do that is to get his memory back, straighten out this romance that the boss has gotten into, which means enlisting her cooperation. Oh and it turns out Torlakh has picked up a hobby, he's a serial killer.

Things get complicated after that. The second Zygon decides that the only thing to do is bring her in to their world and make her one of them. He figures he needs a psychologist to help his boss remember, and come to terms with being a monster from outer space. He'd take her form and do it himself, but apparently just copying someone doesn't give you the subtle nuances of skill he needs. So better for her to do it. He introduces her to Zygon tech, teaches her the ins and outs of shapeshifting or body copying. At first she goes along with it, and her boyfriend gets back on the Zygon track - except that they rebel.

The Second Pirates History, Page 211

Well, Anderson rebels, Michael/Kritakh just seems to go along with whatever personality is strongest. It comes down to Anderson fighting Torlakh, an enemy who knows her every move, and who is intent on destroying her life.

Fair warning - the actual, weird dildo shaped, red squishy, ridged sucker-bearing Zygon actually appears in only one scene, a fight in the dark outside a van. You can tell it's a hard suit to make and get right, because they do all sorts of tricks, low and stark light, quick cuts, shifting angles, etc., to hide the limitations of the suit.

Now that that's out of the way, what we have is a surprisingly taut and complicated little thriller

Carrying the show is Jo Castleton, who plays Dr. Lauren Anderson. She played the same character in the BBV outing *Cyberon.*

I suppose that makes Zygon a sequel, and I should explain this a little. Here goes: Cyberons are basically old style Cybermen with the handlebars filed off – cyborgs in silver suits and helmets with external tubing on their chests and limbs. They first appeared in a BBV audio adventure with Nick Briggs, entirely because they couldn't get the actual rights to the Cybermen.

But once they had 'created' the property, they wanted to do more with them. The result was a film, *Cyberon,* written by Lance Parkin.

Basically an unfocussed version of the 1985 Ron Howard sci fi movie, *Cocoon,* with the Cyberons lurking about as ghostly hallucinations or something.

In *Cyberon,* Doctor Lauren Anderson is treating patients with brain damage or degenerative diseases, there's no hope for them. But then, her supervisor, starts a new drug trial – Cyberon, and it works! The patients start to recover. In fact, they do more than recover, they become stronger, faster, better, you know the drill. They seem to regain their youth, start developing enhanced strength. Meanwhile, Lauren starts seeing these ghostly robots hanging around. Eventually, she realizes, or the ghost robots explain, that it's an alien invasion. The new drug, Cyberon are actually nanotechnology which is being injected into the patients and slowly converting them into Cyberons...

Obviously, didn't really work for me, so I'm reviewing *Zygon* instead. You may want to take a look and maybe you'll think differently. Castleton was good in it.

Castleton seems to have been a BBV regular back in the day, she appeared in second and third Auton films as a psychic, Natasha Alexander; and in *Do You Have a License to Save This Planet* as Gloria.

Apart from these five starring roles, the IMDB lists her in a few minor film or television roles, and she's done audio adventures for both the BBV and Big Finish. She's English, so I imagine that there's a fair bit of stage work hidden on her resume. She's always an utterly charming presence in her films.

Here, she owns the show. Her Dr. Lauren Anderson is the center of the story, and she gives a wonderfully nuanced performance. Dr. Anderson starts off weakly, she's a psychiatrist, but she's rather mousy. Although a workaholic, she's harassed by her boss, and bullied by a more buxom co-worker. The boss and co-worker are having an affair and seem to be conspiring to be rid of her. Even though she's a Doctor, she has to have a roommate. Basically, she's treading water. Which perhaps explains why, put on forced 'vacation' she ends up sleeping with a patient.

Castleton's Anderson is a mixture of strength and weakness, capable in so many ways, but frustrated within her life and wanting more. Michael's terrified of his dreams of being a shapeshifting monster, but she sees it as a desire for power and control, and is almost envious.

Then her life gets weird, terrifyingly weird, as she's catapulted into a world of monsters from outer space, conspiracies, serial killers and shapeshifting. Her roommate is murdered, she experiences life and sex as a man, her very sense of identity, of who she is shifts like sand under her feet and her life is literally taken away from her when Torlakh, wearing her form, murders her coworkers on camera.

And yet, she copes. She's terrified, horrified, intrigued, there are moments when you can see she's utterly lost, but somehow, she copes and adapts, using the tools given to her to outwit an enemy who knows her every move. In the end, she leaves her old life and identity, including perhaps the man she loves, behind. But she's also become something more.

Daniel Harcourt, who plays the Zygon Commander, Kritakh, disguised as Michael Kirkwood, is probably the weakest performance, and according to IMDB the most inexperienced actor. Or perhaps merely the weakest character. He reminds me a little bit of Cavendish from *Daemos Rising*, a weak man out of his depth. He's the Zygon who has completely lost his identity in his disguise. He's an average guy in every sense of the word, not physically remarkable, not particularly brave or brilliant, somewhat indecisive. Despite that, he's also the most moral character, troubled by what he has done and is doing, recognizing that he's living on stolen lives and stolen identities. In contrast, Torlakh doesn't mind it at all, and Anderson is almost lost in the power and opportunities.

There's a hint Michael wasn't always this way, Torlakh/Bob Calhoun at one point complains about his ruthless dedication to the mission, never allowing time off. A bit of a hard nose. But this is no longer that person; he's shapeshifted so long he's lost, not only the sense of who he is, but the sense of being anyone. He's become a cypher, which, I think is part of the reason that Lauren Anderson sleeps with him.

He remains weak throughout, troubled, ambivalent, mostly going along with the stronger personality, whether it's Lauren or Bob, and hapless when caught up in the struggle between them. This consistency of weakness reinforces the sense of Lauren's growth.

The third part of the triumvirate is the satanic mentor and nemesis, Torlakh, disguised as Bob Calhoun, played by Keith Drinkel, who is a very accomplished actor. Torlakh is a working bloke, staying on the job, on the mission, vaguely frustrated to be trapped in a world of talking monkeys. He's got the mission, and he does what it takes, which includes killing people. Bob Calhoun is a serial killer, there's a hint he was one all along, but this seems to work for Torlakh. He's got an undercurrent of sadism, but also frustration and loneliness. Most of the action is driven by his efforts to set right a situation that he feels has gone off the rails, he's not really malignant, he just wants things back the way they should be. Drinkel makes his Calhoun an oddly sympathetic, even likable character.

There's a sex scene between Lauren and Kirkwood, and later another where Lauren 'tests out' the male body, that's as close as we come to soft porn, and within the framework of the story, it makes sense. Lauren is exploring shapeshifting, why not the possibilities of another gender. Her male persona looks utterly bewildered having sex. There's nudity and cheesecake, and it's mostly appropriate to the story.

The story moves along quickly, full of logical but unanticipated twists and turns, playing out like a game of chess between two adversaries. Tension builds steadily and the resolution is satisfying. The cat and mouse between Lauren and Calhoun is gripping. If anything, it's too short. There isn't a wasted scene, things progress almost too quickly.

The Second Pirates History, Page 215

I don't think I'd have minded an extra ten or fifteen minutes to breath.

This is low budget, there's no question. The poverty shows through in small ways. The office of the Hospital Director is practically a broom closet, and his nameplate is a sheet of paper on the door. There's continuity glitches all over the place. Special effects are sparse; some of the shots are what you see in low budget productions where there isn't the time or energy to be more ambitious.

And to be fair, there are some odd and off-putting directing choices. I've mentioned the male frontal nudity at the outset. There's also a scene where Anderson, finding her murdered roommates body, strokes it and rubs his hand on her cheek. Not what I'd do on finding a corpse. But to be fair to Castleton and Baggs, Anderson's character does that a few times (with live characters).

What it comes down to with that kind of stuff is you either live with it and look past it, or you let it stop you dead.

The production history on this one seems to have been unusually tortured. The script was originally by Lance Parkin, going through six drafts, until Parkin got fed up and quit.

It then went to Jonathan Blum, and another six rewrites. Then Bill Baggs, the producer director, did some rewrites, adding more sex and nudity. Parkin and Blum took their names off the project.

Baggs soldiered on, shooting most of it in 2003.

And then?

Nothing.

It literally sat for four years, until 2007.

Then in 2007, there are more scenes shot, and another rewrite. It might have been as little as one day's extra shooting, although I'm not sure what that was.

That seems to have been sufficient though. It came out in 2008 as a DVD release, to jeers and catcalls with fans mocking the sexual elements.

It probably didn't help that by 2008, not only was Doctor Who back on the air, with 10th Doctor Tenant at the height of his popularity, but the BBC was doing no less than three Doctor Who spin offs shows - *Doctor Who Confidential*, *Torchwood* and *Sarah Jane Adventures*, plus yet another spin off in Australia, *K9* in the works, plus Big Finish going full blast with all the surviving classic Doctors.

The big selling point of these Wilderness productions was that it was the Wilderness. Doctor Who had been off the air with no return prospects, so fans were willing to accept cheaply made faux Doctors like the *Stranger* and spin-offs in the Who universe.

But if you have a glut of the real thing? What's the point?

I'm not sure what was going on, whether the delay was lack of money, lack of motivation, some kind of creative funk; whether it just sat in the can for years, or there was a slow post-production, or post-production problems.

It seems the impulse to finally finish it and get it out into the world came from *Torchwood*, the adult oriented Doctor Who spin off. That certainly seems to have upped the sexual content.

Oddly enough, it appears sex and nudity was always part of the plan, back when it was being written and rewritten by Parkin and Blum, probably around 2001 or 2002, years before the series was revived, and before the spin off.

Which begs the question, why?

Look, the reality is that the adult and sexual elements are basically fairly tame and no big deal, out in the outside world. Unless you're in a small inclusive community like Doctor Who fandom, at which point, people flip out at the sight of a bare breast. Something like *Zygon* set people on their ear in fandom, but not in a good way? So why? Why would Baggs introduce things like nudity and sexual themes to audience that simply wouldn't accept it? I don't really get it.

But you know what? This didn't have to be a Doctor Who spin off at all. Seriously, if you stripped out the Doctor Who universe references, simply present it as a straight up Sci Fi thriller, it would work. This would have legs as a modest, but effective, and perfectly marketable B-movie. Cable television, direct to DVD, streaming channels and whatever. It's short, but that can be addressed, it could stand to be fleshed out without ending up feeling padded.

So why bother to make it a Doctor Who spin off? The market is basically a narrow subgroup of fans. How does that even make sense?

It would have been nice to have called this Bill Baggs swan song, and if he'd chosen to go out on this one, it would have been a pretty respectable departure, and the BBV could claim some interesting audio and video through the wilderness period, 1990 to 2003.

But Baggs is still around. He seems to have gone underground for a while; the BBV declined and almost disappeared for about a decade. He's still hanging in there, sort of on the far fringes of the Doctor Who universe, recycling or building on intellectual property that he actually owns, like *PROBE,* or Solomon the Stranger, or marginal Who related but independent properties like Faction Paradox.

Maybe he shouldn't. Baggs is, to say the least, unpopular in some circles. He's got a long history of making promises and not paying, there are a lot of artists, including Colin Baker, Nicola Bryant, Sylvester McCoy etc., that claim he owes them fees or royalties. The people that worked with him, and he connected up with a lot of talent, Nicholas Briggs, Mark Gatiss and many others in front of and behind the screen, found him difficult to work with, erratic, prone to micromanagement and generally a pain. Apparently, to know him is not to love him.

I have no direct knowledge, and I'm not really able to say anything one way or another. I've enjoyed a lot of the stuff he's been involved in, and he's certainly a seminal figure in the history of the Wilderness years and the audio Who universe. But it occurs to me, given his track record of working with a lot of people, including several who went on to do things and have futures in the industry, the fact that he seems so extremely marginal now, probably says something.

Baggs seems to have been a bit of a huckster, not uncommon in film and television production. Big promises and bigger dreams, which never quite materialize, never enough money or resources, moving dollars from one pocket to another, paying expenses or pocketing as needed, and shorting people left and right, always building a house of cards.

In this sense, the surprising thing about Baggs is not the legions of people he stiffed and burned along the way, but just how much he managed to accomplish between 1991 and 2008, both in video and audio, it's a hell of a record of video and audio. There are a lot of people who never accomplish anything. Perhaps this is why he's sticking around.

Baggs isn't the most popular person with the BBC, they were kind of annoyed with his treading on their copyrights, and while they're happy to do business with Big Finish, the word is he's persona non grata. This grows more problematic, since the BBC wised up to how messy its copyright situation was and has been sewing up the right to old characters and monsters.

There's just less and less cope for the things he wants to do. He continues to hover around the fringes of the Doctor Who world, picking up more and more marginal scraps, servicing a community that increasingly dislikes him I don't really see a future for Bill Baggs and the BBV, and that's okay. Everything ends. Sometimes there's nothing to do but put on a hat and mosey towards the exit.

Do we even need these Doctor Who spin offs anymore? By the time the BBV released Zygon, as I've pointed out, the real thing was back with a vengeance. We have the show, we have innumerable spin offs, a thriving audio universe, was it necessary? Is there any room for the BBV or any point?

But he's still in the game, which in a roundabout way gets us to a semi-sequel to *Zygon: When Being You Just Isn't Enough*.

A little background. In Jon Pertwee's first season as the Doctor, way back in 1970, his companion was Doctor Liz Shaw, played by Carolyn Johns. John's character only lasted one year, before being replaced by Jo Grant, played by Katy Manning.

Fast forward to the Wilderness Years. Baggs has released the *Airzone Solution*, a non-Who video, which features former Doctors Jon Pertwee, Colin Baker, Peter Davison and Sylvester McCoy, and a host of former Who actors. It's basically a reunion video, and it goes over fairly well. Well enough to want to try it again.

Meanwhile, Mark Gatiss is an up and coming young writer. It turns out that Carolyn Johns is available. The BBC gives permission to use the character, or at the least the name of Doctor Liz Shaw, and the *X-Files* is really big around this time.

All this comes together to create *PROBE*, an *X-Files* style secret government organization charged with solving paranormal situations, headed up by Doctor Liz Shaw, formerly of UNIT, and a story called *The Zero Imperative*, in 1994, with Pertwee, Baker, Davison, McCoy and other Who folk guesting. This lead to *The Devil of Winterborne*, in 1995, then *Unnatural Selection* and the *Ghosts of Winterborne* in 1996.

I'll be honest, the *PROBE* stuff was not to my taste, which is why I haven't reviewed it. But it did create an intellectual property which the BBV and not the BBC actually owned. So why not dig it out of mothballs?

Mark Gatiss moved on to bigger and better things, Carolynn Johns retired and passed away at the age of 70, in 2012, but Baggs noticed he still had the rights to *PROBE*. So he recast Hazel Burrows as Liz Shaw and released another *PROBE* video, *Time to Die*, in 2015. I can't imagine anyone in the world was waiting for that one, but it did signal a genuine comeback by the BBV.

Then, lately, starting in 2020 or 2021, Baggs dispensed with the character of Shaw, and created a new wholly owned character, Giles, to head up *PROBE*, played by Bill Baggs himself. It's pretty low fi - in each short, Giles, standing against a blank background, talks about an adventure or encounter with the abnormal, punctuated with stock footage from some previous BBV productions. It's an ultra-cheap format, but then again, it's also the age of Covid.

One of these, is called "*Lauren Anderson.*" That's right, we have a tiny backdoor sequel to Zygon, wherein we get to find out what happened after. It's only six minutes, and mostly, it's Baggs playing Giles, telling the story, interspersed with a few highlight clips from Zygon and Cyberon. There's no new footage from Castleton, not even old deleted scenes.

Anyway, it turns out that Lauren Anderson and the Zygon Michael Kirkwood did not live happily ever after. Eventually, Kirkwood became (or was replaced by) a literal emotional vampire. Anderson reached out to *PROBE* for help, and Giles helped to run him off. Anderson became an associate of *PROBE*.

Lauren Anderson is referred to a couple of episodes later in a another six or seven minute recounting by Giles of an adventure involving a sick alien and an injection of Cyberon serum. Anderson is a supporting character here, a kind of consulting physician.

It's either Baggs tying his continuities and properties together, including *PROBE*, the Cyberons, Anderson, etc. or finding a way to recycle some of his older, better, footage, or maybe there's some plan in the works. Who knows?

Baggs does seem to have staged something of a comeback, in the last few years, even making a mainstream (low budget) non-Who romantic comedy. Baggs has made deals with small publishers to release novelizations or anthologies of old BBV videos, has published new eBooks and print books himself, is marketing all the BBV's old works, and working on new projects in video and audio, trying to create new characters and properties, and re-acquiring rights to the *Faction Paradox* franchise.

Baggs has also gotten into trouble once again – the usual allegations of people being hired and not getting paid, issues over rights, involvement of unsavoury persons (specifically a voice actor accused of pedophile inclinations), and a scandal or two. Despite, or perhaps because of his track record, Baggs remains a controversial figure, so we'll see if the comeback lasts.

I find myself wondering if I'm a bit harder on groups like the BBV and Reeltime, who are at least nominally in it to make a buck and have some pretensions of professionalism, than I am on outright fan productions. I don't know. I don't think so, in both cases, I want to talk about the best or the most watchable, I feel no need to promote stuff I find sub-par or tangential

I admit, my tastes are eclectic, but I genuinely enjoyed *Do You Have a License to Save This Planet*, or *Zygon: When Being You Just Isn't Enough*. I can acknowledge low budget, hand to mouth productions, and all the compromises and missteps and crudities that come with that, including Baggs' now rather dubious reputation and still like them and find them worthwhile.

CREW: *Bill Baggs (producer/director/writer), Lance Parkin & Jon Blum (writers-uncredited by request), Alistair Lock (editing and music), Richard Hookings (cinematography).*

CAST: *Jo Castleton (Lauren Anderson), Daniel Harcourt (Michael Kirkwood / Kritakh), Keith Drinkel (Bob Calhoun / Torlakh), David Roeciffe (Ray), Becky Pennick (Joanna), Alistair Lock (Samms), Nigel Peever (Officer Mcutcheon / Zygon Creature), Matt Montgomery (Wealthy Man), Lucy Lockly (Wealthy Wife), Nathan Hamlett (Doctor), Georgina Windsor (Inspector), Blaine Coughlan (Police Officer), Richard Hookings (Police Officer), Nigel Fairs (Police Officer), Marian Baggs, (Patient), Joan Hewlett (Patient), Richard Hewlett (Patient), Chris Bell (Patient), Ralph Baggs (Patient), David Castleton (Patient)*

Review: Sil and the Devil Seeds of Arodor (2019)

An Old Villain in a New Story, It Works

STORY: Sil, pirate capitalist, obnoxious green slug-lizard and nemesis to the Doctor, is in trouble again. It seems that the seeds of Arodor that he's been selling to Earthlings have turned out to be very toxic. Now he's on trial for his life, and his friends and superiors want to make sure he takes the fall.

REVIEW: Doctor Who started up again in 2005, and you would think that would probably be the end of these gray market productions. It's hard to see how they could compete with BBC money and talent.

But oddly, there were still a few efforts - Bill Baggs and the BBV we've already talked about. Reeltime, the big rival in the gray market or productions and documentaries, for its part produced the *White Witch of Devil's End*, in 2017, *Sil and the Devil Seeds of Arodor* in 2019, and *Anomaly,* scheduled for 2023.

We're here to talk about Sil and the *Devil Seeds of Arodor*, capably produced and directed by Keith Barnfather, who, in contrast to Baggs, seems universally admired and respected, written by Philip Martin, and starring Nabil Shaban, Christopher Ryan and Sophie Aldred.

Full disclosure, I was all set to hate this.

Seriously.

Sil is a classic Doctor Who villain who appeared twice in the Colin Baker era of the classic series. He shows up in series 22, in *Vengeance on Varos*, and then in series 23, *Trial of a Time Lord*, in *Mindwarp*, both written by Philip Martin. Considering that the Colin Baker era was really only two seasons and eleven serials, that's really impressive, almost a fifth of Colin's work.

There's a third contemporary Sil story from that era, *Mission to Magnus*, also written by Philip Martin and commissioned for the original version of series 23. Due to the cancellation and hiatus, that was scrapped, but Martin turned into a novel a few years later, and then a Big Finish audio in 2009. The character shows up in another Philip Martin audio from Big Finish called *Antidote to Oblivion*.

So that's the history – four prior Sil stories, all written by Philip Martin, all featuring Nabil Shaban playing the role.

I loathe the little slug. He's actually a slug. Sil is a green, fin headed, half humanoid slug with a sort of tadpole tale instead of legs, lying back on a sort of couch, constantly in danger of drying out. The creature design is chees and ugly in a 'let's keep pouring on latex until we get tired' sort of way.

The character is horrible – unctuous, sadistic, avaricious, Sil has no redeeming qualities whatsoever. He's a classic middle manager, kissing up and kicking down, dialed up to eleven… hundred.

Sil was created and written by Martin for and during the Thatcher era, and he's literally a comment on the unrestrained capitalism and maliciousness of the Thatcher 80s, an era of depravity, selfishness and callousness that we can barely comprehend today. Thatcher was all about systemic shock, taking an axe to social programs, unlimited greed, and gleeful cruelty. It was class war by the nouveau riche against everyone else. So Martin writes Sil with the nastiness of an Englishman nursing a grudge.

It's pretty hard to take. You have to hand it to the English, when they vent, they don't hold back, and Martins had a lot of venting to do. The Thatcher era was utterly unrestrained in its nastiness, on the part of both the Thatcherites and those who opposed them.

It makes for a thoroughly appalling character. And it gets worse; Sil is portrayed by Nabil Shaban, a disabled Jordanian-British actor. Shaban's been in a number of productions, way back, I watched him in *Born in Flames*, and by all accounts a wonderful person.

I absolutely hate the performance, there's such a thing as being too successful. Shaban takes Martin's over the top character, and aims for the stratosphere. His Sil is a shrieking, eye rolling, smirking, scheming, nasty piece of work, oozing malice, utterly unapologetic. The character and performance is like being trapped in a world of fingernails on blackboards, it's that hard to take.

It's awful.

So, when I heard about *Sil and the Devil Seeds of Arodor*, coming out in 2019, my immediate impulse was to conclude that God had died. Why? What depraved cosmic malice, would pick that character, out of 50 years of Who? And really, weren't we long, long past the era of these semi-legit, unauthorized Doctor Who spin offs?

It just seemed so…

Unnecessary.

And horrible.

And it just got worse. It was going to be four 25 minute episodes. A hundred minutes long. That sounded excruciating. And long monologues? I have a lifetime of

Fringe Festivals, listening patiently to endless monologues in 'one person shows.'

Could it get worse?

But you know how it is, sometimes when you pass a car wreck you have to slow down and see the wreckage, just to see how much I could stand, how bad it was.

And you know what?

It won me over.

Seriously, I would not have believed that was possible. I was set to hate this. I wanted to hate this.

And it turned out to be really good.

Go figure.

It's not just me, either. I didn't have a stroke or a head injury, I checked. Sil and the Devil Seeds of Arodor was a success, it did the festival circuit, apparently it's won over fifty awards. It came off quite well.

The basic plot is that Sil's in trouble. The entire story takes place in a detention center on the moon. Sil is an employee of the Universal Monetary Fund, and in the course of his work, he's sold alien fruit to Earth, the Devil Seeds. Bad luck, those seeds turn out to be horrifically toxic and addictive. Millions of lives are ruined, Sil is going on trial, he's guilty as hell and the penalty is death. It looks bad, in the first episode, he tries to bribe two guards into helping him escape, a failed attempt that make matters even worse. In the next episode, his boss, Lord Kiv, from the Universal Monetary Fund, shows up make sure he takes a fall to save the company. Then after that, his former partner, Mistress Na, arrives to throw him under the bus. He's guilty as hell, has no friends and everyone wants him dead. Poor Sil, looks like he's done for. Or is he?

So what makes it work? Sil is as horrible and grating as ever, the character is damned near unwatchable, and the performance is as screeching and over the top as it's ever been, and there's a lot of him. There's absolutely no reason to like it at all.

What makes it work? Hard work. It's a good solid script by Philip Martin and a virtuoso bit of writing. He takes a character that is never sympathetic or likable, and with the perseverance of an ant rolling a boulder up a hill draws us into his world. This Sil is an underdog; things have turned out very badly, through his own fault of course. But now he needs to literally worm his way out from under disgrace and certain death, even while his superiors lie through their teeth and plan to leave him holding the bag. Sil is awful, but he's unapologetically awful, gleeful in his nastiness, and his co-stars are arguably even more awful than he is.

The one appealing thing about Sil is that he's smart. And he needs to be, because really, it's the entire little slug has going for him. Despite myself, I was steadily drawn into his world, watching as a scheme to bribe the guards fails, and then intrigued as he begs, pleads, spots hidden traps and schemes and slowly squirms past all obstacles to emerge triumphant, all without moving an inch from his couch.

Sil has two things going for him, both in terms of the story, and in terms of engaging his audience. First, Shaban's Sil is utterly a creature of Id. He doesn't ever pretend to be nice, and even if he did, no one would believe it for a second. He's a slimy little backstabber, utterly unapologetic about it, and very happy to be that way, and he isn't anything else. He's definitely repulsive, but he's repulsive in a fascinating way. You can't stop watching him, and after a while you come to appreciate, even admire, his point of view. Sure, he's distilled sleaze, but in his world, so is everyone else, he's just the only one who is honest about it.

The Second Pirates History, Page 228

The other thing is that Sil is smart. The character is genuinely clever, and some of the high points of the story are watching him, all alone, monologuing as he meticulously deconstructs the plots against him and figures out how to overcome them. It's genuinely fascinating to sit there and watch him be clever. I'm a sucker for clever characters.

The other half of it, of course, is Nabil Shaban, who literally does the impossible in making Sil compelling. No easy thing, considering he's working under more layers of latex than Ron Perlman in *Hellboy,* and trying to give voice to a screeching nasty little alien. Truculent, arrogant, condescending, wheedling, deliberately nasty – Sil is never likable, but he's watchable. Shaban expertly conveys the appalling character of an amoral alien slug with almost no human sentiments.

It's heavy lifting for Shaban. His character is literally in every scene, and maintains the lion's share of dialogue. Literally every other character is there to interact with Sil. The entire script is on Shaban's shoulders.

In the end, it's that collaboration that wins out. Martin and Shaban's work fit each other like hand and glove. You can tell that Martin knows the character inside and out, he's written him four times previously, and as I've said, he's been using Sil to grind an axe to a very sharp point.

And Martin writes for Shaban's voice, he writes for Shaban's performance. You can tell that when Martin was sitting at his word processor, he could hear Shaban's voice in his head and visualize Shaban's mannerisms and performance. On the other side, Shaban picks up everything that Martin gives him, and runs with it with absolute confidence.

This is a synergy that really can only come about from a collaboration born of experience. Both have been down this road with this character several times, they both know Sil, and better, they're both passionate about the character and the situation. This isn't a nine to five project; there's a depth here to both the writer's and the actor's investment.

And between them, they do the impossible. This is a wonderful example of how a really good collaboration can elevate the material.

The rest of the cast don't rise to the same heights. Christopher Ryan, best known for his work in the *Young Ones* and *Absolutely Fabulous*, shows up as Lord Kiv, a member of Sil's race who has transplanted his brain into a human body. Ryan actually played Lord Kiv before, that time in full latex, in the second Sil serial, *Mindwarp*, back in 1986. That serial ended with Kiv's brain transplanted into the Doctor's companion, Peri. This time, Ryan is clearly not willing to wear the latex. Sophie Aldred appears as a Draconian, lady, Mistress Na, wearing fairly crude latex appliances and no gloves. They acquit themselves reasonably well as Sil's frenemies, but basically, they're there to be foils for Shaban's Sil.

Apart from that, the cast is the Adjudicator, a prosecutor and a couple of guards. There are a small handful of extras for some hallway scenes. This plays as a courtroom drama, so everyone is stiff and formal, particularly the trial officials, and there's not a lot of room for personality and nuance.

Overall, despite the use of a number of camera angles, this production is very static; it feels very theatrical and formal. That comes with a courtroom drama, the roles are all extremely defined and narrow, and everyone literally stands in place. Except for the first segment, when Sil is being wheeled through corridors on his failed escape, there's very little movement or action. It really does come across like a stage play.

Beyond that, the production is sparse. There's very little in the way of effects, some occasional CGI shots of a Moonbase to establish location. Interiors are unadorned, flat walls and doors, without adornment. These are very basic sets or locations, basic concrete.

Compared to Reeltime's earlier work, notably *Downtime* and *Daemos Rising*, the production values on display are a big step down. Both those productions featured kinetic stories with a number of characters interacting, action sequences, outdoor shots, multiple vivid locations. Of course, there productions were a lot more expensive, particularly *Downtime*.

In comparison, *Sil and the Devil Seeds* is Spartan to the point of being threadbare. They give it a shot, and there are CGI moonscape inserts, but there's only so much you can do with the format of a courtroom drama, and only so much camera artistry or angles you can manage when it's all literally in one or two identically nondescript rooms. Criticism of the production invariably comes back to these production values, which are admittedly sub-par, and I can respect that.

I put that down to financial limitations. Keith Barnfather did a far more polished job of directing in *Daemos Rising*, so he's got the chops. The reality is that limited budgets and a constrained format doesn't give him a lot of room to show directorial or cinematic flair. There are only so many places you can put the camera. So he settles for a basic, workmanlike job.

Oddly, this actually works for the production, again, coming back to Martin and Nabil. Within the stuffy confines of a courtroom drama, Sil looms larger than life. Everyone plays their assigned court drama roles, except for Sil, who schemes, begs, snivels and boasts nonstop, always subverting both the proceedings and the form. Everything and everyone else is literally stoic and colourless, so Shaban's Sil literally pops in every scene. Martin and Shaban take the limitations of the production and literally turn it around. As I said, it won me over, and I was prepared to be a hard audience, I still hate Sil, but I admit he's a watchable little slug.

Sadly, Philip Martin passed away after Sil and the Devil Seeds of Arodor was released, on December 13, 2020. I'm glad he got to see his work go over well. Apparently, before he passed, he'd written a sequel, and there's some talk of doing that one. Nabil Shaban is still around and doing well, at 69 years of age, it's not clear that he's up for playing Sil again, who knows, it's certainly a character he's embraced, and truthfully, I can't imagine anyone else carrying it off.

We'll see what happens next. Sil remains a bit of an atavism, he's very much a character spawned in the Thatcher-esque 80s, and this production is something of a throwback to the wilderness 90s. It's a venture that treads around loopholes in Doctor Who intellectual property to produce a gray-market product. Released in 2019, it feels antique, and old fashioned, the product of bygone times and sensibilities, and entirely unnecessary and supplanted in what is now a super-saturated Who universe. Honestly, I can't imagine the BBC doing something like this at all. This could only come out of an outfit like Reeltime, or some similar group. And honestly, I don't get the economics, that makes no sense to me, which probably explains the threadbare production values - there's not a lot of big money to go in, in, nor reasonably expect to come out of it.

Really, the only reason I think this exists, is that it was and is a labour of love, for Philip Martin, for Nabil Shaban, for Sophie Aldred and Keith Barnfather and the rest of the people who were part of this. And you know what? That's fine. It's better than fine, it's glorious.

Perhaps that really is all the justification that is needed. As much as I question the business model, or the need, maybe it's not about either one of them, but simply finding a way to create something you love, in a world they love.

That means that the entire weight of the project rests on the script by Philip Martin, on Keith Barnfather's direction, and on the shoulders of Nabil Shaban himself, playing Sil, and chewing the scenery for all he's worth.

CAST: Sil - Nabil Shaban; Lord Kiv - Christopher Ryan; Mistress Na - Sophie Aldred; Adjudicator - Janet Henfrey; Larnier - Sakuntala Ramanee; Monk - Jim Conway; Piers - Jay Ramanee-Murphy; Joh Michael Rook - Guard.

CREW: Producer & Director - Keith Barnfather; Writer - Philip Martin; Cinematographer - Rob Thrush; Art - Ray Phillips; Makeup - Begona Martin; Animation - Chris Thompson; Music - Alistair Lock, Colorist - Sarah Buxton.

CHAPTER 13:
EVERYTHING OLD IS
WHO AGAIN

Sometimes a story takes a long and winding road. For every movie or television series, for every novel, the path is seldom straightforward. Instead, littered everywhere along the path are things lost, possibilities cast aside, roads not taken. This is particularly apparent in television. Almost every television series is littered with compromises, things that could not be achieved are replaced with what could be done stories and characters that were abandoned, loose ends that are never picked up and projects that fell through.

In its fifty year history, Doctor Who is littered with these, starting with the very beginning. The original script for the pilot was called *Nothing at the End of the Lane* - the Tardis wasn't a police box, it was invisible, and the Doctor wasn't an alien but a time traveler from the far future. That was a very different show.

Even with the Doctor we knew, the second serial was going to be *Masters of Luxor*, by one of the key creative people involved with the show, Anthony Coburn. Masters of Luxor never quite came together, instead the Daleks were rushed into production, and Doctor Who was never the same again.

The Second Pirates History, Page 234

It went on. Stories were pitched; some of them were even written, but ultimately dropped. An acrimonious dispute with writers resulted in the Quarks, the Yeti and the Great Intelligence vanishing from the series. A gap opened up in the transition between Troughton and Pertwee. Even for the show that was actually produced, entire seasons were aired and then the tapes wiped away by the BBC. Despite recovery efforts, sixteen serials are lost forever.

When Roger Delgado, who had played the Master, died in a car accident, his final story died with him. Tom Baker's movie about the *Scratchman* never got off the ground. *Shada* never aired and was almost lost completely due to a union strike. The cancellation crisis of 1985 resulted in the abandonment of an entire season's worth of stories, including commissioned and completed scripts. Another planned season vanished away for 1990 when the show was cancelled in 1989.

The years following 1989 saw dozens of attempts to revive the series - a succession of proposed movie projects that never quite went anywhere. *Lost in the Dark Dimension* wasn't just the title of an abandoned anniversary project, it described the many efforts to revive the series or make a movie or do something, anything with the property.

A chronicle of all the lost and abandoned Doctor Who projects - all the serials that were pitched, or commissioned, or written but abandoned, the Peter Cushing *Doctor Who radio series* of 1966, the *Nelvana animated series*, *Terrance Dicks radio series*, *Terry Nation's Dalek series*, the abortive revivals, all the movie versions that fell by the wayside and so on... They could fill their own book. Perhaps they should. There are several web pages that chronicle the ones that never got made.

So, inevitably, fans would end up exploring these roads not taken.

The Second Pirates History, Page 235

I'll be up front. The champion here is Big Finish Audio productions, which, in addition to a staggering amount of original programming, has made something of a fetish of tracking down these lost arcana, and either adapting existing scripts as audio stories, or commissioning full scripts from the stillborn proposals and projects, or re-mounting forgotten stage plays as audio adventures. Big Finish and the fan audio community probably deserve a book of their own.

In the meantime, however, there have been some very interesting and significant efforts to recapture those gaps and abandoned projects, and to breathe new life. The gestation period is immense; decades may pass between the original project and its fan realization. But they form a fascinating reflection of the show's history.

In particular, the next four fan films represent projects that crossed a span of decades....

Review: Marco Polo (1963-2015)

Loose Cannon Productions and Reconstructions

STORY: The malfunctioning Tardis lands in Tibet in the 1200s, almost directly in the path of Marco Polo's caravan. Polo is transporting the Princess, Ping Chou, along the Silk Road to the Court of Kublai Khan. Accompanying him is the warlord, Tegana, also on a mission to sign a peace treaty. The Doctor and his companion become involuntary guests, when Marco Polo seizes the Tardis, intending to make a gift of it to the great Khan. Meanwhile, Tegana, realizing that with a magical tool like the Tardis, he can overthrow even the mighty Kublai Khan, begins to plot in secret.

REVIEW: Doctor Who lists ninety-seven missing episodes from the 1960s, and sixteen serials that are entirely or mostly lost, probably forever. The earliest of the sixteen lost serials is *Marco Polo*, the fourth serial of the first season, following immediately after the Daleks.

Oh, and by the way, you can watch a colourized version of it today.

Wait! What? How is that possible? What happened? Why were all those episodes lost? And what's the deal with being able to watch them today? Colourized even?

The Second Pirates History, Page 237

Once again, we go back to the early days of television. All this stuff now that we take for granted as the business of television and entertainment, reruns, residuals, a lot of that hadn't been worked out then, or it hadn't really caught on in England way back then.

Television, back in the 1960s in England, was still an ephemeral medium. When you think about, it really had been only a decade or so that television was around and common. The BBC had taken its inspirations for television from Theatre and Radio. This notion that it could or should be recorded and broadcast again and again, that wasn't really in place. A lot of television, especially in the fifties and early sixties, was live.

Honestly, no one really saw that there might be a market for that. Television was something you watched once, and then moved on. It was just entertainment. It wasn't seen as something special or unique to preserve. It was like a stage play - you put it on, if you were lucky, it worked, and once it was done, you moved onto something else. This modern notion of permanence just wasn't really there.

Even when it was videotaped, as was beginning to happen, a lot of performers and creative people looked kind of askance at the idea that a performance that they'd been paid to give once might be shown again and again and again... without them being paid for it. In fact, the contracts for actors, and perhaps for writers and directors, specified that their performances could only be shown twice in England.

Which meant that back in those days, Doctor Who was good for only two television airings. If you were a fan, you collected the novels. If it was really popular, as were the first two Dalek stories, the BBC licensed it out to people made theatrical movies out of it.

But the rule was, and the contracts said, only two television broadcasts, and that was it.

What happened was a lot of videotapes, not just Doctor Who, but dramas, specials, cop shows, mysteries, varieties, comedies, all sorts of things, just ended up sitting in Warehouses collecting dust, unseen and unremarked. Warehouse space costs money, maybe not a lot, but it does cost money. It adds up, particularly the more you need and the longer you need it. And videotapes were very expensive, but they were re-useable, if you were willing to wipe. It didn't necessarily make sense to have all of this stuff that you would never use again, long past any legal or conceivable use, piling up, eating storage costs, when it could be disposed or recycled. Particularly when there were more and more videotapes of programming accumulating, every day, every week, every year.

Maybe the BBC, when it started out, might have wanted to keep a library of its programs. That would have been fine for the first few years. But after ten years, you've got a lot of stuff. After twenty years you have vastly more. You'll need to keep renting new warehouses to store it all. Huge piles of programs that no one ever looks at.

Expensive videotapes, that you can never legally broadcast again, that takes up space that you can wipe and record something more useful over.

What would you do?

What the BBC did was institute a recycling/clearing policy. They made up a policy and a schedule, and periodically, when something had sat for long enough, they got rid of it. This was not uncommon. It happened in Canada, in Australia, in the United States. There are vast amounts of early television and early movies that are simply gone forever.

Now, a certain number of serials of Doctor Who lasted a bit longer than usual. That was because the show was marketable.

That two showings only rule? There was a loophole in the contracts. It only applied in England.

You could sell the show, and air it, in international markets - Nigeria, Algeria, Canada, Hong Kong, Australia, wherever.

Back then the technology was so rudimentary, that they couldn't copy videotape. Well, they could, but it was expensive and there were issues of incompatible formats internationally.

Instead, what they did for international sales was that they'd run the program, and stick a 16 mm film camera up to the screen and film it. The films would then be shipped off. Sometimes, if demand was good, you might make several film copies of a serial. Or if a serial was late coming back from wherever you'd shipped it, it was easier to strike a new copy for the next customer than it was to miss a shipping date.

A lot of the lost episodes that have been recovered aren't videotape but film, from film canisters that got shipped off somewhere and misplaced or forgotten.

The thing was, it often wasn't a good idea to just wipe popular videotapes, because someone might need them for overseas sales, so a lot of them hung around just a bit longer, or copies of them lingered here or there. Videotape you could erase and recycle film stock tended to stick around longer.

The first erasures actually began in August, 1967, when the master tapes from the first season were purged and recycled.

There was another round of junkings in 1969, then in 1971.

This didn't mean that they were automatically all gone. International sales for the Hartnell era were strong and there were copies floating around many of which got returned and put into storage at different warehouse sites, to await their own eventual destinies with the dumpsters.

Unfortunately, international sales of for the Troughton serials were weaker, sometimes only one or two countries were purchasing, or perhaps none. This meant that fewer film copies were made, or none at all for the Troughton era. Fewer copies meant fewer locations they were kept at, less demand, and easier junking.

Doctor Who's old episodes hung around, but without anyone realizing it, they were slowly vanishing away. Some serials and episodes were wiped away entirely when videotapes were wiped and there were no film copies. Other, luckier episodes had film copies for international sales, those copies returned, sat in different warehouses, eventually slated for destruction when they went long enough unrented.

Those termination dates were coming up, more and more of them. Even Pertwee era serials were being wiped and discarded.

Fast forward to 1977: What's going on then? Well, Tom Baker is at the height of his popularity, and Doctor Who is a genuine phenomenon rivalling its Dalekmania days. Star Wars is sweeping the world. And maybe people in suits around the world are noticing that there's money to be made off this Sci-Fi junk.

And there's a fan named Ian Levine, who desperately wants to collect Doctor Who. He has the books, the autographs, souvenirs, merchandise, scripts. You name it, he's got it. But what he wants is to actually own a copy of a serial, maybe more than one.

Levine, in the middle of 1977, purchased six episodes of *Frontier in Space*, an otherwise pretty standard Pertwee serial, in the first ever BBC sale to a private individual. Previously, they'd only sold to other television stations internationally.

Truthfully, they didn't actually sell to foreign television, they just rented them out, and the foreign stations were supposed to eventually return the film cans so that the serials could be rented out somewhere else.

So Levine's purchase was really a big thing. The episodes had to be specially recorded for him on the U-Matic format, the predecessor of Beta and VHS. He paid 3000 pounds for them. According to online inflation and currency calculators adjusted for inflation, that's an astonishing 16,000 to 32,000 pounds today, and $23,000.00 to $46,000 American. That's a year's income for a lot of people, or the price of a really good car, or a low-end home.

Levine set out to purchase more, but was told that the BBC didn't sell episodes more than seven years old. Undaunted, he kept at it and eventually obtained special permission to collect old episodes from the 1960s.

I think that Levine's quest to collect his own episodes may have sent some shock waves through the BBC. It was a wake-up call that maybe, somehow, these old serials from the 60s might have some value. Levine had spent real money, 'sit up and pay attention' money. At the very least, there was a very obnoxious, aggressive person knocking hard on the door about all those forgotten serials. That has to set something rolling.

Beta and VHS had just come to the United States in 1976 and 1977, and they were starting to show up in England. There was a new format, and perhaps a sense that the world was changing again. It was just possible that all those old programs, sitting in dusty boxes on video and film in warehouse might be worth something.

So, following on Ian Levine's agitation, the BBC took an audit of what it did and didn't have for Doctor Who from the

1960s. A mere 47 episodes existed, and very few complete serials. 206 episodes were listed as missing.

In response to that, in 1978, the BBC decided to officially end junking (although due to poor communication, some junking continued until 1981). They started getting serious about trying to organize their old library.

Sue Malden was appointed, and she chose Doctor Who as her pet project, and set about trying to seek out and recover old episodes from various sources. She discovered that there were no master tapes left from the 1960s, but by hunting about here and there, she could track down copies created or set aside for one reason or another.

Meanwhile, in that same year, Ian Levine, who was now legally able to buy episodes, was also on the hunt himself. Following up on a rumour, he went down to the Film Vault at Villiers House, where the BBC kept their material for overseas sales and distribution. He discovered a staggering 79 episodes, including many listed as missing. According to the story, they were sitting there waiting to be junked before Levine's intervention.

Between Levine and Malden, 70 lost episodes were rediscovered in 1978. This was the beginning of a crusade by Levine, Malden and fans all over the world to track down and recover as many episodes as they could. Over the next thirty-five years, another thirty-nine episodes would turn up, including nine in 2013. Most likely, the remaining ninety-seven are lost forever.

Or were they? Were they completely and truly gone forever in any form?

The still-missing Film and video copies are almost certainly gone. It's possible that an episode might turn up, but none has in almost a decade.

Back in the 1960s, Beta and VHS didn't exist, there were no laserdiscs, no DVDs. But there were reel to reel audio tape recorders, back then. Fans could set up their audio recorders in front of the television, wire it into the speakers, and actually record the voices off the television.

Why bother? Well, because at best, the episodes would only air on television once or twice and then be gone forever. Reruns were not a thing back then. The BBC's own contracts provided only for two broadcasts in the United Kingdom. The only way to enjoy a good episode of Doctor who was to audio record it, then at least you could listen to it and share it with your friends any time you wanted.

Believe it or not, there was a real culture of audio recording back then, in both America and Britain. Episodes of *Star Trek, the Lone Ranger, Space Patrol, Gunsmoke, Dragnet*, comedy series, you name it, people were making their own recordings. It helped, I guess, that television in those days was pretty talky.

Big spectacular visuals, lots of nuance on screen, that was for movie theatres. Television, back then, was a small eight or twelve inch screen, black and white, low resolution, and made on relative shoestring budgets with static sets and fixed cameras. It wasn't the lush visual experience we have today with 40 or 50 inch flatscreens, full colour, pristine digital 4k. The television image was poor, so compelling dialogue and music was pretty important. It translated to audio only recording coming off better than you would expect nowadays.

The outcome is that just about all of the missing episodes of Doctor Who, every single lost episode, still exists as an audio recording, thanks to the dedicated fans of the era, in particular Graham Strong, David Holman, Richard Landen, David Butler, James Russell, Allen Wilson. These youths preserved what the BBC didn't value, that we have audio records, reconstructions, animated classic episodes and serials comes down to them and their peers.

This fan practice of audio recording and sharing would in turn lead to creating audio adventures of their own, but that's another chapter.

There's another part to the story. Back in the 1960s, there was a fellow named John Cura. Cura was a photographer who developed an interesting business.

Now remember, no VHS, no Beta, no DVD or TiVo. If you wanted to record a television program, you either made an audio recording, which was pretty limited. Or you stuck a film camera in front of the television... and film was expensive. To rent its shows to international markets, the BBC actually did that – they'd stick a 16 mm motion picture camera in front of the television set, and then they'd ship those films all over the world. But that was a high end commercial undertaking.

But for various reasons, there was a need for reasonably priced visual records of an episode - for continuity, for promotions, for directors or actors, there was a market.

What Cura did, was he figured out how to adjust the shutter stop timing and focal length of his cameras, to account for the scanning and curvature of a television image. This meant that he could take pictures off a television without any distortion or scan lines. Cura then set up a bank of cameras and started taking pictures at the rate of seventy to eighty shots per episode. He called these Tele-Snaps and he'd offer them to whoever was willing to pay. I'm sure that the BBC, among others, weren't thrilled by this. But it was a unique service and Cura made a good living from it.

By the time he passed away in 1969, he is estimated to have taken well over a quarter of a million Tele-Snaps. Despite much of it ended up being thrown away. Nevertheless, his surviving work is the only surviving visual record of a lot of programs which are otherwise completely lost.

Of course, among Cura's files of Tele-Snaps are the visual records of many of the Doctor Who serials from 1963 through 1968. Not all of the lost episodes were recorded by Cura as Tele-Snaps, but a good number were.

Ultimately though, Tele-Snaps, were quickly obsolete. No one followed in Cura's footsteps. Technology moved on quickly. It became easier to record and edit videotape and to print images. By the 70s and 80s, Tele-Snaps ended up as a minor curiosity, an interesting footnote for archivists and historians.

Then, around 1987, someone got a very bright idea.

There were all these audio recordings of the lost episodes. There were all these Tele-Snaps of many of the lost episodes. Why not synch them up together, so that the audio track accompanied a moving slide show of the images from the Tele-Snaps?

That way, you could literally 'Reconstruct' the old episodes. With a bit of tweaking here and there, maybe some pans and scans, zooms, you could even add a limited degree of pseudo-animation to liven things up. You could spice it up with other authentic photos or clips, sometimes even shoot or animate bits. It wasn't quite the same as having the live action episodes, but it was the next best thing.

This isn't nearly as easy as it sounds, by the way. Think about it. You have an audio track. No video. Instead, all you have are a series of ninety photographs that you have to try and match to the dialogue, essentially guessing at what goes where or how long it should last. If you're lucky, you have the novelization to guide you. If you're really lucky, you have the shooting script. But even these are imperfect guides, and there's a lot of guesswork and art involved.

The first known Reconstruction, matching Tele-Snaps to the audio record, was probably Richard Landen, back in 1987, who re-created Episode Two of Power of the Daleks. He released an upgraded version in 1990. Then, in 1995, a man named Richard Develyn began to do Reconstructions of entire serials. In 1996, Michael Palmer, and a group calling itself 'Change of Identity' began doing their own Reconstructions. In 1997, Harold Achadz released a Reconstruction. It was definitely a movement.

The most successful and famous Reconstruction artists were a group that called themselves *Loose Cannon*, founded by Rick Brindell and running from 1997 to 2015. The group also included Dean Rose, Russ Port, Derek Handley and Stuart Palmer, among others. Over the years, they've become very close to synonymous with the art-form. If you've watched a Reconstruction, it was probably a *Loose Cannon* project.

Reconstructions were an art form almost unique to Doctor Who. The technique has been used here and there to fill in gaps on old movies like *Metropolis,* or as a device in art house films such as *La Jetee.*

Doctor Who presented a perfect storm of a successful series with a huge backlog of lost stories, a wealth of Tele-Snaps, an almost complete audio record, and a cult following with the creativity and inclination to put it together. No other series or production really filled those requirements.

But now we've drifted a bit afield, we were talking about *Marco Polo.*

Marco Polo has a special status in the world of Doctor Who.

It was the first of the historical serials that were part of the original concept of the show and featured heavily through the Hartnell and Troughton years. In many ways, it was intended to be a showcase serial, and extraordinary time and care was lavished upon it. On top of that, it just missed out on becoming the first Doctor Who theatrical movie, when Disney's London Office expressed interest in acquiring the rights to the story. If they'd actually made it, they would have probably stripped the Doctor Who elements out though, and just went straight up historical - no time travelers.

It's also the only serial lost from the first season (although a couple of episodes are still missing from the *Reign of Terror*), and the oldest serial to be completely lost.

In 2013, the Internet went wild with a rumour that *Marco Polo* had been found. It hadn't been.

Finally, it's the last Reconstruction done by Loose Cannon, released in 2015, and the first to be colourized.

Watching the Reconstruction, I'm struck by how this story really must have been the original big showcase project for the Producers and Directors. The culmination of the original vision for the show as a cerebral guided tour through history. *Unearthly Child* was the concept test pilot, the Daleks were a last minute replacement and a lower class pulp potboiler, and *Edge of Destruction* was a couple of 'ship in the bottle' fill-in episodes.

But with *Marco Polo*, you can tell, this is where they planned to go big from the start. This was going to be their masterpiece, their breakthrough. One episode after another, it's just a succession of elaborate, sumptuous, gloriously detailed and beautiful sets, props, costumes. The story is overrun with cast members and extras. It has a feel of an old style movie epic.

I was initially uncertain about the decision to colourise a black and white serial. That sort of thing sometimes smacks of being annoyingly 'special,' and quite often, colourising something that was designed to be shot in black and white can steal a bit of magic away. But in the case of *Marco Polo*, although the Tele-Snaps photographed off a television were in black and white, there was a huge wealth of production photographs in colour which gave accurate reads for hues and tones. Each of the Tele-Snaps used was individually hand coloured, which must have been an immense amount of time and effort.

But it works magnificently. If you're going to colourise, this was the production to do it, because it allows us to appreciate these magnificent sets and costumes in their original glory. Even the Tele-Snap format, the succession of still pictures, works well for *Marco Polo*, because without the distraction of moving characters, we can appreciate just how stunning the production design for this serial was. You can appreciate how extraordinary it was visually, and understand why Disney might be interested in remaking it.

As to the Tele-Snaps themselves, by and large, you get used to them. I thought it might be difficult. After all, it's really just a slide show with voices. They do use a few tricks now and then to liven up proceedings - the map shown in the narration sections is animated. In a scene with a sandstorm, they CGI in some fog and sleet effects onto the image. There are a few zooms and close ups, some pans to give an illusion of motion, at times, the camera shifts back and forth in close ups of figures that are clearly in the same original picture, but surprisingly, there's not that much of it. There are occasional subtitle crawls describing some action which isn't clear from the pictures. Mostly though, the Reconstruction artists are content not to be tricky, but just to try and match the images to the dialogue and let the story tell itself.

The narrative itself is no great shakes. We aren't talking Swiss-watch plots, full of complexity and interlocking elements. This is almost painfully straightforward and completely bereft of any science fiction elements except the presence of the time travelers themselves.

The Doctor and his companions end up in Tibet and become involuntary guests of Marco Polo. Polo is on his journey to see the great Khan, in company with a warlord and a princess. Basically, it's a travelogue, every episode sees them further along on the journey. But that's okay, because this almost leisurely pace allows the characters to develop and it showcases its gorgeous and intricate production design.

One thing that helps the Reconstruction is that the visual element is uniform - they're all Tele-Snaps, same style, same quality. In some of the other Reconstructions, *Power of the Daleks,* for instance, surviving motion clips are inserted, as are photographs and other material with the Tele-Snaps, perhaps different reproductions of Tele-Snaps, so the visual quality is all over the place. Here it is beautifully consistent.

The Tele-Snaps format seems to work best when people are tranquil, when they're just hanging out and having conversations. There's any number of tense scenes that are depicted well, and the Doctor's backgammon tournament with Kublai Khan is so rich in image and expressions it might as well be live action.

But the Reconstruction doesn't handle action terribly well - a fight with bandits falls flat, a climactic swordfight between the villainous Tegana and Marco Polo in the final episode fails utterly. But that's a small flaw.

A nice touch is that the *Loose Cannon* people tracked down Mark Eden, the actor who starred as Marco Polo, several decades prior. He consented to return to the character to do a couple of wraparound bits - the aged Marco Polo, sitting at his writing desk, looking back on the decades and writing about his experience with the Doctor. It's a live action prologue and epilogue that adds a bit to the production. Eden also narrates a short documentary about the life of the real Marco Polo.

It's not the same as watching the real 'live' video episodes. But it's closer than you might think. By this point in time, between *Loose Cannon* and others, many lost serials now exist as Reconstructions, sometimes in multiple versions.

It's tempting to think of *Loose Cannon's* work as definitive. But inspired by *Loose Cannon* and the Reconstruction artists, other fans have tried to build onto that work, using the audio tracks for different kinds of animation, sometimes even using the Tele-Snaps as backgrounds, sometimes using the Tele-Snaps for collage animations, or simply experimenting with different ways to make their Reconstructions more vital. It comes down to evolving technology and interest and dedication. It's hard to say where things will end up.

Since then, there have been other fans and groups of fans that tried their own hands at Reconstructions. Josh Snares, who made a number of his own fan films, has produced several semi-animated Recons, including an animated version of *Evil of the Daleks*.

Then there was Ian Levine himself, who used the format to recreate never-made Doctor Who stories, including *Yellow Fever and How to Cure It* and *Lost in the Dark Dimension*. Levine in these efforts set out to recreate, not just serials that had been lost, but famous stories that had never actually been made - something that would have been near impossible as a film. But the Reconstruction genre gave him a format, "an audio track accompanied by a slide show of stills," which made it workable.

Even the BBC got into the act, using 'official' Reconstructions to fill in missing episodes for its DVD releases of incomplete serials like the recent release of *Underwater Menace*. A 'reconstruction' version of the The *Faceless Ones* is included on the DVD release of the animated re-creation of that serial.

On another front, BBCi, the online division of the BBC ran the Reconstructions as part of its 'cult television' website in the late 90s.

These webcasts eventually inspired BBCi to run a series of semi-animated new productions, *Death Comes to Time* with Sylvester McCoy, then *Realtime* with Colin Baker, and finally Shada with Paul McGann and Lalla Ward - audio stories accompanied by sequences of artists' drawings, very similar to the Reconstructions in style. Building on that, BBCi launched their own animated Doctor Who with *Scream of the Shalka*, featuring Richard E. Grant as the Doctor. It's fascinating how one thing leads to another, how each step inspires new innovations.

In 1977, the BBC was down to 47 episodes from the sixties. Since then, 109 have been recovered. Without Ian Levine stirring the pot, the junkings may have continued uninterrupted. Without Ian Levine and Sue Malden and dedicated networks of fans all over the world, people who actually searched for lost episodes, and people who recognized what they came across, most of those lost 109 episodes would never have been recovered.

Without fans, there would not have been an audio record of all of those lost episodes. Without Richard Develyn and Michael Palmer and Richard Brinnell, reconstructions of all those lost serials would not exist. Fans preserved and recovered so much that was lost, re-created what couldn't be recovered, and in the era when the show was gone, they were the sole authors of a wonderful burst of creativity and accomplishment.

In the modern era, we're probably seeing the Reconstructions fading away. The BBC has been steadily creating, or commissioning, fully animated re-creations of the lost serials. Now you can watch the lost adventures of William Hartnell and Patrick Troughton as cartoons, rotoscoped, using the

Tele-Snaps as references, and relying on extra sources from Director's notes and shot lists, to set photos, etc.

You can still find them. The wonderful innovation and creativity behind the Reconstructions is being forgotten. Left behind as the world marches forward.

I hope that the colourized Reconstruction of *Marco Polo* hangs around for a while. It is so visually gorgeous; I can't imagine an animation doing it justice.

But even so, all of the BBC's animated re-creations are still based on the audio recordings created and preserved by fans. That's a good legacy.

CAST: *William Hartnell - Doctor Who; Carol Ann Ford - Susan Foreman; William Russel - Ian Chesterton; Jacqueline Hill - Barbara Wright; Mark Eden - Marco Polo; Derren Nesbitt - Tegana; Zienia Merton - Ping-Cho; Paul Carson - Ling-Tau; Tutte Lemkow - Kuiju; Martin Miller - Kublai Khan; Peter Lawrence - Vizier; Claire Davenport - Empress (Abridged)*

CREW: *Verity Lambert - Producer; Warris Hussein - Director; John Lucarotti - Writer; Tristram Cary - Incidental Music; Darek Ware - Sword Fight; Daphne Dare - Costume; Ann Ferriggi - Make-up Supervisor; David Whitaker - Story Editor; Barry Newbery - Designer; Mervyn Pinfield - Associate Producer; (Abridged)*

RECONSTRUCTION CREW: *John Cura - Telesnaps; David Homan, James Russell - Audio Recordists; Mark Eden - Additional Scenes as Marco Polo and Narration; Derek Handley, Dean Rose, Rick Brindell - Reconstruction artists; Derek Handley - Editing; Derek Handley and Dean Rose - Colourisation Composites and Special Material; Mike Fillis - Music; Steve England - Web Support; Dean Rose - Historical Research; Thanks to Tony Clark, Jan Vincent-Rudzki, Richard O. Landen; David Howe, Barry Newbery, David Miller, David Brunt; Julian Knott; Peter Ware; Ron Handley; Margaret Rose; Loose Cannon Productions, 2015.*

Review: Masters of Luxor (1963-2014)

The Lost Story Made Real

STORY: The Tardis is drawn to a strange empty city on an alien world. There they encounter a humanoid Robot, the Perfect One, and his golem-like Derivatrons. The Perfect One explains the fate of the prior inhabitants, a fate that awaits the Doctor and his companions....

REVIEW: Okay, here's the skinny. Way back in 1963, when Doctor Who was starting up, it was working out stories, taking pitches, hiring writers, etc. The first script they did was *Unearthly Child*, written by Anthony Coburn. It was a success, thankfully.

Coburn was a friend and associate of Sidney Newman, and he'd actually been involved in the development of Doctor Who. I think he was the one who came up with the word 'Tardis.' So of course, they invited Anthony Coburn to do a second script, and slated it into the production process as the second serial. It was originally going to be the follow up episode.

But there were some problems with it. It wasn't ready. The producers weren't completely happy. It got pushed back, with the *Edge of Destruction* being written at the last minute to give a bit of breathing room.

Even then, it still was not ready. So Terry Nation was called in and whipped up something in no time at all, and the *Daleks* took its place. The rest is history, as far as Doctor Who was concerned.

As for Anthony Coburn, he found the *Masters of Luxor* kept getting pushed back and pushed back. *Marco Polo* came next, instead. I think that they just didn't want it, but were having trouble saying no. Eventually, they did say no. Coburn chose not to be associated with the show any longer. That seems a bit high strung if you ask me. I imagine that there was some sense of betrayal. It's a hard thing to go from the inner circle to 'your script is tosh, sorry.' Still, we all get faces in the asphalt sometime. You got to get back up and keep going.

Oh well.

There, the story should have ended. But the *Masters of Luxor* got published in August, 1992, by Titan Books, as part of a series of Doctor Who script books, for used and unused scripts. Note the date. The show's over, but we're coming up on the 30th Anniversary. There's buzz and hoopla, and Titan is hoping to cash in with any Doctor Who themed product it could generate.

Now available to the public, the script floated around for another nine years, until 2001, when a group of Chicago area fans led by Frank Smialek and Anthony Sarlo decided to mount a production of it. I think they chose it partially because it was such an iconic script - the planned second serial, by one of the key creative people involved at the beginning. And partially because the ambitions of the script seemed achievable - small cast, indoor production, not a lot of action.

I think there was also a fascination with the idea of bringing a '*Lost Doctor Who*' to life. There was a certain allure, given how early the *Masters of Luxor* dates in the series history, and how pivotal the Daleks that replaced it, turned out to be. A Doctor Who where the *Masters of Luxor* rather than the *Daleks* ended up getting made could be quite different, the trajectory of the show might have been very different.

So they got together, and put on a production. But the finished episodes were shown only a few times, the complete serial in total was shown only once, and that was it. From there, the fan edition of the *Masters of Luxor* itself passed into legend. Rumours circulated about a lost masterpiece. Along the way, an 'official version' of *Masters of Luxor* was produced as an audio adventure by Big Finish Productions.

Finally, in 2009 – the same year that Fire and Ice came out – *Masters of Luxor* was submitted to the Fan Film Database on YouTube. Immediately following that it was released to DVD as a two disk set, with extras, including commentary.

So here we are.

Now, before I start my review, I have a caveat or two.

This *Masters of Luxor* is not exactly the entire and complete *Masters of Luxor* that Anthony Coburn wrote. Keep in mind that Coburn was writing at the very beginning of the series history. A lot of things had not gelled. In his original script, he had the names a bit different. He threw in some religious themes that were pretty foreign to the show, and likely made his script harder for the show's producers to buy. So even with the Titan Books script, there were adaptations from the original.

Then, when the fans were workshopping and preparing to shoot, they made some further adaptations. At that early point in the series, Ian and Barbara were intended to be the heroes, and the Doctor was just the vaguely untrustworthy guy who delivered them to situations. Not quite, but close to that. Of course, as the show went on, the Doctor became much more central, much more quickly. So they touched it up to emphasize the role of the Doctor. There was a much younger actor for the role of the Doctor, Anthony Sarlo, so the relationship with Susan changed and he became her uncle.

They cut stuff out. The original script was for six episodes. They got it down to four. I am seriously okay with that. The black and white serials of Troughton and Hartnell tended to run long and tended to be seriously padded. There was a repetition and slowness to the pace of the old serials that modern audiences can find difficult. Honestly, sometimes I like the old Cushing films better than the original stories, because the original seem to drag a bit. It was a different era, different standards.

So yes, this is a mediated script, an interpreted script. You know what? I'm fine with that. The production process is a complicated thing, full of adjustments and compromises. Very few scripts make it to the screen exactly as written. There are a hundred reasons for changes, ranging from scheduling, to actors availability, to things making sense on a page that don't make sense when you try to film it. From what I can tell, there were no adjustments or adaptations that lost the spirit of the script, what ends up on screen is clearly a rendition of what Anthony Coburn wrote.

Not that I've read the original *Masters of Luxor* myself, mind you. But it feels authentic, watching it.

So, on to the review…

Okay, the thing I celebrate about the best fan films is that they capture the look, the feel, the style of Doctor Who, in its particular era. You watch them, and it feels like you're watching some alternate universe version of the BBC series. Or they feel like you can just slip these stories in among the BBC DVDs and no one would ever notice.

Masters of Luxor is like that. This feels so much like a Hartnell serial, it's uncanny. The lighting, the sets, the pacing, that formal theatrical style of dramatic acting that was a staple of the first decade or so of British television, it's all there, and masterfully done.

The 'voices' or performances are spot on. Honestly, I'd have to go back and watch something from Hartnell's first year, to distinguish this 'Susan' from the real one. Her look and performance are so finely tuned that they blur together.

Partly it's because this is an actual script from that season, so Coburn was tapping directly into whatever there was available. He was an intimate part of the brain trust. He may have met the actors, seen their work, perhaps even attended rehearsals or stood in the television studio and watched them play the characters, so he had their voices down. Hell, he helped to create these characters. So if the Susan from *Masters of Luxor* is talking and acting like the one from *Unearthly Child*... Duh!

On the other hand, this was literally the second story they were going to do, so I'd think that a lot had not fully gelled. No matter how good Coburn was, I can't see him writing to the idiosyncratic voice of the actress. Coburn couldn't write to that level because it just wasn't there to draw on yet. I think a lot comes down to the actress, Samantha Eaton, just nailing it.

All the performances are spot on.

Again, there are some caveats. Anthony Sarlo, who plays the Doctor has much more of a role than the original script would have allowed him. On the other hand, Sarlo doesn't bring the edge to the character that Hartnell does. Hartnell was the definition of crotchety bastard, and Sarlo simply isn't a bastard.

Then there's the Matt Ellegood who plays 'The Perfect One' kind of robotically, but he's a robot so that's the point. Kirk Jackson playing Tabon as the bushy bearded Dr. Zarkoff type scientist is probably the weakest link, but that's inherently a factor of the script. An older more intense actor would have brought more to the role but it wouldn't have worked – Jackson's character is essentially stereotypical and I can't say it's a bad decision to play it with restraint. There's a formal quality to the performances, which in modern terms would be a liability. But it's very much in keeping with the strongly stage and theatrical foundations of the BBC of that time.

Of course, there is the fact that they play with American accents – well… get over it. After a few minutes, I stopped noticing.

The production design is exemplary. That's partly a matter of the script's gift and the productions talent and commitment. You have a very impressive Tardis console and set. It looks very authentic to the period. The costumes, props, the sets and robots are all well done, and authentic to the period. The Police Box shell was actually borrowed from the Federation, creators of *Save Who* and *Reign of Turner*, apparently. There was a minor aggravation, when they painted it darker, to ensure it would show up better in black and white, without thinking to ask for permission.

As I've said, the script calls for very static sets and settings: No jungles, no ruined cities, nothing too exotic, instead it's just mostly rooms and corridors, featureless and sterile. The script feels very stage bound, very static sets, nothing too exotic. If you were a fan group looking at a script to adapt, and you looked at the Daleks…. well, you'd say 'we're boned mateys – we have to build jungles, we have to build caves, we have to build a Dalek city with several rooms and corridors, we're going to be building sets till we're all old and gray.'

If you're looking at *Masters of Luxor*? Well, there are only a limited number of sets, just rooms and halls, not a lot of set dressing, and all the action takes place indoors. Much easier to build and shoot for.

The Second Pirates History, Page 259

In the end, its cheap – tinfoil, duct tape, odds and ends, you can spot the cheapness. But it's well done, well-shot cheapness.

Of course, this period was 1963 Doctor Who. The original show back then was shot on black and white and broadcast on low res TV, with a BBC production budget that was pretty shoestring and a production background that was heavily theatrical. When they did crazy ambitious stuff, you sometimes got stories like the *Web Planet*, impressive but flawed. So if you are copying that era, the bar is kind of low to start with.

Apart from the Tardis interior walls and console, the most impressive production design are the robots, called 'Derivatrons' You can tell there's a lot of duct tape and aluminum foil in their DNA. They're not the standard 'tin can' variety of robots – that's the universal default for robot and that's always hard to carry off well. What they've done here is gone for a more 'golem' style of bot, very roughly humanoid, without facial features. They're almost like crude clay effigies, half formed and half finished, without the bother of detailing. Visually that works.

It also works in terms of design concept. The 'Derivatrons' are literally imperfect clay, crude reproductions of humanity, whereas the 'Perfect One' is the finished product. The script is loaded with ideas of imperfection and perfection, of refinement from basic forms to elevated detailed creations. It's nice when the production design expresses and works with the ideas in the script.

Which, I suppose, takes us to the story itself. What's it about? Basically, it's about a Pinocchio's quest to be a real boy, by dismembering other real boys and wearing their skins…

Okay, not really. Although you have to admit, that's a humdinger of a B-movie plot. But actually, this is what it is in a nutshell, although in a deeply philosophical way. *Masters of Luxor* is really the story of the 'Perfect One' and his own oedipal longings. The Masters have gone away, leaving behind their robots, including the most perfect, the most exquisite, the most nearly human creation – the 'Perfect One.' But although he's perfect, he's not quite perfect enough. In religious terms, we'd say his problem is a lack of soul. In technical terms, we might say he's unable to exceed the boundaries of his programming. In social terms, we'd say he's a self-absorbed git with a giant stick up his butt.

The 'Perfect One' is alternately contemptuously dismissive and oddly worshipful of the vanished society that created him. From his description, they were a nastily arrogant, utterly self-absorbed bunch of gits. Much like him, come to think of it, although that may be all he managed to perceive. They created robots not just to serve them, but to worship them, which is a bit creepy.

But the Perfect One also aspires to be more like them, and so he's picked up the habit of grabbing passing space travelers and disintegrating them in an effort to absorb or grasp their 'human essence.' It's futile, it won't work, can never work, but he's a robot, and he just doesn't have the programming to realize it or understand it. The 'Perfect One' is as human as he can get, but he doesn't have a clue.

Which is sadly human, when you think of it.

As you can tell, this is a deeply philosophical story. There are literally only two guest speaking roles, Tabon and the Perfect One after the central quartet of the Doctor, Susan, Ian and Barbara. So add it up – sparse sets, no real shifts of location, tiny cast. What else is left to the cast? Except to talk to each other, and talk, and talk. It's very reminiscent of a rather ponderous stage play.

There are a lot of spiritual and religious overtones; it's very metaphysical and philosophical. What is life? Where do we come from? Where are we going? What makes a machine a machine, and what makes a person a human being? Anthony Coburn was, by all accounts a deeply religious man, and this shines through. Apparently the original drafts were heavier on religious subtext, and he had to tone it down for the BBC. He couldn't tone it down enough though.

Honestly, it could have been death. Can you imagine six episodes of philosophizing back in 1963? This was for a children's show – how many 12 year olds are working on their Masters degrees in theology? That's not to say it's an out and out bad script. Anthony Coburn was a competent writer, and he was writing about things that were important to him. But it definitely comes from a very theatre oriented, very introspective/contemplative tradition. It doesn't really take advantage of the opportunities of the television medium at all. I can understand why Verity Lambert ultimately passed on it.

What saves it is the central character of the Perfect One, who is a complete deadpan whack job. Not malicious, per se, but uncomprehending. His massive cluelessness becomes fascinating. He's like this giant boulder of obstinate stupidity rolling down a hill. All the other characters are just trying to get out of his way, trying to reason with him, overcome him, escape him, and he's just impervious to it all.

Oddly, I think that the script may have revealed more than Anthony Coburn intended to. He was a very devout man, faith was a large part of his life. But faith is ultimately like programming: It is unreasoning and embedded, setting boundaries on our consciousness. The limitations that he was exploring in the Perfect One, I think entirely unconsciously, reflected the limitations imposed by faith.

So what do we have? Not the *Daleks*, I'll tell you that. I can see how Coburn would have been upset to be dumped for

Terry Nation's brainchildren; the Daleks are pulp adventure, potboilers all the way. Masters of Luxor is very consciously 'art.' That would have to grind some gears.

In terms of Hartnell's serials, I think it probably most closely resembles *Edge of Destruction*, or the *Sensorites*, or the *Ark*. But really, it's its own creature. Although it feels just like a Hartnell serial, there isn't anything in there quite like it. Which, when you think of it, makes it an accomplishment for both Coburn, and the fans that produced it.

I'm pleased to say that for now, the lost masterpiece is a found masterpiece.

CAST: *Doctor Who - Anthony Sarlo; Ian Chesterton - Clyde Scott Goble; Barbara Wright - Stephanie Gloeckler; Susan Foreman - Samantha Eaton; The Perfect One - Matt Ellegood; Tabon - Kirk Jackson; Robot - Kirk Jackson, Frank Smialek; Proto - Ric Horejs*

CREW: *Written by Anthony Coburn (1963); Script Editors - Anthony Sarlo, Ric Horejs, Frank Smialek, Director/ Editor/ Incidental Music - Frank Smialek; Camera Operator - Dan Graczyk; 2nd Editor/ Sound - Ric Horejs; Costume - Will Wiseman; Assistant Director/Costume Designer - Jamie Ramsay; Designer - Bryan Whyte, Ed Dawson, Pete Papavasiou; Line Producer - Kirk Jackson*

Review: Devious and the Secret Season (1969-1991-2025)

Season 6B and the Thirty Year Quest

STORY: At the end of War Games, the Time Lords force the Second Doctor to regenerate into his Third incarnation, but midway through the change, the Doctor is abducted by a group of renegade Time Lords who take him to a hidden world as part of a test. Unfortunately, the Daleks and Cybermen are already there...

REVIEW: Devious is probably the most famous and storied fan film out there. It is, or it is going to be, a six episode serial made in the classic style, with 25 minute episodes. The finished story, when it plays, will be 150 minutes, on a par with the serials of the sixties and seventies.

They started in 1991, and it's still only half released. After almost thirty years in development, the first episode has only been released three years ago. Since then, it's been an episode a year. Assuming they keep to that schedule and nothing goes wrong, we should have the whole thing no later than 2025. Cross your fingers.

The Second Pirates History, Page 264

Apart from that ambitious size and complexity, what makes it famous?

For one thing, they managed to get Jon Pertwee to reprise his role as the Doctor back in 1995, a year before his death. That was his final performance as the Doctor, and perhaps his final performance ever. For that alone, it would be a part of history.

That scene from Devious appears as an extra on the War Games DVD. It's one of the few times that the amateurs 'go pro' – that a fan film makes it into the BBC official releases. Possibly, it's the only time.

Jon Pertwee's dialogue was later sampled with permission by Big Finish Productions, which had obtained a license to do Doctor Who audio productions. Pertwee's voice appeared in Zagreus, Big Finish's multi-Doctor epic audio story.

Props from the fan film – the Tardis Console, used by the Doctor and the Master, as well several Daleks were borrowed by the BBC itself for use in 1999's Curse of Fatal Death. It says something when the British Broadcasting Corporation is knocking on your door with its hand out.

The Devious production also supplied props, including Daleks, for a couple of stage plays – Evil of the Daleks and The Dalek Masterplan, both starring Nick Scovell as the Doctor, and adapted for stage by Scovell and Rob Thrush, back in 2006 and 2007.

Count in convention appearances, exhibitions, coverage in mainstream and fan media. It's probably one of the most famous Doctor Who fan films ever… And it's never been released.

So what exactly is *Devious*?

Devious is a Doctor Who serial set during Season 6B.

And what the heck is season 6B?

It's a sort of 'ghost season' between the Troughton Doctor's end and apparent forced regeneration in The *War Games*, and the Jon Pertwee Doctor's first appearance in *Terror of the Autons*.

Now just to be clear, there wasn't any gap in scheduling between Troughton and Pertwee, where a whole bunch of planned episodes fell into the void.

That happened in 1985, with the cancellation, uncancellation and hiatus, where a whole season of stories, some already paid for, were cancelled in favour of something else.

And that happened in 1990, when the cancellation of the show resulted in another season of episodes in planning being abandoned. This was different..

What happened is that when Patrick Troughton left the role of the Doctor, he didn't stick around for the regeneration scene to morph into Jon Pertwee. Instead, you just get the end of the *War Games* with Troughton screaming and spinning at the end of season six.

Then at the start of season seven, you begin with *Terror of the Autons,* and the Police Box landing and Jon Pertwee falling out, wearing Troughton's clothes. The implication is pretty clear that Troughton regenerated straight into Pertwee. But we don't actually see the morphing from one to the other, as we did with Hartnell to Troughton, Pertwee to Baker, Baker to Davison, etc.

At first, nobody gave it much thought. The trouble started up with Troughton's later appearances as a 'guest Doctor' in the *Three Doctors*, the *Five Doctors* and the *Two Doctors* which created continuity issues.

In the *Five Doctors* and the *Two Doctors*, particularly, he's obviously older and creakier. In *The Three Doctors*, December,

1972, Troughton was only three years older than his last appearance as the Doctor in June, 1969, that's easily overlooked. But in the *Five Doctors* and *Two Doctors*, it's 15 and 17 years after he left the show, and he wasn't a young man on the show, so it's impossible not to notice he's a lot older.

There were other signifiers. The Troughton Doctor always had companions, but in the *Three Doctors* he's alone.

In the *Five Doctors*, he runs into two companions, Jamie and Zoe, and notes their memories were wiped in *War Games*, so he knows they're illusions. But if he knows that, then that means he's from after *War Games*, where he supposedly regenerated, immediately, so there's a gap.

In the *Two Doctors* he's clearly working as an agent for the Time Lords, which runs contrary to the entirety of his three seasons where he's on the run and hiding out from them. He's got doodads he didn't have before and which his successor doesn't, like a remote control for the Tardis. There are various contradictions and loose ends.

This is the sort of thing that us fans love to dig into.

Although the Doctor Who comic strips weren't canon, it was pointed out that Troughton had an entire summer of strips where his Doctor is stranded on Earth for six months after the War Games. That added to the mix.

No one in the BBC really had much of an answer for all the glitches.

Neither Bob Baker and Dave Martin who wrote the *Three Doctors*, nor *Terrance Dicks* who wrote the Five Doctors, ever seemed to give any thought to the continuity issues.

Truth was, no one in charge cared that much. Remember that fandom as an organized movement of nit pickers and archivists was late in coming into existence. And remember that for the first decade or so, there were no re-runs, they couldn't legally do reruns, there were no collections of videotapes to compare, and the BBC had so little regard that it was junking the old episodes. The junkings were so thorough that Hartnell's appearance in the *Three Doctors* is literally the only Hartnell appearance preserved on the original video recording, everything else was junked and eventually recovered or not recovered.

Robert Holmes, who wrote the *Two Doctors* just assumed that the Doctor had been under the thumb of the Time Lords the entire time. All the time he was running and hiding from them, they'd known exactly where he was. Effectively, he was a secret agent for the Time Lords, occasionally doing dirty deeds on the sly. This idea was later elaborated on by Chris Chibnall in his 'Timeless Child' story thread in the Whittaker era.

"Continuity," someone said, *"is whatever we happen to remember on a given day."* I'll caveat that – it was whatever they happened to remember that happened to be useful – if it wasn't, they'd just ignore it and do whatever they needed to. To be fair, they were writers doing a job they were getting paid for, not nerds parsing the text like you and me.

The Season 6B theory may have been floating around for a while in fandom, but it was formally articulated by Paul Cornell, Martin Day and Keith Topping in their *Doctor Who Discontinuity Guide*, published in 1994.

The theory goes that Troughton didn't regenerate directly into Pertwee right away. Rather, the Time Lords kept him around as their monkey-butler to do missions for them, resulting in his later appearances in the various numbered Doctors. Eventually, once his usefulness was over, his memory was wiped and they regenerated him into Pertwee, but just not right away.

Season 6B was so cool and worked so well that the BBC got up off its rump, ambled over, gave it a look see and mumbled *"Makes sense. It's official."*

Indeed, the Season 6B theory was even more fluid.

Sure, the Troughton Doctor definitely lasted a lot longer than anyone suspected. The various team ups were clear proof of that.

But even so, we still don't see the Troughton regenerating into Pertwee. Those look like his clothes, but can we really tell from clothes? Troughton's outfit wasn't particularly distinctive, not compared to later costumes.

Hypothetically, you could have Troughton regenerate into someone, who then regenerates into Pertwee. You could have an intermediate Doctor between Troughton and Pertwee.

You could have a bunch of them, as many as you *wanted*. An infinite number of secret intermediate Doctors.

The Time Lords, after all, were more than capable of handing out extra regenerations, or wiping the knowledge from minds.

That's actually one of the possible explanations for the Ruth Doctor, aka the Fugitive Doctor, aka the Black Woman Doctor who appears a few times during Jody Whittaker's run as the Doctor on the BBC – that she's a hidden 6B Doctor. Or possibly not, it's up in the air.

Which brings us to Devious:

Basically, the story in Devious is that half way through his regeneration from Second to Third, the Doctor is plucked out of the time stream by a group of sneaky Timelords watching from a nearby asteroid. Seems they have some ulterior motives. They place the half-regenerated Doctor on this planet to run some situational adventure tests, I dunno, just checking out his heroism or cunning or something. Then the

Daleks and the Dalek Emperor and even the Cybermen show up, and everything just goes to hell.

That's where Pertwee comes in. At the end of *Devious*, he shows up to meet his half-regenerated Doctor self, and explain that he's supposed to continue morphing into the Third Doctor.

There are a couple of other sweet cameos – Anneke Wills shows up briefly as Troughton's companion, Polly. And there is also Peter Tuddenham and Hugh Lloyd, who back in the day played the Time Lords who passed sentence over Troughton.

Devious has been in production for over thirty years now. Filming started in 1991; principle photography was mostly finished by 2005. Since then, they've been messing about with post production for the last decade or so, editing, tweaking the sound mix, doing CGI touch ups.

In fact *Devious'* shooting took place over such an extended period of time that the actors visibly aged. Ironic, given that Troughton's aging in the *Five Doctors* and *Two Doctors* helped inspire the 6B series.

Luckily, they apparently managed to insert a plot point – a 'time glitch' that sometimes caused the characters to be artificially and temporarily aged – sort of like in *Time Crash*, or in *Death Takes a Holiday*. Time: You got to watch it, or it will turn on you, that wibbly-wobbly bastard.

Back when I wrote the first edition of this book, it was 2017 and *Devious* had literally been in production longer than the original series existed. While there were regular updates on the *Devious* web site, there was still no sign of it actually being released, and it seemed quite possible it would never be released. A project endlessly discussed, endlessly in production, but never actually appearing. A kind of fan film experience of *Waiting for Godot*.

But to everyone's astonishment and joy, the first episode was released in 2020. Since then follow up episodes were released in 2021 and 2022. We're now half way through, and there's a real prospect that it will all be out in the world someday.

So is it any good?

Well, so far what we've got are three of the six episodes, plus a handful of teasers and promos. In addition to the three episodes, there was a sixteen minute 'stand-alone' tribute to fan films called *The Never Was*; an edited twelve minute mini-episode from the end of *Devious* which featured Jon Pertwee's last appearance (it can be found on the *War Games* DVD); an unofficial three minute trailer; perhaps four minutes of other clips; a lot of photographs; and a detailed web site. Not enough to give us the complete story, but enough to at least give us an idea of what we've got.

We can't fault the sets and props. If you've got Daleks, Cybermen and Tardis consoles rugged enough and good looking enough to appear on television and on stage, then that speaks for itself. If you visit their website, there are ample pictures of props, sets, costumes, all of it to a highly professional standard.

The CGI effects also seem effective and professional, though the CGI monster from the first episode is kind of wonky.

The story concept seems okay to me. The notion is even ingenious. But hey, there are plenty of slips between the cup and the lip. There's a big gulf between a good idea and a good script, and another gulf between a good script and a good execution.

At this point, the Doctor has been plucked from between regenerations, and landed on a world without his memory or Tardis by a group of Time Lord Renegades.

But I'm not really being fair – in the first episode, the story starts in media res – in the middle of an adventure. The

Doctor and his companions drop out of a time bubble; it's a brand new Doctor who immediately passes out. There's a lot of stuff going on. Medieval barbarians are attacking; the Doctor's companions are trying to keep him safe.

But there are immediate signs something is weird, the Doctor is being watched, both by ground observers and by a group in a Tardis up in orbit tethered to an asteroid. It appears that they're choreographing the Doctor's adventure.

But almost as soon as this becomes clear, things start going wrong for the watchers. The ground observer senses she's being watched by something. It turns out she's right. Meanwhile, the orbiting Tardis is attacked and perhaps destroyed by a mysterious force from the planet.

The Daleks make an appearance, which appears to have been in nobody's plan, and it turns out, there are quite a lot of them. An entire factory of them. The complications are accumulating, and things are heating up rapidly. So far, it's developing nicely.

Meanwhile, there's the Doctor in the middle of it all, oblivious to the scheme that surrounds him, and equally oblivious to the fact that the scheme has gone badly off the rails. Or the fact that even that is part of some other, larger, deeper plot. But over the first three episodes, he's starting to unravel it all.

As new Doctors go, Tony Garner's version is a genial sort. At first, he seems slow, his style of speech is careful and soft-spoken. But as the story goes along we see that this Doctor is as smart as all the rest, his amiable simple-mindedness is just a cover for a brilliant, observant mind.

Garner's is the friendliest version of the Doctor we've seen. His character is filled with a childlike glee. Even when he's sarcastic, it's simply not hurtful, there's just no meanness.

The Second Pirates History, Page 272

There's a line in Tony Garner's interaction with Jon Pertwee... *'All those people who died...'* That's quite nice, regret and sadness and compassion all rolled up.

Of course, the renegades plot depends on plucking the Doctor out of the Time Lord's grasp, and inserting fake memories of themselves as his companions. Sometimes, this gets confusing, the Doctor has flashbacks which may or not be real memories, and these flashbacks can disrupt the narrative flow, to the point it's hard to keep track of what's going on.

This is a complicated story even by the standards of the classic era serials, and the flashbacks and flash forwards, real and imaginary, the cutaways, mean you have to watch it very carefully. It also means that repeat viewings are well rewarded; you'll keep picking up new insights with extra viewings.

And I suspect that each new episode released will contain new revelations or new visuals that will send us back to rewatch the previous episodes in a new light.

Some of the visuals are flat out intriguing. The Police Box drops out of the air next to what looks like a pirate galleon. There's an implanted memory sequence to insert the Doctor's fake companions that is built around an extraordinary CGI of a translucent sailing ship and funeral ceremony. There is a cutaway to a Dalek assembly line. The orbital attack in the first episode could be the climax of any other serial. Another, possibly implanted memory flashback features a tense moment with Polly and some *Tomb* style Cybermen.

Basically, the nested format, half Matrushka dolls and half *Inception* allows for all kinds of eye-candy scenes. And they've had thirty years to come up with it.

It's not all great. There are rough spots of course – that's inevitable in something that's been in development this long.

The Second Pirates History, Page 273

Some bits – dodgy amateur acting or costuming, that's an inevitable artifact. Other bits are factors of technology, evolved or evolving CGI, or camera resolution so detailed you can see the scratches on a Dalek's dome. But even in professional, multi-million dollar productions, there are wobbly bits.

My advice is don't get wrapped up in that. For every dodgy bit, there's a lot that's complex, intriguing, visually arresting and extraordinary.

Bottom line, there is more than enough there that I would want to keep watching.

Why is it taking so long?

I don't know. Limited resources? Limited free time? Perfectionism?

Or maybe... Just maybe... The journey became the thing. If you look at the website for Devious, it stretches over decades, featuring all these showings, activities, demonstrations, there's coverage, there's a hundred little side trips. It is just endless stuff.

You almost get the feeling they've fallen in love with the process of making it, and they don't want to stop making. That while Devious is in production, it gives them a reason to hang out, a common cause, a social life, it's a mission, a goal, a purpose?

If and when *Devious* is finished then that's over. Perhaps making Devious became more important than finishing Devious. Perhaps Devious the process took over as the goal, the source of meaning and accomplishment, from *Devious* the result.

But hopefully, it will be finished. Even halfway through, there's no guarantee. Any number of things could happen. Copyright strikes on YouTube, Cease and Desist letters or suits from the BBC, hard drive collapses as happened with *Fire and Ice's* second production, or the *Forgotten Doctor's* second series, personal melt-down's, flame-out's, sickness or death, a worldwide pandemic, collapse of civilization, acrimonius internal disputes… Who knows? It's not over till it's over. We just have to wait and hope.

Assuming it is finally finished on or before 2025, what will people make of it? It is very much the ultimate Season 6B movie, its style and feel so intimately bound with classic Doctor Who, so profoundly reminiscent of both the Troughton and Pertwee eras.

And yet, we'll be over sixty years into Doctor Who, over twenty years into the new era, post-Eccleston and Tenant, Smith, Capaldi, Whittaker, Gatwa. Post Davies, Moffat and Chibnall.

Literally, all of New Who, all of Big Finish, all the Virgin novels have literally come and gone while Devious was in production.

The show, the standards and expectations, the fans and fandom will have changed so much. Hell, most of the fans wouldn't even have been born when *Devious* started production.

Will it be obsolete on completion, born only to be forgotten? Or will it be appreciated for the incredible accomplishment it represents? Will the story be fresh and current?

Bottom line: So far, we have an engaging, charming, unique Doctor. We've got a wonderfully elaborate set of nested plots. And accompanying all that, we have series of extraordinary visuals.

I think it will hold up.

CAST: Tony Garner - The Between Doctor; Jon Pertwee - The Third Doctor; David V Clarke - Bradley / Auriga; Anthony Townsend - Phillip / Callisto; Lynette East - Amber/Adreinna; Heather Cohen - Aquilia; Karl Mayne - Luxulyan; Ian Edmond - RalibArthur Harrod - Aturo / Villager; Richard Kingshott - Nilan / Uist; Stephen Cranford - The Covellitor / Villager; Ashley Nealfuller - Chaldar / Imberhorne; Anneke Wills - Past: Polly; Hugh Lloyd - Present: Scribe; Peter Tuddenham - Present: Voix; Amanda Evans - Brogar the Archer; Steve Mayhew - Orkzet; Neil Jones - Observer Teleko; Chris T. Kirk - Observer Vardrah; ? - Observer Valerian; Tim Pieraccini - Third Doctor's stunt double; 'SCUM Fight Re-Enactment Group - Villagers and Clan Marauders; Andy Shaw and 'cyberfriend' - Cybermen; Ian Watts, Ashley Nealfuller & Sylvester McCoy - Black Dalek (radio controllers); Ashley Nealfuller - Claw Dalek; James Quinn and James Quinn Jr. - Tech Dalek; Alia Halstead, Ashley Clarke, Kris Vincent, Colin Vincent, Cori Samuel, Francis Wetherilt, Laura Clarke, Lauren Wetherilt, Nicola Keith, Paul Hayes, Ringo Dhansay, Rob Horne, Rowlie Darby, Simon Goble, Sylvie Winn, Simon Baker and Steven E. King - Silver Daleks.

CREW: David Clarke - Director; David Clarke & Ashley Nealfuller - Writers; David Clarke, Stephen Cranford & Ashley Nealfuller - Producers; Martin Johnson - Music; Many, many others, various production positions; In Memory of Hugh Lloyd, John Nathan-Turner, Jon Pertwee, Peter Tuddenham.

Review: Yellow Fever (and How to Cure It) (1984-2012)

The Lost Story from the Lost Season

STORY: The Autons are on the move and have taken over the British Prime Minister in London. The Doctor's struggle against the alien invaders takes him to Singapore, and a confrontation with his old enemy, the Master.

REVIEW: Like the Dark Dimensions, *Yellow Fever* is one of those infamous lost 'never made' episodes. It's also the most controversial with bitter disagreements over everything from who would have been in it, to how far it got, to what it would have been about, to what the title really was.

Cast your mind back to the first months of 1985. Doctor Who, along with several other shows, was secretly being cancelled by the unsympathetic senior management of the BBC.

No one knew that yet though, season 22 was still being aired and wouldn't complete its run until March. John Nathan-Turner and the production crew were hard at work on season 23, scripts and stories were being commissioned, some were even completed, budgets prepared, casting was in progress.

The stories for the upcoming season included *The Nightmare Fair,* by Graham Williams, commissioned September 25,

1984; *The Ultimate Evil,* by Wally K. Daly; *Mission to Magnus* by Philip Martin; *Yellow Fever and How to Cure it* by Robert Holmes, the first episode commissioned October 26, 1984, the rest commissioned on February 6, 1985; the *Hollows of Time* by Christopher Bidmead, commissioned November 21, 1985; and *Children of January* by Michael Feeney Callan, commissioned on February 5, 1985; a final story, *Gallifrey,* by Pip and Jane Baker was commissioned March 11, 1985.

Then the axe fell and the show was being cancelled, and then the axe unfell, sort of. The BBC decided to cancel the series in January and February. But as rumours of cancellation reached a crescendo, the BBC Senior Management beat a diplomatic retreat and formally announced formally on March 1, 1985, that Doctor Who was not cancelled, merely put on hiatus for 18 months, bumped into the 1986 fiscal year. It also stated that Doctor Who was going back to a half hour format.

The other shoe dropped in May, 1985. Doctor Who would not be returning to a full slate of 24 to 26 half hour episodes, but rather, the show was were cut back to a mere 14 episodes. Reduced numbers of episodes and reduced budget meant that the planned season and stories was unworkable. It was back to the drawing board through June and July. A new concept was developed, the Doctor on Trial. By July 9, 1985, the original season plans and stories were abandoned.

Several of the lost stories eventually saw the light of day in some alternate form. In 1990, Virgin Books published novelizations of *Nightmare Fair, Mission to Magnus* and *Ultimate Evil.* Later, Big Finish would do audio adaptations of *Nightmare Fair, Mission to Magnus and the Hollows of Time. Ultimate Evil* was released as an audiobook separately. *Children of January* was almost a Big Finish audio, but there were scheduling problems.

This left *Yellow Fever and How to Cure It* and *Gallifrey*, forever lost in the abyss, neither of which seems to have made it to a full finished script. *Gallifrey* doesn't seem to have amounted to anything, and there's no indication of any writing or work done, not even an outline. But *Yellow Fever?* There's a tale of ambition and hubris, blind alleys and ignominious defeat.

The writer of Yellow Fever was Robert Holmes. His work on the show spanned five Doctors, starting with Patrick Troughton and ending with Colin Baker. He wrote eighteen serials, and seventy-eight episodes including the *Krotons, Spearhead from Space, Terror of the Autons, Carnival of Monsters, Ark in Space, Pyramids of Mars, Brain of Morbius, The Talons of Weng Chiang, Deadly Assassin, Caves of Androzani, the Two Doctors, the Mysterious Planet* and the *Ultimate Foe.* He was script Editor between 1974 and 1977, considered the high point of the series. His stories regularly dominate top five and top ten lists. He created the Autons, the Sontarans and Sarah Jane Smith. Not all of his stories were memorable, but he's generally credited with some of the best stories, and was considered the best writer in the series history.

Thanks to Eric Saward, he, along with Terrance Dicks, was one of the only classic writers to find his way to the John Nathan-Turner age of the 1980s.

That's pretty much the only kind thing I have to say about Eric Saward.

While working on the final serial of the Trial of a Time Lord, the *Ultimate Foe*, Robert Holmes passed away of liver disease on May 25, 1986.

Yellow Fever and How to Cure It was Robert Holmes great lost story. The great lost story, from the great lost writer, from the great lost season. For this reason alone, it's a significant part of Doctor Who lore and history.

As to what it actually was, that's less clear.

The Second Pirates History, Page 279

According to Shannon Sullivan's web site: *"John Nathan-Turner hoped to take Doctor Who on a location shoot to Singapore, where two episodes of the BBC drama Tenko had been filmed. He and production manager Gary Downie travelled there on October 19th, 1984. After viewing their footage, Robert Holmes was commissioned to write the first episode of "Yellow Fever And How To Cure It" on October 26th. All three episodes were commissioned together on February 6th, 1985. On February 27th, 1985, production of Doctor Who suspended until Spring 1986, with the programme then returning for a season of twenty-five-minute episodes. Holmes was asked to rework his storyline for this format... But the programme's reduced budget precluded location filming in Singapore. Doctor Who Magazine Special Edition #3, Doctor Who: The Trial Of A Time Lord DVD Production Subtitles."* (Abridged quotes)

Yellow Fever, was planned for three 45 minute episodes. How far did it really get? Sources vary. There may have only ever been an outline for the first episode. Another suggests that the first episode was completed and an outline done for the whole story.

Ian Levine, posting on Facebook has a very different take on it: *"As for Yellow Fever, I had a photocopy of the original scene breakdown of all three episodes, given to me by Eric (Saward). Indeed at one point Eric was hired to write it for the Doctor Who book range, and got paid an advance, which he later returned."*

Note Levine's use of the word 'had', I'm not sure that anything currently exists of *Yellow Fever*. Or if it does, it's locked away and forgotten somewhere.

As to the story - according to John Nathan-Turner, in an interview published in Doctor Who Magazine in the early 90s, *"Yellow Fever and How to Cure It would have involved Peri hankering for a trip home to the United States, and began with her seeing the Statue of Liberty through the TARDIS screen. Then she discovers it's a replica in an ornamental garden. That was just one of a wide variety of* locations we planned to use in Singapore. The story would have involved Kate O'Mara as the Rani."

Building on that, this seems to be the most commonly circulated synopsis online, provenance unknown: *"The Doctor shows Peri an image of the Statue of Liberty on the Tardis scanner. Venturing outside, they find that they are not in the United States of America, but in a collection of miniature famous landmarks from around the world situated in Singapore. Walking around, they notice statues which then begin to move and the Doctor recognizes them for what they really are - Autons! The travelers investigate and discover that the evil Rani has allied herself with the Nestenes, who, since the Doctor's last encounter with them have developed an affinity for rubber as well as plastic. The new Autons are now armed with bullets that bounce around corners and hands that can melt over the face of an adversary. However, their troubles are not confined to the Rani and her new allies who are using a travelling street circus for cover. The Master is also in Singapore, jealous that the Rani is working with the Nestenes, as he had previously done in Terror of the Autons, and he determines to stop her plans. Can the Doctor and Peri aided by a holidaying Brigadier Lethbridge-Stuart defeat the evil Time Lords and the Nestenes."*

For what it's worth, this feels authentic, something that fits in with Holmes style and the sort of thing Nathan-Turner would have liked.

On the other hand, Levine's Facebook posting says, *"The Rani was never to be in this story. Kate O'Mara was still doing Dynasty, and there was no mention of her in the story breakdown. This was a story about The Master, The Brigadier, UNIT, and Benton. The first half was set in London, with an Auton Prime Minister, the second half in Singapore. It would have been wonderful, especially with Graeme Harper directing.... That imagined cover featuring The Rani is just plain WRONG on so so many levels . ....Yellow Fever's tag "And How To Cure It", was a Bob Holmes joke and never seriously intended to be a part of the title. ."*

I'm not entirely sure about that. It doesn't seem consistent with Nathan-Turner's interview, or the apocryphal synopsis, both of which start in Singapore and definitely feature the Rani.

Going back to Shannon Sullivan, *"Shortly thereafter, Nathan-Turner asked Holmes to add the newly-introduced Rani to his storyline, alongside the Autons and the Master. .....Spring 1986, with the programme then returning for a season of twenty-five-minute episodes. Holmes was asked to rework his storyline for this format, with the Master no longer appearing."*

My impression is that the story seems to have been driven by Nathan-Turner. He had the idea for Singapore. He, or he and his spouse Gary Downie, went there and took some photos or shot some footage. Or maybe he just wanted to vacation in Singapore, and shooting some footage and suggesting a story was his way of getting the BBC to pay for it. Assuming that the Singapore garden of miniatures was Nathan-Turner's inspiration, it's likely that he was inspired to go with an Auton story. It's just a natural fit - plastic men for a faux plastic garden of monuments. Anyway, he commissioned Holmes for the story. From Sullivan's description, it seems that originally it was just the Master and the Autons.

Then the Rani gets introduced into the story. John Nathan-Turner seems to have liked the Rani and definitely wanted to do more with her. He'd brought back the character back for Time and the Rani, and again for Dimensions in Time. By this time, the Master had been used a lot, he was getting pretty overexposed. The Rani had been freshly introduced, and I think her drag-queen flamboyance and archness appealed to Nathan-Turner. I could see him wanting to wedge the Rani in there.

Or perhaps the Rani, the Master AND the Autons? Not impossible. Turner wasn't really a storyteller; he was a showman at heart. He thought in terms of stunts and coups.

Big 'events.' Things that rocked people back on their ass and got them talking. He wasn't really one for nuance or plot. In the previous season, he'd brought together two Doctors and the Sontarans. I could see two great Villains and the Autons being his idea of an event.

Of course the Master and the Rani had already appeared together the previous year in Time and the Rani. It also appears that the Master was going to appear in the Hollows of Time, and that would have been two appearances. I think Turner would have wanted to avoid overuse: These would have been the ninth and tenth appearances for the Master in five short years. This might indicate further executive meddling in February, to write the Master out of the story altogether, and give it entirely to the Rani.

Regardless, there seemed to be some drive to hold onto the story. As late as May, 1985, *Yellow Fever* was still being considered as part of the shortened fourteen episode season, which would have probably meant pruning the six episode story down to three or four. Given budget cutbacks, location shooting in Singapore was no longer viable, which had been the whole inspiration for the project.

In May, Robert Holmes took the very unusual step of asking to withdraw the story, after apparently being commissioned to write it for months.

Why? Well, the likely budget cuts, loss of Singapore locations and reduction of episodes would have probably gutted the story.

But I think there might be more to Holmes withdrawal; this story seems to have been micro-managed to death by Nathan-Turner.

It was Nathan-Turner's idea to use Singapore, and he chose Singapore locations. Nathan-Turner decided it was a Master story, then changed his mind and made it the Master and the

Rani, Then he changed his mind again, to just the Rani and the Master is out. Nathan-Turner drops Singapore.

It's almost a Nathan-Turner story; his fingerprints are all over the place, with Holmes as the jobber. Word is that sometimes Nathan-Turner could be capricious and very hard to work with. I suspect that Robert Holmes just got sick of it. I suppose given Nathan-Turner's heavy hand, the question becomes was it really a Robert Holmes story?

Apparently, something very similar actually happened on the Two Doctors, with Nathan-Turner changing locations from New Orleans to Spain, introducing the Sontarans, and basically doing a lot of micro-managing that probably had Holmes tearing out his hair. Holmes may simply not have been up for a round two of that kind of treatment.

That was where things lay, until somewhere around 2010, give or take a few years, when Ian Levine gets involved in the story. Levine decided to start creating, or re-creating his own versions of Doctor Who stories.

As we've noted elsewhere, Levine is a major figure, albeit controversial, in Doctor Who fandom. Without taking anything away from the man, I freely acknowledge that he was a part of Doctor Who's history for years, and perhaps a crucial part in certain respects. There's much to admire.

I also acknowledge that there's an incendiary and contentious history, that Levine might be a touch difficult at times, and perhaps he might be best admired from a distance.

Around 2010, Levine began getting involved with re-creations of Doctor Who. His first project was working with David Busch to create an animated version of *Mission to the Unknown*. This was the lost 'single episode' story from the Hartnell days, which featured none of the regular cast. Rather, it was kind of a backdoor pilot for a Dalek TV series, and lead in for the *Dalek Masterplan*. Like many other serials from those days, it had been lost. But there weren't even Tele-Snaps, so it was especially lost. You can find this online, it's not half bad.

There have been other attempts to do *Mission to the Unknown*, eventually culminating in a group of students from University of South Lancashire, who re-enacted and re-created the episode live with approval from the BBC.

Concurrently, or shortly after, he produced and funded an unofficial completion of Shada, the great unfinished Tom Baker story. The unfinished sections were completed with animation, and Levine reunited most of the cast, excluding Tom Baker, but including Lalla Ward, to supply voices. Apparently, he had some thought that the BBC would pick it up from him.

This seems mad to me.

The BBC is a corporate bureaucracy, and that's just not how places like that work. I find it difficult to see someone like Levine being that naive about business. I could see doing *Mission* as a demonstration project to sell the BBC on the concept, but if they weren't buying that, I don't see a next step.

Ultimately, the BBC would take the step of actually getting Tom Baker, and doing their own version of *Shada* with animation filling in the gaps

That means there are at least four or five versions of *Shada* out there. There's an original official version from 1992 by John Nathan-Turner, with Tom Baker showing up to narrate or explain the missing bits. There's a Plymouth Productions fan version, where live fan-actors act out the missing bits. There's a Big Finish semi-animated version where Paul McGann joins Lalla Ward to retell the story. There's Ian Levine's new version, sans Tom Baker but with animation. And the final BBC release, with Tom Baker and animation.

Levine's version of *Shada* is out there. It's not easily available, but it can be tracked down. It's actually fairly comparable to the BBC version. It suffers a little from having to substitute Tom Baker, but it's definitely worth it.

From there, he seems to have gotten right into it, indulging in a bewildering variety of projects, using everything from traditional animation, to CGI, to Reconstructions, to collage animation, to live action.

Some of it is simply peculiar, he hired Sylvester McCoy to shoot additional prologue scenes as the Doctor for *Downtime*, which is profoundly, extremely unnecessary, and detracts and distracts far more than it adds.

He did the same thing *Destiny of the Doctors*, a 1990s computer CD Rom game. In addition to computer graphics of various scenarios featuring a whole list of monsters from Cybermen and Daleks, to Sontarans and Sea Devils, the game featured audio clips from all the surviving Doctors, plus 'stand in' voices for Hartnell and Troughton, and archival voice clips from Pertwee, and a series of short live action film clips of the Master, played by Anthony Ainsley, taunting the game player. There's a narrative story, of sorts, but it's basically a computer game. Levine enlisted Sylvester McCoy to shoot additional scenes and dialogue … to be added to the game, to transform and re-edit it into a fan film? That's beyond odd.

Between 2010 and 2013, he had a dozen projects, mostly private and unreleased. According to Levine's Facebook posts, he was working on Yellow Fever in 2012.

In 2013, Levine released a 45 minute 'Trailer' containing snippets from his various Doctor Who projects, including *Yellow Fever, Gallifrey* and *Dark Dimensions*. A couple of scenes of *Yellow Fever* appear through almost seven minutes at 16:04 to 22:50 of Levine's compilation, as well as bits of *Gallifrey* and *Dark Dimensions*.

The actual whole films themselves, with the exception of *Mission to the Unknown* and *Shada* are unreleased, and will probably remain unreleased. Another of Levine's strange choices. Why go through all that trouble, the time and money, to create these things and then hide them away? Why release only this 45 minute teaser?

Strange.

So here we are. With a dozen Ian Levine fan films to discuss, why focus on *Yellow Fever*?

It's true, there's not a lot to base a review on. But there's a lot of historical significance to Yellow Fever, which earns it some attention.

Of course, there's significance to *Mission to the Uknown, Shada,* Mission *to the Unknown* and even *Evil of the Daleks* but in various forms, other versions of all those stories exist or have been created, and have superseded Levine's productions. *Downtime* and *Destiny of the Doctor*s seem surplus to requirements, pointless embroidering of existing works.

Yellow Fever, on the other hand, is unique, there's no other version out there, there's no book, no script, novelization, no episodes, no CD Rom game, nothing really except the story of its rise and fall, and Levine's claimed memory – it may be Levine's single, unique 'sui generis' production.

Finally, Levine is doing some interesting things technically with *Yellow Fever*, which makes me pick it over his other projects.

For *Dark Dimensions, Yellow Fever* and *Gallifrey*, Levine decided to adapt the format of Reconstructions - creating or collaging a series of still pictures, accompanied by an audio track. Reconstructions are an art form almost peculiar to Doctor Who, used by groups such as *Loose Cannon* to recreate most of the lost serials.

Here, Levine is using this technique or art form to create brand new stories, or to re-create stories that had never actually been filmed. With *Dark Dimensions*, it's pretty much a straight on 'Reconstruction style' project. With *Yellow Fever* and *Gallifrey*, there's increasing efforts to move or crudely animate the components of the image.

There are no short cuts. Shooting live action is extremely difficult and expensive, you need sets and locations, lighting, equipment, synch sound, actors, directors, editing... It's a huge undertaking. Animation is theoretically simpler, but is also time consuming and expensive.

The Reconstruction format offered a viable means to re-create or create stories. But it's a very distinctive, very quirky thing. You would actually have to understand the history of Reconstructions, to be able to appreciate their use in re-creating the lost serials.

More than that, you have to get used to appreciating Reconstructions in and of themselves, to make those allowances, to invest in being entertained by what is essentially a slide show with voice over. To really understand or appreciate what's been done with *Yellow Fever*, you actually have to be invested in the language and style of a very peculiar and narrow art form. That's not saying it succeeds or fails, we'd have to first learn to appreciate the genre before we could even begin to evaluate it.

In applying the 'Reconstruction style' to original unmade stories, Levine has created something fairly new here, but it stands on the shoulders of what has gone before, is an extension of what's gone before. And it is an extension. Levine's *Dark Dimensions* seems to be a straight faux Reconstruction, with photographs and compositions or collages of photographs. *Yellow Fever* takes things a step further, crudely animating bits of the collage or composition, so that some of the elements move.

The Second Pirates History, Page 288

Call this collage animation, very similar to Josh Snares *Evil of the Daleks* animation. Gallifrey takes this even further, crudely animating talking heads in the style of some of Terry Gilliam's *Monty Python* work, or the experimental children's show *Angela Anaconda*.

This 'collage animation' is neither fish nor fowl, neither still pictures nor anything resembling real or natural movement, not live action, but not traditional forms of animation either. It can be quite off putting. Definitely, it takes a bit of getting used to.

Regarding *Yellow Fever's* 'Reconstruction,' I'm not sure whether any photographs were taken specifically for the project, as seemed to be somewhat the case with *Dark Dimensions*, or how many. In the case of Anthony Ainley, playing the Master, he'd passed away in 2004, so all of his images are definitely stock. Photographs of the Brigadier, the Doctor, Sargent Benton and Peri are certainly not modern. Levine seems to be raiding archives, or perhaps screen captures and then trying to fit it into his script.

At least with John Cura's Tele-Snaps for Reconstructions, they were all in order and following a developed narrative. There was a pre-existing script, director's notes and production photographs for episodes which had been shot and broadcast on television by an actual cinematographer and director.

In contrast, this is much more an assembled narrative. For that reason, perhaps, a lot of the photographs themselves are collaged together, foreground characters from two or three different pictures isolated and jammed together, with yet another photograph used as background. You can tell that the photographs are taken from all over and just mashed together. The lighting and shadows of the faces are wildly inconsistent, the *Frankenstein* stitches are showing everywhere throughout the story.

There's a sort of animation. Characters are marching about, leaning, and displaying more of a sense of physical motion. Not much, but it's enough. Images tend to be static and posed, but a bit of computer pokery gets them to lean forward or back, shift positions slightly, reminiscent of people's natural fidgetiness. So it feels weirdly authentic.

As often as not though, the effort to bring real motion accentuates the stiffness and unnaturalness. It can lead to unfortunate results - one of the shots on the seven minute section which tries to depict the Master and Doctor engaged in desperate battle makes it look like they're humping. Talk about awkward sexual subtext!

Watching the seven minute segment of *Yellow Fever*, it feels overly written. The dialogue seems to go on just a little too long or to be too windy. Possibly that's just the way Levine writes, or possibly he lacked a good script editor to tighten things up.

The voice actors filling in for the Sixth Doctor and Brigadier don't even try to sound like them, and their delivery is.... peculiar. Very peculiar. Oddly, the voice actor for the Master sounds and inflects very much like Anthony Ainley, so either they sampled his old dialogue, or found a very good sound-alike.

Between the excesses of dialogue and performance and the awkward parts of the collage animation, I have a sneaking suspicion that we might well be looking at an inadvertent masterpiece - kind of Doctor Who's '*Plan Nine From Outer Space*' or '*The Room*' where ineptitude manages to hit just the right notes to make something hilariously funny.

I'm not entirely sure I'm comfortable with that though.

I'm pretty sure that camp classic wasn't what Levine was going for. This version of Yellow Fever is Ian Levine's own script, based on whatever documents and recollections he had, or once had available to him, or claims to have had or seen. It's likely that time of those documents was likely around October, 1984, before Nathan-Turner seems to have started pushing the Rani into the story. It's clear that Levine regards the Master-only version as the truest, most authentic, perhaps the only version.

Levine claims to have a photographic memory, I'm a bit skeptical, but it's at least possible that he absorbed enough to write his own version, or to create notes for someone else to write.

But I don't think it sounds like Holmes voice at all. And, with all due respect to Levine, I don't think he's really a polished writer.

I have no doubt whatsoever that Levine was completely earnest about this project. In his mind, he was faithfully recreating Robert Holmes vision.

"I Reconstructed three of the missing stories myself on audio, and did detailed visual Recons on DVD of all six stories, with Nicola Bryant, Julian Glover, Milton Johns, Jon Levene, Waris Hussein, John Leeson, Nigel Plaskitt, Ian Fairbairn, and many many more. I am incredibly proud of them. Both Yellow Fever and Gallifrey were totally faithful to the original storylines.

Nicola Bryant played the Colin Baker Doctor's companion, Peri Brown. Jon Levene is known as Sargent Benton from UNIT. John Leeson did the voice of K9, though I doubt that K9 would have appeared here. Waris Hussein is best known in Who circles as the Director of both the Unearthly Child and Marco Polo. The rest are working actors who have taken various roles, including on Doctor Who.

I'm entirely prepared to give him credit for his effort in recruiting people. And to give him credit for a genuine effort. This was important to him, he wanted to do something good. He wanted to make a tribute to Robert Holmes.

The Second Pirates History, Page 291

He was sincere and I respect that.

Sincerity wouldn't save him from being terrible though.

Seven minutes isn't really enough to pass judgement. It's a fan film, and a certain number of mistakes or foibles should be allowed for in a fan film. The truth is there's little in the way of money or resource. People are learning as they go. So sometimes, you just make a mistake or pull a boner and keep on going.

Overall, of the little we've seen of it, it's far from perfect. But there's a certain engaging quality to it. I actually found myself being drawn in to the short segment. I was watching, I was interested. I was willing to forgive its glitches. I think it would be worth watching the whole thing. It might very well be brilliantly good. It could just as easily be brilliantly bad.

My advice to Ian Levine is have it screened in a large room of Doctor Who fans and see what their reaction is. If they love it as a sincere work of innovation and storytelling, a tribute, then that's terrific.

If they laugh their asses off, take the Tommy Wiseau route, and take credit for creating a work of a subversive comic genius. The only failure is to be boring.

Somehow, I don't see Levine's *Yellow Fever* as likely to be boring. I suspect though, that few of us will ever see it.

CAST: *Nicola Bryant - Peri Brown; Jon Levene - Sargent Benton; Julian Glover; Milton Johns; Waris Hussein; John Leeson; Nigel Plaskitt; Ian Fairbairn; (incomplete)*

CREW: *Ian Levine; (incomplete)*

AFTERWORDS

Where Do We Go From Here?

Welcome to the second edition of the second volume. I'm absolutely thrilled that you've made it this far. Have you read the first volume? I think it's terrific. If you haven't, maybe think about giving it a shot.

In the first volume, I explain what a Pirates History is. I talk about the general history of fan films or unauthorized pirate films.

We start with the first woman to play the Doctor, Barbara Benedetti, who did a series of films from 1984 to 1988.

I explore the earliest fan films from the Super 8 days of the 70s – films like Son of Doctor Who, Ocean in the Sky, the Image Makers and Doctor Hoo that have been almost completely lost.

In terms of Doctor Who history, there's the cancellation crisis of 1984, the fan rebellion that 'uncancelled' the show, the slow war of the BBC to destroy the show between 1984 and 1989, and the failed revival of 1993.

Then we look at the evolution of a fan culture in the 1980s, the impact of technology, particularly videocassette recorders and camcorders on shaping that culture, and the emerging fan film tradition, along with the best fan films of that time.

Finally, we go into the wilderness years, the 1990s – when Doctor Who was gone and off the air, and when fans started making serious and high quality films.

But here we are at the second volume, so what I really want to do is tempt you to the next step.

If you haven't gone there already, could I persuade you to back up and take a look at Volume I?

A PIRATE'S HISTORY OF DOCTOR WHO

REVISED AND EXPANDED

BY
D.G. VALDRON

VOLUME I

The Second Pirates History, Page 295

On the other hand, if you've already read Volume One and Two, I have one more....

THE LAST PIRATE'S HISTORY OF DOCTOR WHO

NEW AND EXPANDED

BY D.G. VALDRON

VOLUME III

The Second Pirates History, Page 297

Alongside video, there's an entire universe of Doctor Who audio productions, official and unofficial, going all the way back to Peter Cushing, Jon Pertwee and Tom Baker. We'll chart the failed official attempts to do the Doctor as radio or vinyl adventures.

Parallel to that, we'll explore the emergence of a lively and thriving fan audio adventure movement, the rise of the Audio-Visuals and how they in turn spawned the BBV and Big Finish Audio Adventures.

2000 to 2004 was the end of the Wilderness years and the cusp of the revival of the show by the BBV. At the same time, there was an explosion of creativity, and a series of brilliant new fan films that even tempted official Doctors to come back and revisit their roles in a series of homages and recreations of the classic series.

This would continue with the films of the modern era, with a new series of ambitious fan films inspired by the revival – enthusiastic fans, new technologies, and a new show inspired: Fire and Ice, How to Stop a Timelord, Project Fifty, The Forgotten Doctor and the Ginger Chronicles.

Finally, modern technology has profoundly changed both fan clubs and fan films. Gone are the days of meetings and clubs, Super 8, and bootleg videotapes. There's a new era of Cons, video platforms, computer based editing and sound mixing, CGI and greenscreens and new platforms, that have given fans better tools than ever before and unimagined access to audiences.

It's terrific. Tell your friends. Buy copies and give it to them. Have fun.

ACKNOWLEDGMENTS AND THANKS

This is a book about fan films. In a sense, it's a book about a television show that people enjoyed and were so inspired by that they decided to make their own. It's a book about the people that made these fan films.

Fans can be a persnickety bunch. That comes with the territory I suppose. When I began this project, I could see two major problems. No way was I going to make everyone happy.

First, I was going to get called out for mistakes and omissions. If I got a date wrong, or mentioned that The Dalek Masterplan was 10 episodes rather than twelve, spelled names wrong, locations, years. Someone was going to be coming down my throat for something.

Second, I was going to get grief for all the films I didn't review. The ones I didn't have time or space for, the ones that got overlooked or dismissed or didn't make the cut. There are so many films out there....

In the meantime, I need to acknowledge the people and institutions that have made this book possible. First and foremost are the film makers themselves. Mark Sinclair, Nigel Woodley, Kevin Jon Davies, Ryan K. Johnson, Peter Fagan, Rob Warnock, Jennifer Adams, Nigel Peever, Kevin Taylor, Ian Taylor, Paul Ferry, Rob Thrush, Dennis Kuhn, Nick

Scovell, Rupert Booth, Randy Rogel, Barbara Benedetti and on and on. These names, as important as they are, are the tip of the iceberg. I've gone to great lengths to list cast and crews because these films are communal efforts. There are literally hundreds, even thousands of people who have invested time and effort, love and talent in these myriad productions. I wish I could acknowledge and thank each one of you. I can only say: Thank you, your work is appreciated.

Beyond them, the Ian Levine's, the Mark Humphries, the Richard Brignell's, the multitude, the fans, the culture, the network, the clubs and associations, all of it individual that created the environment where these films could emerge, that volunteered time and energy, that were both inspiration and audience, that preserved and circulated, copied and distributed. Thank you, thank you so much. If not for you, these films would not have come down to us. I would not have been able to see them.

This is primarily a book of reviews. The comments and critiques mostly deal with my views and impressions from watching the films themselves. My opinions, of the films, of the show, of the BBC and politics and culture are my own.

Information about the productions themselves usually comes from online sources, primarily from the film makers themselves. Ryan K. Johnson, the Federation, Ad-Lib Productions have all maintained detailed web sites. Bedlam Productions has a Facebook page and has posted extensively on YouTube. There is actually a web page devoted to the Ultimate Adventure. Online searches have often turned up comments from people involved in production. In some cases I've been lucky enough to have made direct contact with some of the creative people themselves.

Beyond that, I've tried to place these films and their reviews within various contexts - of the history and politics of the show itself, of the culture of fans and fandom, of changing technology.

This has involved a lifetime of experience, from learning about and watching and even shooting super 8 films, in my grandparent's basement, to wearing a lizard man suit for a short film, to discovering VHS and Betamax and being part of fan culture and trading networks. There are more sources than can be counted easily.

As for the show itself, Doctor Who, with more than fifty years of history backstage and onscreen, and a cult following entering its third generation is incredibly well documented. There is an infinity of books, magazines, magazine articles, fanzines, professional and amateur publications; there are newspaper articles and quotes, online threads, documentaries which seem to canvas every aspect of every moment of production. Having lived through some of it, having been a fan for going on thirty years, I am immersed.

For the record, most of my quotes are taken from online sources - imdb.com, chat threads and comments, newspaper articles online, etc. Relatively few quotes are from direct personal correspondence. I've attempted to at least acknowledge these sources, but if I've overlooked stuff, then no harm was intended and no infringement or theft contemplated.

For the record, there are particular sources that I want to acknowledge which allowed me some context or insight, or were useful references or compilations.

First, **Shannon Sullivan's Doctor Who website**, incredibly thorough and well researched was often a 'go to'.

Dalek 63-88 is the definitive Website, Podcast and YouTube series for the surprisingly fascinating and detailed history of Dalek props. You wouldn't think such dry subject matter would be so riveting, but it's an absolutely engrossing site.

Wikipedia, Imdb.com, and numerous personal web sites and chat threads were invaluable.

The BBC's own Doctor Who DVD releases were an essential tool, not only for the stories themselves, but for an incredible volume of documentary bonuses and literally hundreds of hours of commentary which in many cases were startlingly honest.

A few books I specifically want to point out: **The Nth Doctor** by Jean Marc and Randy Lofficier, published through Virgin Books, 2003. It chronicles the efforts to bring Doctor Who to the Silver Screen beginning in the 1990s, with synopsis of a dozen or more abandoned scripts. I made minimal use of it. But I love it to pieces and you should buy this book.

The Doctor Who Discontinuity Guide, by Paul Cornell, Martin Day and Keith Topping, published in 1995, is an essential and thoroughly charming reference work. Again, just go and buy it. If you already have it, buy another one and give it to a friend. I actually got to meet Paul Cornell once.

Finally, Richard Marson's **The Scandalous Life and Times of John Nathan-Turner,** published 2013, is, I think, the definitive chronicle of the career of a controversial figure, and the last word as to the politics and maneuvering behind the hiatus. The Johnathan Powell quote is taken directly from this book.

I'm very, very pleased to be able to recommend and plug **Downtime, The Lost Years of Doctor Who**, by Dylan Rees, published 2017, by Obverse books. It is a marvelous chronicle of the gray-market video and audio. Although we cover some of the same ground, our approaches are quite different. His book is marvelous. If you like mine, please go buy his.

In the meantime, thank you.

More Books from the Author

Have you made it all the way here? Have you actually read all this way

Wow. That's amazing. I'm very flattered. I want to give you a hug or something.

Seriously. Thank you! Thank you so much!

I'm going to assume that if you've made it all this way, you've enjoyed yourself. You've learned some juicy new gossip about old Doctor Who, you've found some insights into technology and how it affects what we do, and maybe you found some of the reviews really entertaining.

I will repeat, almost everything I've written about you can find out there, if you look around hard enough. I strongly recommend you do so. I genuinely believe that these films and these Doctors deserve to be remembered.

And I hope you liked my writing and writing style. Because if you did, then I have some non-Doctor Who books, both fiction and nonfiction, that I think you'd love.

They're available on multiple platforms as eBooks, and in some places as print books or audiobooks. Lots of choices.

Please feel free to visit my website: denvaldron.com.

Or just let me tell you about them right now…

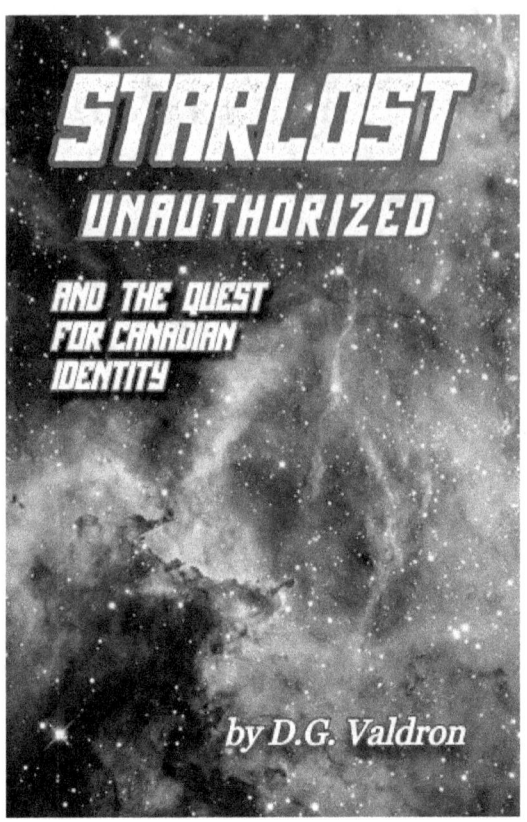

STARLOST UNAUTHORIZED
And the Quest for Canadian Identity

The series that was Harlan Ellison's nemesis. The most
controversial series in the history of sci fi television. This
exhaustively researched book, based on interviews with some
of the stars and writers, brings a fresh new interpretation of
of the Starlost, and a re-evaluation of the series and its themes
in the context of the 1970s crisis of Canadian nationalism.

The Second Pirates History, Page 305

LEXX UNAUTHORIZED

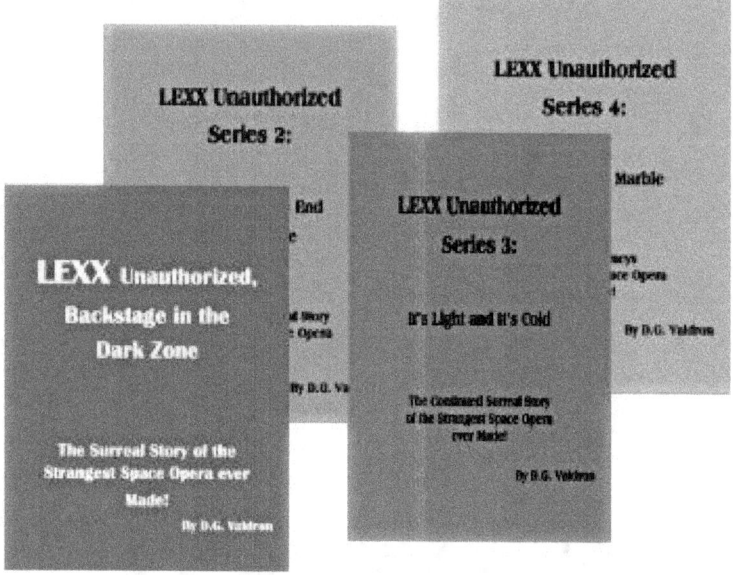

LEXX a show about a giant space bug that blows up planets, the cowardly security guard who is its captain, and the undead assassin, runaway love slave, and robot head who form its crew.

Originally billed as 'Star Trek's Evil Twin,' the cultiest of cult sci fi, LEXX's forte was black humor, startling visuals, big ideas, and a sensibility that had more to do with surrealists like Jodorowsky or Bunuel than mainstream science fiction. And, as unconventional as it was onscreen, the story of how it came to be is even more bizarre.

A Dark Fantasy
of Murder and Redemption

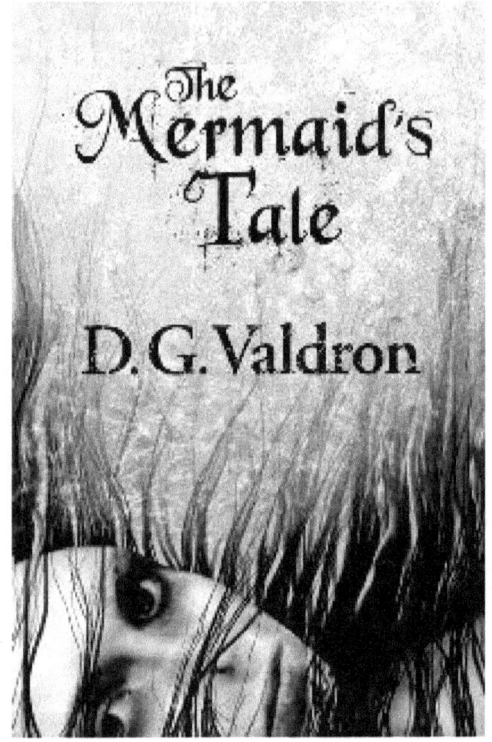

There's a City where all the races come together uneasily, Civil War gathering, and dark powers assembling.

There's a Mermaid, murdered cruelly, her people distraught. There's an Orc, to solve the murder, before it all comes crashing down.

And there's something else: this world's first serial killer.

The Second Pirates History, Page 307

FUNNY FANTASY
And COMIC SCIENCE FICTION

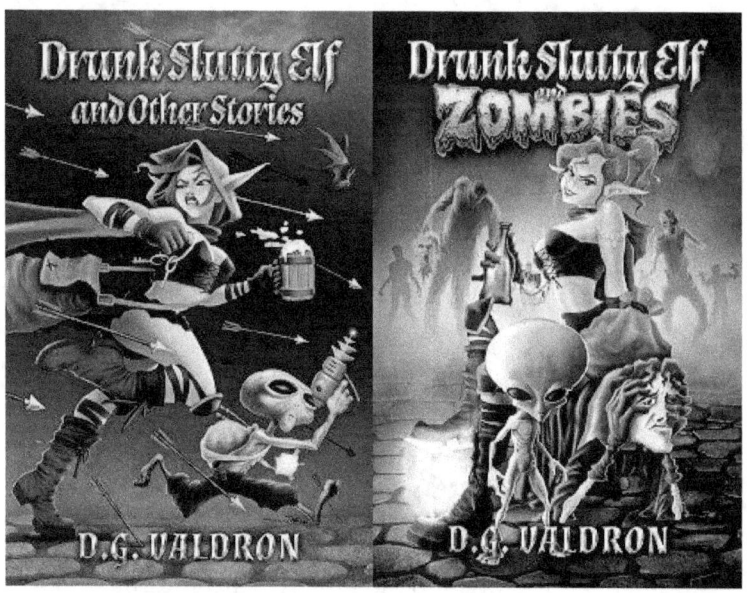

DRUNK SLUTTY ELF AND OTHER STORIES
Plus
DRUNK SLUTTY ELF AND ZOMBIES

Two volumes of savage, satirical, subversive wicked, funny, frantic science fiction and fantasy. Demented ghost hunters, frustrated aliens, horny giants, drunken elves, sneaky ghosts, wayward barbarians and many more.

The Second Pirates History, Page 308

HEARTS IN DARKNESS
Three Collections of Horror Stories

Featuring riveting stories about a man's cancer learning to talk to him, the ultimate serial killer; Allison, a paralyzed pregnant woman feeling her fetus taking control of her body, a desperate single mother lured down a dark path; the army enlisting the unkillable men in the masks; Silence about a thief hiding in the home of a killer; a ghost that haunts the people around its victim, and many, many more. Melancholy darkness, chilling horror, dark visions.

AXIS OF ANDES
NEW WORLD WAR
A History of WWII in South America

Berlin, 1937, Adolph Hitler and his cabinet meet with a strange delegation from Ecuador.

The delegates from the small South American nation beg for help, fearing an impending invasion from their rival, Peru.

What happens at that meeting sets in motion a chain of events that sets the entire continent on fire. By the time it's done, millions are dead, nations are in ruins, and the map of Latin America will be changed beyond recognition.

The Second Pirates History, Page 310

ALTERNATE REALITIES
A Trilogy of Strange New Worlds

The Fall of Atlantis includes a geo-historical exploration of a real Atlantis ending in a different kind of tragedy; the Retroverse, a fun the accidental cinematic universe of 50s sci fi films, Ancient Rome plausibly crossing the Atlantic, because of coffee(!!!), and the saga of an Alternate Greenland that was never covered by ice.

The Dawn of Cthulhu, an exploration of lost continents, real and legendary; the secret history of the Cthulhu Cult as a genuine religion, and the biology, evolution and linguistics of muppets and their friends.

The Bear Cavalry, the True (Not!) History of the Icelandic Bears, chronicles a history where travelling Vikings domesticated North American Bears and eventually learn to forge them into the most terrifying medieval fight force ever – with excursions into history, biology and art along the way. Bonus story – the Sharebear Apocalypse, is it really just a hug that feels so good.

The Second Pirates History, Page 311

TWILIGHT OF ECHELON

Published by

AT BAY PRESS

Based on the work of famed artist Robert Pasternak the book
features paintings from Pasternak's Echelon series,
accompanied by stories written independently by D.G.
Valdron, Lovern Kindzierski, Alex Passey and Blaise Moritz.

The Second Pirates History, Page 312